THE NEW COMPLETE BOOK OF THE
HORSE

THE NEW COMPLETE BOOK OF THE

HORSE

JANE HOLDERNESS-RODDAM
OLYMPIC TEAM GOLD MEDALIST

INCLUDING PHOTOGRAPHS BY BOB LANGRISH

SMITHMARK

This edition published in 1992 by
Reed Consumer Books
part of Reed International Books Ltd.,
Michelin House, 81 Fulham Road,
London SW3 6RB

First published in the United States by
SMITHMARK Publishers Inc.,
16 East 32nd Street, New York, NY 10016

Reprinted 1992

SMITHMARK books are available for bulk purchase for sales
promotion and premium use. For details write or telephone the Manager of
Special Sales, SMITHMARK Publishers Inc., 16 East 32nd Street,
New York, NY 10016; (212) 532-6600

Editor: Anne Crane
Design and Art Direction: Alyson Kyles
Production: Nick Thompson
Picture Research: Jenny Faithfull

Illustrations by Gillie Newman

ISBN 0 8317 6303 5

Printed in Hong Kong

Half-title: 4th century mosaic

CONTENTS

FOREWORD

I was brought up with horses from the word go, and at six months old was being taken for rides every day on my brother's pony, Tickle. I eventually graduated to the Pony Club, enjoying all the many activities encouraged by that splendid organization, as well as how to look after my own pony.

At the age of six, and later at eleven, I went to the U.S.A. to ride in their pony classes, causing a bit of a stir by riding sidesaddle because it was the only way my mother could ensure I would not fall off! This was the start of the pony exchanges, which took place for several years between Britain and the U.S. — a far cry from today when horses and ponies regularly fly across the Atlantic.

After a win at the Badminton Horse Trials in 1968, I went on to ride for Britain in the Olympic Games in Mexico on my ex-Pony Club pony, Our Nobby, who I had virtually grown up with since I was 14. From him I learnt so much about riding, self-preservation and generally how a horse thinks, or does not think, as the case may be. Gradually I started to really understand horses, which has been of such benefit over the years as I have continued to compete, judge, teach and ride in various disciplines at shows and events around the world.

This book is designed to give practical information on how to prepare for the many equestrian activities of today. However, the reader must be warned that it is impossible to cover everything in the space available. Hopefully, there is something for everyone, whether trekkng across vast expanses of land, or vaulting on the lunge in a confined area.

The horse provides us all with so much to watch and enjoy, as well as care for, and has always proved to be a delightful and faithful companion, giving so much pleasure to so many and, I am sure, will continue to do so for generations to come.

Jane Holderness-Roddam.

Left and title page: the author riding Balingreen at Gatcombe Park Trials 1991

INTRODUCTION

For centuries the horse has had a unique relationship with the human race. It has been used as a work horse, war horse, messenger, display animal, for sport and recreation, in mines, on ceremonial occasions, for entertainment, and for hunting. It has also been the subject of many outstanding works of art around the world.

It is known that the horse was descended from the tiny little *Eohippus* which stood little more than 12 in. (30 cm) high. This animal had pads on its feet (four in front and three behind) and roamed across the huge land-masses, living in the forests and wandering on the marshy ground some 40–60 million years ago. The *Mesohippus* was descended from the *Eohippus* and was a little larger. It had three toes on each foot and more efficient teeth, enabling it to eat more varied vegetation. This species existed between 40–25 million years ago. The *Miohippus* followed, then the *Merychippus*, nearly as big as a donkey, which had an enlarged central toe allowing it greater speed and the ability to move farther afield. The *Pliohippus* lived between five and two million years ago and was the first species to have properly formed hooves, the two outside toes having by this time completely disappeared. With the coming of the ice age, however, the horse's ancestors were greatly reduced in number, and eventually they became extinct on the American continent about eight thousand years ago. Those that survived spread across Europe and Africa from Asia and started to flourish as direct ancestors of the modern horse – *Equus caballus*. This appears to have emerged into four basic types from which the various breeds of today have evolved.

They were the Forest horse, the Plateau horse, the Steppe horse, and the Tundra horse.

Coldbloods and warmbloods

The Forest horse was a heavy solid type with a large head and feet and was most likely to have been the founder of the coldbloods and heavy draft breeds. The Plateau horse was a finer type, and it is known that the tough little semi-wild Mongolian horses of today are descended from this strain. The Steppe horse was of a lighter type and was probably the originator of the oriental breeds such as the Arab and the Barb, which were the forerunners of the Thoroughbred of today. The Tundra does not appear to have had much influence, but was a large, heavy strain of animal, and the Yukat – the huge horse of the Polar regions – may be the only

descendant likely from this type.

The nomadic Eurasian tribesmen were possibly the first humans to realize the potential of the horse. They moved along the regions beside the Black and Caspian Seas, and there is evidence that they domesticated the horse about five to six thousand years ago. Records in China show that raids on horseback took place four thousand years ago. Egyptian tomb paintings vividly portray the horse, which is shown being driven and ridden, while the first ridden horse race to be held at the Olympic Games took place in Greece in 648 B.C.

A reconstruction of the probable appearance of *Eohippus*, the earliest known ancestor of the horse. It lived about 40–60 million years ago and was about 12 in. (30 cm) high.

The evolution of the horse

The horse we know today is descended from the tiny *Eohippus* of some 40-60 million years ago. It has since grown tremendously in size, and its feet in particular have adapted from the original four toes so that there is now one single hoof encasing the pedal bone supporting each limb.

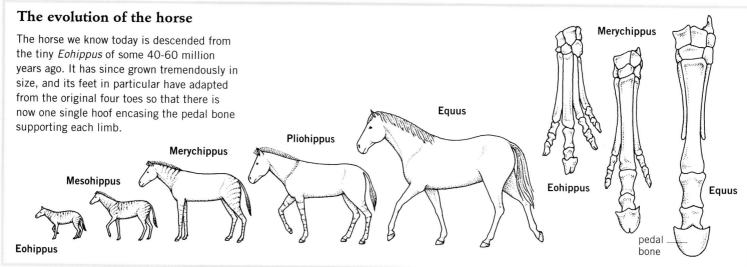

Mesohippus

Eohippus

Merychippus

Pliohippus

Equus

Merychippus

Eohippus

Equus

pedal bone

The horse in art. Far left: a detail of a frieze from the Parthenon showing two young horsemen about to join a procession. Left: a Greek vase, circa 460 B.C., depicting a sculptor modeling a horse. Center: a knight prepares for a tournament, from the 14th century illuminated manuscript, the Luttrell Psalter. Bottom: Horsemen advancing into battle, from the Bayeux Tapestry.

Xenophon (431-350 BC)

The great Greek horse trainer and cavalry officer, Xenophon (431-350 B.C.), wrote an astonishingly detailed book on the training and management of horses, much of which is still relevant today and includes details on many of the current high school dressage movements. Although organized jumping was not practiced until very much later, Xenophon also wrote about how to take a horse across country over the natural obstacles likely to be encountered.

By the thirteenth century, following the wars of the Crusades and the capture of oriental horses, selective breeding appears to have been practiced with special emphasis placed on breeding for performance in war, racing, and for work on the land. The influence of the Arab breed had been enhanced by the prophet Mohammed, who had noted its importance and had given orders for its development and management to his followers. The Arab was bred throughout North Africa and was eventually brought to Europe. Interbreeding with the

Above: The Byerley Turk

The Darley Arabian

The Godolphin Arabian

Arab greatly improved the European breeds already in existence.

The founding of the Thoroughbred

In England the Thoroughbred was founded on breeding from three imported Arabs: the Byerley Turk, the Darley Arabian, and the Godolphin Arabian. They were used on the existing "running horses," which had been used extensively in betting in England up to that time. The enhanced standards led to more organized racing taking place, first at Newmarket, which remains the home of Thoroughbred racing in Britain and later, in 1711, at Ascot. In 1793 the General Stud Book was set up, from which all Thoroughbred horses can be traced.

Tremendous enthusiasm for the training of horses started in Europe during the Renaissance, and in 1532 the first riding school of note was set up in Naples under Federico Grisone, where many of the more complex dressage movements were evolved and practiced. In Britain William Cavendish, 1st Duke of Newcastle, inspired many by his book, *A General System of Horsemanship,* first published in 1658. In the late sixteenth century, a riding school was set up at Versailles which was frequented by the nobility, and in 1735 the Spanish Riding School opened in Vienna, using the book *Ecole de Cavaliere,* written in 1773 by the great French trainer de la Guérinière, as its bible. This school places great emphasis on classical training for both horse and rider, and to this day it is renowned for its performances in Vienna and displays given around the world with its exclusive Lipizzaner horses, "the dancing white horses" of Vienna. In 1768 the French Cavalry school was set up in Saumur, and it too has had considerable influence worldwide. Known as the Cadre Noir, its riders wear a distinguished black uniform and have had a considerable influence on riding and dressage.

Many of the high school movements practiced to this day in the Spanish Riding School have evolved from movements used in war to escape the enemy. Most of these movements are natural to the horse as a means of escape to avoid trouble. The *levade, capriole, corbette,* and *croupade* are famous for their ability to show the power and magnificence of the horse.

Left: "Un manége sous Louis XV." An engraving from de la Guérinière's book *Ecole de la Cavaliere*, first published in 1773, showing riders in Louis XV's riding school performing some of the exceptionally graceful *haute école* movements known collectively as "airs above the ground." The *levade* is demonstrated on the left and the *capriole* on the right. Below: The Spanish Riding School of Vienna and the Cadre Noir in France are the only two schools which perform *haute école* in its complete form. Here the Spanish Riding School is seen giving one of their dressage displays on their famed gray Lippanizer horses.

Jumping as a sport

Jumping was a late starter in the equestrian scene, and it was probably when land began to be fenced in England in the early eighteenth century that it became necessary for the horse to have to jump more than fairly simple natural hazards. Hunting then became a natural training ground, along with riding for the cavalry, as increasing use was made of firepower and horses were required for reconnaisance and pursuit. This necessitated the ability to jump cross-country quickly and successfully. In this respect, the Irish were probably the most inventive. The first known competitive jumping event took place in Ireland for a wager in 1752 when two hunters were raced over 4½ miles (7.2 kms) from one village church to another, that is, from "steeple" to "steeple." Hence the word "steeplechase," and the beginning of the sport which thrills so many in its present form in the racing world today.

The "leaping" competitions which were practiced over high, thin poles or wide fences eventually became popular enough for the Royal Dublin Society to include such an event in its show in 1864. In 1866 Paris also had a jumping competition, which included a cross-country course, mostly outside the arena. Various rules began to emerge in different countries and at first this led to some confusion. Eventually, however, in 1912, show jumping became an Olympic sport and since then has been organized with the rules laid down and standardized by the FEI (Fédération Equestre Internationale). Show jumping is now practiced throughout the world, and horses and riders at the top of the sport are household names.

Federico Caprilli (1868-1907)

The person who has had the greatest influence on jumping was undoubtedly the Italian Cavalry instructor Federico Caprilli (1868-1907). Until the late nineteenth century, riders had a very stiff and upright style of riding with a backward pull on the reins, particularly over fences. Caprilli realized that this was tiring and inhibiting for his officers, who needed to be able to jump quickly over fences and ride freely cross-country. The method of riding used also restricted the horses.

Caprilli made his riders shorten their stirrups and sit more in balance with their horses and ride with a forward seat over the fence, allowing the hand forward rather than back. This gave horses the freedom to use themselves over fences. Previously they had been made to conform to their riders' wishes, but Caprilli's training made the rider conform to the natural carriage of the horse. Since 1907 Caprilli's style of riding has been known as the "Italian" seat. His early death meant that he was probably unable to execute all of his revolutionary new ideas. However, he, along with Xenophon, has undoubtedly made the greatest contribution to the world of horsemanship.

Pomp and ceremony

The horse in battle is thankfully a sight now rarely seen, but even so the horse still plays a major part in national security. The Royal Canadian Mounted Police are world famous, as are the British Household Cavalry. Part of the Household Division is regularly seen on London's streets acting as escort to monarchs and visiting dignitaries, and it performs outstanding displays around the world.

The pageantry of state occasions would be incomplete without the horse. Majestic horse-drawn state carriages are very special, and who can forget the amazing spectacles seen on such occasions as the wedding of the Prince and Princess of Wales, coronations, and the funeral of President Kennedy.

The world of racing has produced some outstanding performances of speed and sometimes sheer guts when a tight finish is battled out to the line on the flat and over fences. Thoroughbred horses continue to dominate the breeding of future champions of the track and also influence competition horses.

There can be few more magnificent sights than the sheer beauty and power of racehorses in tip-top condition, seen here on the track at Paradise Valley, Phoenix, Arizona.
Right: Pageants and parades are immensely popular worldwide. Here the Royal Canadian Mounted Police draw huge crowds in Calgary.

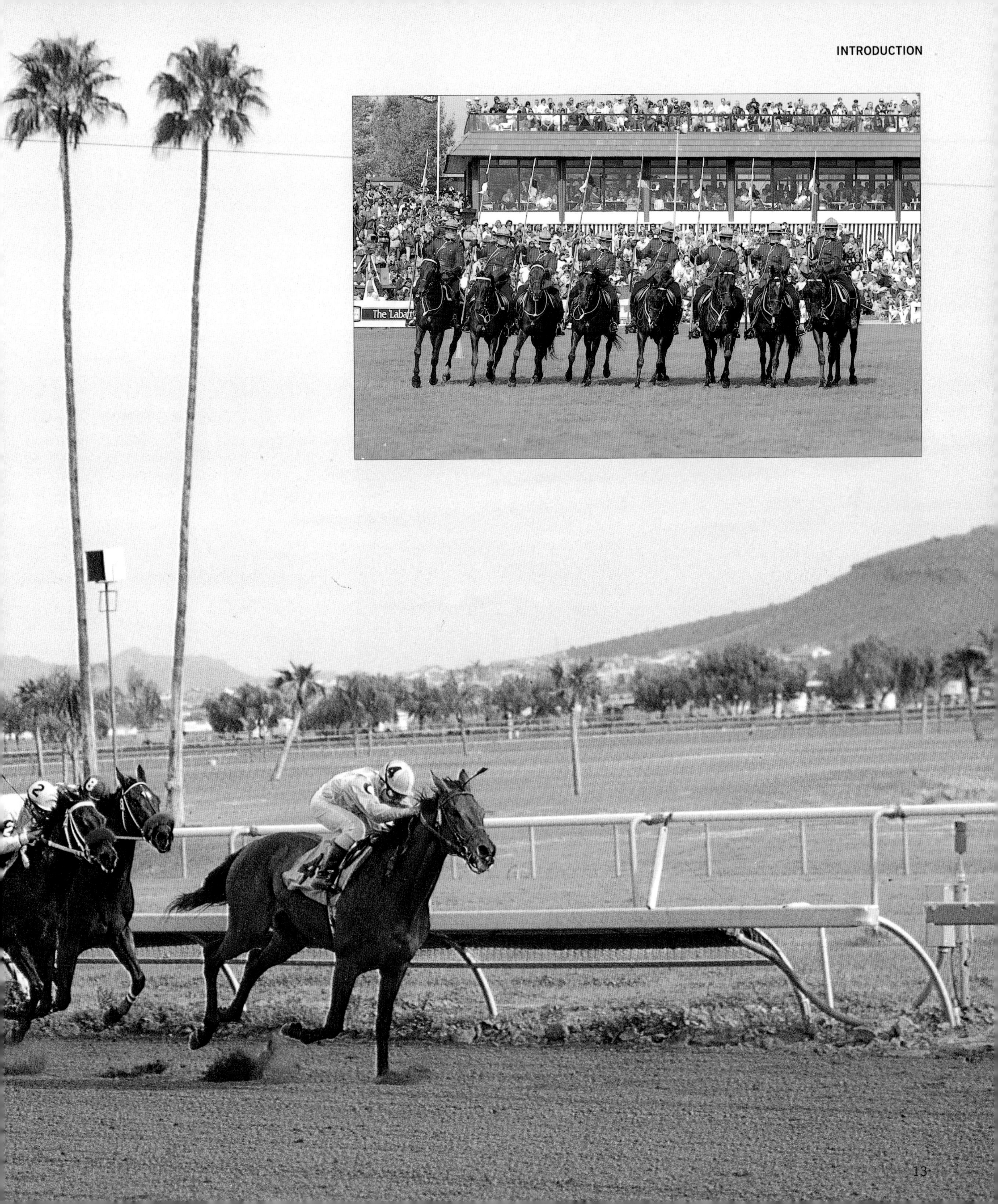

The horse in fiction

The horse has been immortalized in many different ways. Equestrian statues around the world adorn parks and cities, while great paintings of magnificent steeds hang in art galleries. In millions of homes there are pictures of horses, both big and small, which adorn the walls.

Children have read of Napoleon's magnificent gray Marengo, or Alexander the Great's Bucephalus and the Duke of Wellington's diminutive chestnut Copenhagen, which carried their riders into battle. Story books have enthralled youngsters with such tales as Dick Turpin's ride from London to York on Black Bess. Perhaps the greatest book ever written about a horse is Anna Sewell's *Black Beauty*, first published in 1877. Poems in their thousands have covered just about every equestrian pursuit, and many television programs and films have featured horses or have been based upon a story about a horse. Tales from the Wild West, starring cowboys such as Roy Rogers on Trigger or the Lone Ranger on Silver, or a story about the horse and life in the Midwest provide a huge choice of stories which depict horses of every shape and size in numerous different roles.

The horse in battle. Left: Napoleon on Marengo at the Battle of the Pyramids, July 1798, during his Egyptian campaign. Below:The Charge on the Sun-Pole, a study of North American Indians on the warpath by Frederic Remington.

Heavy draft horses are the much-loved gentle giants of the equestrian world.
Left: A team of Clydesdales, the Scottish draft horses which have become so popular, at the Royal Highland Show in Scotland, in 1990.
Below: The Drum Horse of the British Household Cavalry draws all eyes at the Royal Windsor Horse Show.

Europe is rich in history which includes the horse. In the U.K. alone there are no less than sixteen white horses cut into the chalk hillsides. Some of these horses are fairly modern, but some are very old, such as the Uffington White Horse in the Vale of White Horse in Oxfordshire. This is thought to date from the first century B.C. and is the same tribal symbol of the horse which was used on coins of the Celtic Belgae tribe.

While motorized transportation has overtaken horse power, nevertheless the horse is still used to carry large loads to inaccessible areas. Although the days of the stagecoach and the mail runs have long since gone, the art of driving horses in harness still continues, though nowadays in a more competitive atmosphere, with carriage driving becoming more and more popular.

The U.S. has wonderful horse parks, none of which is more outstanding than that in Lexington, Kentucky, in the heart of the famous bluegrass breeding and stud farm area, where triple crown champions from the racetrack breed to reproduce their out-standing talents. The horse parks regularly hold spectacular parades of ridden, driven, and led horses of all breeds, colors, and sizes. Perhaps none is more breathtaking than the eight-horse hitches of, for example, the Budweiser Clydesdales.

A return to the past

Heavy horses are making a triumphant comeback from their decline of yesteryear and are now in great demand, with shows holding more and more classes for these magnificent animals. Plowing contests are increasing in popularity, and some small farmers are returning to old methods of farming which include horses; in some instances, they are proving cheaper than modern machinery. Breweries too are once more using horse-drawn wagons for local deliveries as it is realized what an impact horses have on tourists as a means of advertising in the big cities. Farm sales can provide old equipment and harnesses, and the collector can have a field day restoring them to their former glory.

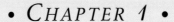

CHAPTER 1

LEARNING TO RIDE

'When Allah willed to create the horse
He said to the South Wind –
"Condense thyself.
I will that a creature should proceed
from thee."
Then came the Angel Gabriel and
took a handful
Of this matter and presented it to Allah,
Who formed of it a dark bay and
chestnut horse.'

Arab legend

Riding a horse can be an immensely beneficial and enjoyable experience. Once you have mastered the art, there are many very different activities you can choose from, ranging from hunting to eventing.

Riding provides a very special form of exercise as it requires not only physical prowess and skill, but also mental alertness. Continuous concentration is essential, as is the ability to control an animal which may not always be willing to agree to your instructions. Bear in mind that there is always an element of uncertainty about riding. After all, you are interacting with a live animal which has feelings and a mind of its own, not an inanimate machine that will always instantly obey your commands.

Riding is only now becoming truly appreciated, not only because it is a sporting and leisure activity, but also because it acts as a therapy for those who want to improve their skills of coordination, balance, alertness and concentration.

When to start riding

The sooner you get started, the sooner you will master the art of riding. Some parents acquire a pony and teach the child to ride when he or she is very young as mine did, starting me out at six-months-old in a basket-chair saddle. Children's leading rein classes are very popular, and youngsters from the age of three up can be seen in the show ring.

Children learn very quickly when playing with their friends' ponies, and this can be one of the best ways to learn to ride, as long as they are under constant supervision and wear suitable footwear and correct riding hats. The latter are absolutely essential. Older riders do best if they start at a riding school until they are reasonably confident and competent to manage alone.

Where to start

Even if you have your own horse, the best place to start is at a reputable riding school where there are suitable horses or ponies and qualified instructors to start you off on the right lines. Some people find riding is easy while others may find it more difficult to learn. Balance and coordination are two vital qualities needed. With some good instruction it should not be too long before the rudiments of riding are mastered.

If there is no good riding school nearby, it may be possible to learn to ride on someone else's horse or pony, provided you are taught by a person who really knows what he or she is doing. It is essential that at first you have someone to help you mount and start you off, as well as a second person to hold

Riding is an enjoyable pastime for all age groups. There is nothing better than a good ride in lovely surroundings in perfect weather, as seen here.

on to the horse. The animal must be quiet and sensible and not likely to be frightened of the inevitably unorthodox antics of the beginner.

The riding school

There are a many riding schools which offer a wide variety of lessons and activities, but it is always best to join a riding school which has been approved and officially recognized by a registered equestrian society or club or recommended by word of mouth.

Your instructor should be fully qualified to teach and should hold at least an Assistant Instructor's (A.I.) or equivalent certificate. If you can, choose a helpful and reassuring instructor who is willing to take time to build up your confidence and provide full explanations and clear instructions during the lessons, which should offer a balance of practical and theoretical instruction.

First impressions of the riding school must be that of a well-kept, clean, and neat stable run by friendly yet professional staff. Most stables choose Monday as their rest day after a busy weekend, so it is always best to telephone beforehand to make certain of your visit. A great many riding stables have open days during the summer months which are ideal for making a close inspection. The stables should be clean and airy with no foul

smells, and all the doors and windows should be safe and thoroughly secure.

The horses or ponies should appear fit, well shod, healthy, and content. If horses are kept standing around tacked up for long periods in between lessons this is a sign of bad management. Even though the horses should have been hand-picked, always approach them with care.

The tack room should be clean, neat, and well-organized, with no signs of damp. Usually the tack is lined up under individual name plates indicating the name of the horse or pony. It is important that all the tack should look clean with the leather parts supple. All buckles and keepers should be secure and all girths, pads, and blankets clean and dry.

Facilities These are probably the most important factor to consider when choosing your riding school. Check if there is an indoor school for the colder months, and a floodlit school for winter evenings. All the school's floor surfaces should be well prepared and soft enough so as not to jar the horse's legs or hurt the falling rider. The surface should be raked and sprayed regularly to smooth any divots and reduce the amount of dust kicked up by the horse's hooves.

Check what sort of lessons are available. You may find that it is impossible to have private lessons at weekends or at other busy periods. If there are group lessons, there should really be a maximum of six people per ride and all of an equal standard.

More advanced riders should check if the riding school specializes in the field they wish to pursue, be it dressage, showjumping or cross-country. Many rural riding schools have their own novice cross-country courses and outdoor facilities, whereas riding schools in built-up areas and inner cities may have restricted space and a single indoor school. In either case, dressing rooms, restrooms, and even lecture rooms are usually available.

Dress

The riding school may lend you a suitable hat and stick and will insist on the correct footwear, which should be a sturdy, well-soled boot or shoe with a small heel to prevent the foot from slipping through the stirrup iron. If you decide to buy your own riding hat, check that it is fitted correctly and of the approved standard to comply with insurance regulations. Today, all hard hats must be fitted with a safety harness which includes a chin-strap, and your instructor should insist that this is worn at all times. It is essential whenever and wherever you are riding to wear clothes which cover your arms and legs for added protection. To ride at your best, you must never get cold and wet or, at the other extreme, overheated, so choose your clothes carefully.

It is important to keep all garments, especially jackets, buttoned or zipped up securely so that they do not flap and startle your horse or pony. Open zippers often cause damage when allowed to flap about and may scratch the saddle.

Most instructors insist on clothing which is close-fitting without being restricting, to allow them to see clearly how you are using your back, seat, and leg aids. Denim or other sturdy cotton jeans are suitable to ride in, but many people change to jodhpurs as these are much more comfortable, being specially designed for riding. Most riders prefer to wear gloves at all times to avoid painful sores on tender fingers.

In all schooling situations you will find it necessary to carry a stick, never to be used as a form of punishment, but rather as an extra artificial aid to back up your natural aids (see p30). Your instructor will advise you on the type and length of stick required for your standard of riding, and the particular horse you will be riding.

A career with horses

If you are considering a career with horses, perhaps as veterinary surgeon, a groom, a farrier or even as a professional show jumper or eventer, or a jockey, whether or not you have your own horse, a riding school should be your first port of call as it should offer the help and guidance necessary to help you study the subjects you need for the exams. Some people study stable management and horse knowledge without ever having ridden a horse or wishing to ride, and go on to make excellent teachers or judges in the show ring, or to help charitable groups that provide riding facilities for the disabled. There are also numerous exams at different standards qualifying for higher teaching levels.

A recommended riding school where horses and facilities are well suited to the novice rider is the ideal place to start your riding career. Safety must always be a top priority; check on this aspect before embarking on your first ride. The riders and ponies seen below on a group lesson at an outdoor school are well turned out and wearing the correct headgear. They are riding in single file at a safe distance from one another to avoid accidents.

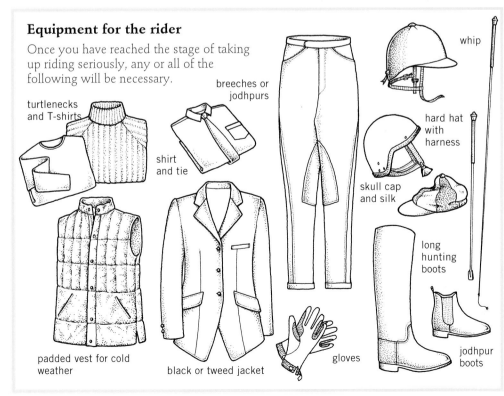

Equipment for the rider

Once you have reached the stage of taking up riding seriously, any or all of the following will be necessary.

turtlenecks and T-shirts

breeches or jodhpurs

shirt and tie

whip

hard hat with harness

skull cap and silk

long hunting boots

padded vest for cold weather

black or tweed jacket

gloves

jodhpur boots

The horse or pony

It is important to know something about ponies and horses, their make-up and shape, color and age, and also the terminology which is used.

The horse or pony is normally led and mounted from the inside, that is, its left side. The outside is the right-hand side of its body.

Age

If its date of birth is not known, a horse's age can be determined by its teeth. It takes some time to learn how to identify the various changes that take place in the teeth, but the diagrams on the right will provide the necessary information. Always take care to handle the horse gently but firmly when looking at its teeth, and do not put your fingers inside its mouth unless absolutely necessary. You must be sure you know what you are doing; otherwise; you may be bitten; and there is the added danger of contracting one of the many viruses prevailing today.

The young horse loses its milk teeth between the ages of eighteen months and five years old; these are then replaced by a second set of permanent teeth which develop certain characteristics according to the age of the horse. The horse has a full set of permanent teeth by the age of six.

A mature horse has 18 teeth in each jaw, top and bottom. There are six incisor teeth in front and twelve cheek (or molar) teeth, six on each side. Males develop four tusk (tush) or canine teeth. Up to four wolf teeth may appear just in front of the molars, but they are usually removed if they interfere with the bit. The front incisor teeth are used for grasping and tearing food, while the cheek teeth grind the food before swallowing. For care of the teeth, see Veterinary care, p. 77.

Colors and markings

Horses come in a huge variety of colors and very often have markings (i.e. white hair) on their legs and heads according to their type or breed. There are sometimes very strict rules as to how much white marking is allowed. Some breeds have definite colors, such as the Cleveland Bay, whereas the palomino coloring (a golden coat with a white mane and tail) appears in any breed or type. The Palomino's splendor makes it highly prized, and it is the only full color that has show classes specifically catering for it. The colored horse is now becoming very popular again. There are two types: skewbalds (white with chestnut or bay patches) and piebalds (white with black patches), and both are very much in demand.

The main colors are set out below. Note

The horse's incisor teeth

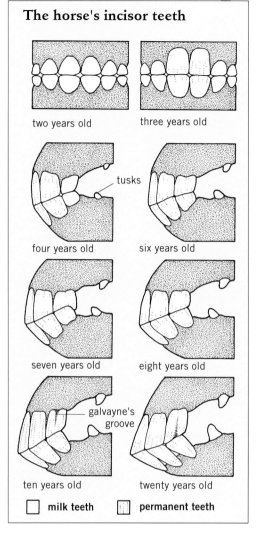

two years old — three years old

tusks

four years old — six years old

seven years old — eight years old

galvayne's groove

ten years old — twenty years old

□ milk teeth   ▨ permanent teeth

that black points refer to the tips of the ears, muzzle, mane and tail, and the lower limbs.

Black is not often seen unless it is predominant in a breed such as the Fell pony. The color, though, is greatly admired and is the choice for many parade horses.

Brown is a solid color, ranging from deepest brown to brown/ black.

Bay is a bright mahogany color with distinctive black points. It may vary from a light bay to a bright or rich blood bay. A bay brown is a mixture between bay and brown, but still showing black points.

Chestnut is reddish-brown to ginger. It can vary from a light golden color to a dark red. The horse will usually have a chestnut mane and tail, with or without white markings on the head and legs, but sometimes the mane and tail is flaxen (straw colored). (Chestnut is often called sorrel.

Grays have white hair or a mixture of white and black hairs on a dark skin. Depending on which color is predominant, grays may be dark in color, iron gray, or dappled with hammer patterns, usually at the quarters, or

Markings

The head may be of the solid color or marked with a star, stripe, blaze, or white face and snip. White markings may appear on one or more of the legs and are generally described according to the part of the leg marked from the pastern down. A sock, stocking, or leg describes the amount of leg from the pastern up that has the markings.

Ermine marks are black dots on a white surface, usually a lower limb.

Zebra marks are black or dark stripes across the back of the forearms and on the front of the gaskins, often seen on duns.

A list, ray, or stripe is a black line extending from the mane down through to the horse's tail. In Norwegian Fjord ponies, this looks particularly dramatic as the rest of the mane is white.

Liver marks are darker spots or shapes which appear on chestnut-colored horses.

Strawberry marks are chestnut patches, often appearing on grays.

Saddlemarks are white patches of hair which appear on the body because of rubbing or pressure. These are usually found around the girth and over the

A chestnut with white markings

A bay with distinctive black points

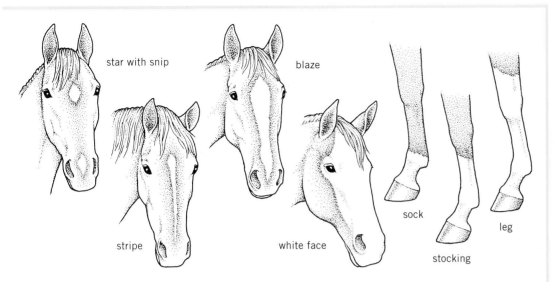

Wall eyes are very distinctive. The horse's eyesight is by no means impaired. They are particularly common in colored horses and those with white faces as well as in some creams.

withers or saddle area.

Flesh marks are areas of unpigmented skin and often appear along with white face marks on what is otherwise a dark skin. Flesh marks are very common on the muzzle area.

Mealy eyes and muzzle Cream-colored hair around these areas. This is a typical characteristic of the Exmoor pony.

Whorls are areas of hair formed around a center spot that look like small wheels. Their positioning is unique to each horse, and they provide a very useful means of identification.

Other markings are sometimes given to the pony or horse by its owner to provide a means of identification. They include branding (usually under the saddle), freeze marking, lip and ear tattoos, and hoof numbering.

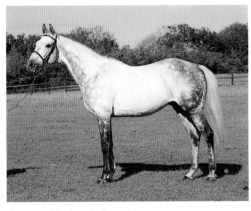

A gray with dappled markings

An Appaloosa with a variety of spots

they may be flea-bitten, where the coat is covered with little dark specks. Except for albino, grays are usually born dark in color; sometimes they are almost black and get lighter with age.

Duns vary greatly. They may be a golden cream or a mouse color or even silver with black points. Many have a list (that is, a black line down the spine), and they often have zebra marks on their legs.

Roans are a mixture of two or more colors. The blue roan has black and white hairs, giving it a bluish tinge. Bay and white hairs produce the bay or red roan. Chestnut and white hairs produce a strawberry roan.

Palominos have a golden coat with a white mane and tail. Ideally the color should look like a newly minted gold coin (see p.102).

Cream is the shade of pale cream to white on a pink skin. The horse's eyes should be dark. If they have blue or wall-eyes, they are usually called cremellos.

Piebalds, often called Pinto, have large areas of black and white. Very often they have wall eyes, especially if the face is predominantly white. (See the Pinto, p.102)

Skewbalds have areas of white with bay or chestnut patches, and often have wall-eyes. Some horses have a mixture of more than two colors, in which case they are known as odd-colored.

Appaloosas or spotted horses or ponies have a variety of spots of all shapes and sizes, but generally fall into one of the five basic patterns: leopard, marble, blanket, snowflake, or frosted. In the U.S.A., great efforts have been made to standardize the Appaloosa as a breed.

Leopard Here, the base color is white with black spots distributed over the entire body.

Near leopard The horse is born with leopard marks, but the head, legs, and sometimes the shoulders are of a darker color, which sometimes fades as the horse matures.

Marble The base color is dark when the horse is born. It can fade almost to white except for "varnish" marks on the horse's legs and head.

Spotted blanket This is a horse with a dark front with a white blanket of spots over the loin and quarters.

White blanket This is a dark front with a white blanket with few or no spots at all.

Few spot Here the horse has leopard markings with very few spots but some blue or red marks. The base color is white.

Snowflake The base color is dark with white spots. The horse is often born with a solid color coat, and the spots gradually appear later as the coat changes.

Frosted Here there is a dark base color with either frost or spots which appear later.

Buying a horse

Whatever method you use to buy your horse, and from whatever source you buy it, it is always wise to have an experienced knowledgeable person to advise you and give a second opinion.

Many horses are bought and sold through advertisements in equestrian journals. Prepare a list of questions before telephoning the owner, and try to gain as much information as possible before making arrangements to see the horse. Horse dealers today run a fairly reputable service, though they can be costly. They often arrange for the horse to be taken on a trial period, subject to strict scrutiny, by the prospective new owner.

The best method of buying is through personal recommendation. Spread the word through your friends and your local riding school that you are looking for a horse or pony. Many equestrian centers act as unofficial dealers, with a number of horses at livery, waiting to be sold on. It is said that all horses are for sale, for the right price, so do not feel shy about approaching owners direct if a horse catches your eye while visiting a local horse show.

How to look at a horse

Once you have found a suitable horse, and one that you can afford, the inspection procedure is always the same. The first rule is to take with a pinch of salt any claims of success in the show ring or competitions unless they are backed up by documentary evidence. Arrive early for the appointment so that you can see the horse in his stall. Take note of his stable manners as you or the groom enter the stall. Ask if he is easy to shoe, load into a trailer or truck and a good traveler.

As he is led out of the stable in a halter, study his outlook. Does he look keen, bright, and alert, or a little headstrong and willful or downright lazy? Watch the horse carefully as he is walked and then trotted in hand past you on both sides, toward you and away from you. Make sure the handler uses a long, free rein so as not to interfere with the horse's action or head carriage. The ears and tail are good indicators of his attitude and general wellbeing; a crookedly held tail can be a sign of back trouble. Now watch the horse being ridden. See how he looks tacked up. Notice how the rider is riding him and how much effort is needed to encourage the horse or quieten him during basic schooling exercises.

Finally, before going to the expense of a veterinary examination, ask yourself, "Is this the horse for me?"

Veterinary certificates

If you are seriously interested in buying a horse, make a preliminary offer, subject to a thorough veterinary inspection. Beware of the owner who offers to supply you with an existing certificate or warranty; you could find yourself expected to pay for this.

Make sure your vet is clear about the purpose for which you are buying the horse. A thorough inspection should take around two hours, after which you will be given a certificate which claims the horse is "sound in wind and limb," (but only for the amount of work it will be expected to do in the near future). The vet will confirm the horse's age and will check all vaccination and worming records and breed certificates made available. If asked, he or she will advise you on future diet and medication, on insurance, your legal rights, and your obligations as the new owner, plus any freeze-marking or other means of identification you may wish to use. The veterinary certificate is valued as good assurance; nevertheless, the onus of the transaction still falls on the new owner.

When trying a horse with a purchase in mind, first look at it in the stable to see if it is quiet, then see it stood up in a halter outside, and watch its behavior to decide if you like its general make and shape. Watch it run up in hand toward and away from you so that you can assess the straightness of movement and its general action. See it ridden and, if you think it is suitable for you, ride it yourself to get the feel of it. Do not let yourself be bamboozled by sales talk if you have any doubts.

Conformation

When choosing a horse, its type and shape need to be looked at very carefully. You also have to consider its suitability for the job you have in mind.

- Is the horse or pony the right type and size? For instance, a light-boned horse is unlikely to be the right horse for show jumping.
- Is the horse well-proportioned with a strong and well-balanced look?
- Does the horse move well? Is its action true and straight, with good flowing strides, or is it very upright with a short, choppy stride?
- Has the horse got good feet and clean, strong legs?
- Do you like the overall first impression, and does the horse really appeal to you?

If you cannot say yes to these five important points, the horse is almost certainly not going to be worth bothering about. If, however, you like what you have seen so far, then it is certainly worth taking a more serious look at each part of the animal in turn and having a ride, if this is feasible.

When checking over a horse, always start at the front and work to the back, as follows: **The head and neck** should be pleasing to the eye and in proportion to the horse's body. There should be plenty of room through the jaw with a nicely arched neck to set it off. The eye is most important, and a kindly, generous expression should be sought out. Too much white or small, piggy eyes usually indicate obstinate or difficult animals. The angle at which the neck joins the head may influence how the horse carries its head, and this will be of paramount importance if you are choosing a dressage horse or one to be successful in the show ring. A head set on too low or too high will always influence the head carriage. A large or heavy head may tip the horse onto its

Conformation defects

There are several defects in conformation which should generally be avoided, some being more serious than others. While no animal is likely to be perfect, most aspects of a horse need to be good if the occasional defect is to be excused.

Ewe necks tend to mean a weakness and in any case will always be rather unsightly and spoil the overall look.

Hollow and roach backs can be caused by weakness, mineral deficiency, or arthritis. (Although unsightly, a horse with a hollow back can still provide a very comfortable ride.)

Goose rumps, although rather strange to look at, often indicate a good jumper, but they would not be acceptable in a show horse.

Pigeon toes (toes turned inward) and **cow hocks** (toes turned outward) tend to lead to strain in the joints.

Sickle hocks denote weakness.

Curbs and thoroughpins (strains in the hock) are caused by strain and weakness in the joint. Minor curbs may not cause too much trouble.

Bog and bone spavins can cause lameness in the hock area, and their seriousness depends on how much they are affecting the hock action. Bone spavins are much the more serious as they are a permanent condition and result in the horse being unable to continue in any serious work.

Illustration labels: ewe neck; long, hollow back; goose rump; roman nose; weak thigh muscles; weak shoulder muscles; sickle hocks; shallow girth; capped hock; cow hocks; long, thin cannon bones; bog spavin; curb; thoroughpin; splint; small, boxy feet

The points of the horse

Knowing the correct names for the various parts of the horse's body is most important. The illustration below provides a comprehensive guide to the different parts of a horse, which are known collectively as "the points of the horse."

forehand. Roman-nosed horses are often thought to be very genuine in character: beware, however, of horses with a bump between the eyes; they are often stubborn and headstrong.

The ears should be alert and usually carried forward. Those horses with ears which are usually laid back may have a bad temper or an ungenerous disposition.

The shoulders should be deep and slope back from the point to the withers. Straight shoulders produce a choppy ride and often get jarred up as well as usually feeling very short in front. The withers should be of a reasonable height, but if they are too pronounced it may be difficult to fit a saddle.

The chest should be fairly broad and strong. Narrow-chested horses are often on the weak side and are prone to brushing. They may also be less footsure than broader-chested horses.

The limbs should be straight and strong, dropping directly from the shoulder to the ground. There should be plenty of bone, measured from just below the knee.

The knees should be flat and straight and not tilting backwards (back at the knee). A slight tilting forward (over the knee) is much less serious and unlikely to cause strain, but if the tilting is excessive, the horse may be prone to stumbling.

The cannon bones should be short and flat, when seen from the side, with plenty of bone; long cannons are less strong. Tendons and ligaments should stand out prominently.

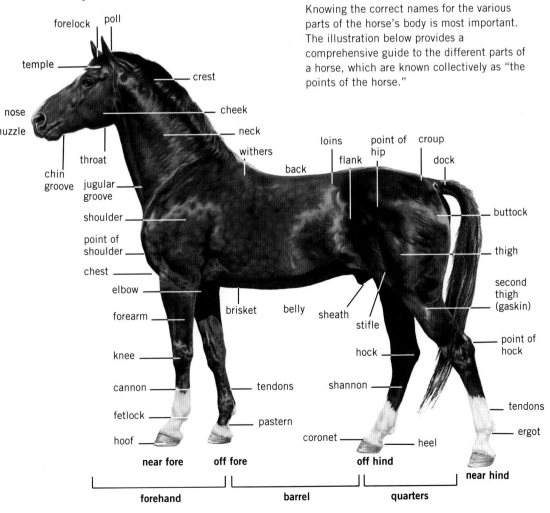

Illustration labels: forelock; poll; temple; crest; nose; muzzle; cheek; neck; throat; chin groove; jugular groove; withers; loins; flank; point of hip; croup; dock; back; shoulder; point of shoulder; chest; elbow; forearm; brisket; belly; sheath; stifle; buttock; thigh; second thigh (gaskin); knee; cannon; tendons; hock; shannon; point of hock; fetlock; pastern; tendons; ergot; hoof; coronet; heel; near fore; off fore; off hind; near hind; forehand; barrel; quarters

The fetlocks should be strong and free from signs of age such as windgalls or puffiness. Very round joints (apple joints) are not favored as they are prone to knocks and strains.

The pasterns should be strong, of medium length, and sloping. Upright pasterns tend to cause jarring and provide an uncomfortable ride. If they are very sloping, while they may make a very comfortable ride, they are also prone to strain.

The feet are perhaps the most important feature of all. First check that both front and hind feet are a matching pair. Front feet are rounder than hind feet and should have a balanced look about them. The angle of the foot should be uniform and slope at approximately 50° to the ground. Feet that turn out may cause brushing, which in turn can cause lameness if excessive. Pigeon toes or the habit of turning the toe in can affect the fetlock joint, but unless this trait is very pronounced, it is generally less serious. Flat feet or feet with thin soles tend to be prone to corns and bruising, and they generally have rather weak, low heels; extra care and the use of pads may be needed.

Narrow or "boxy" feet tend to have contracted heels and seldom stand up to serious work; they may also be an indication of navicular disease. A horse with really unmatching feet should be avoided at all costs, as should horses with roughened or ringed walls in their feet, as this is a sure sign of founder, although mild rings may be caused simply by a sudden change in diet. In extreme cases, X-rays may be required to determine the bone structure of the feet and are often used to diagnose suspected cases of navicular disease, pedal ostitis, or ringbone.

The back and barrel The rib cage should be deep and well sprung, allowing ample room for the vital organs. The back should be short and strong with good heart room (i.e. a large girth), giving the impression of a tough, athletic horse. Long, weak backs with flat sides and narrow chests usually indicate a lack of thriftiness, and these horses are generally poor doers.

Mares are often longer in the back than colts or geldings, but they should still be strong over the loins and elsewhere. Exceptionally short backs may mean the horses provide uncomfortable rides, and they may not have scope over big fences.

The hindquarters should be strong and well-muscled on the mature horse, with well-proportioned angles from hip to stifle to hock. The points of the hip should be square and even with well-formed thighs, and the points of the hock should sit directly under the point of the buttock.

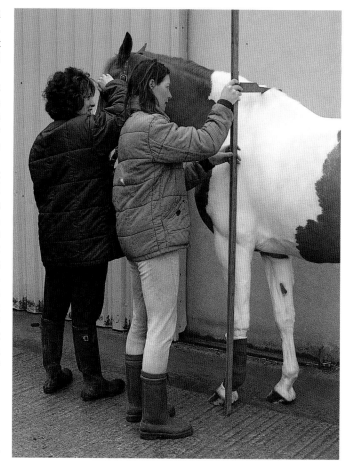
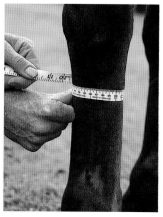

Height is an important point, especially if you intend to enter for shows or competitions where this plays a part. Be sure that you get your horse measured offically before you buy if competitions are to play a major part in your riding career. Having a "lot of bone" is a sign of strength as a horse's legs take a great deal of strain. The picture above demonstrates measuring of the cannon bone. This is always done just below the knee on the foreleg.

The hocks should be large and of a good angle, and the horse should be well-muscled right up under the tail. Those "split up the back" tend to be weak behind. Viewed from behind, the quarters should appear rounded and strong with the hocks directly below and the limbs straight, down to the heels. From the side they should be strong and well-muscled with the hocks well underneath to provide an overall appearance of strength.

The tail should be set at a good angle and not too low down, and it should be carried centrally and straight. A tail that tends to kink, look stiff, or is held to one side can be an indication of back problems. For dressage and showing, the tail position can enhance the performance, so this should always be taken into account.

Height

The size of the horse can make quite a difference to your assessment. It must be the right size for you and for what is required of it. Remember that a big horse may be perfectly controllable in fairly quiet conditions, such as cantering around a show ring or an indoor school, but that same horse might be very difficult to manage when galloping downhill toward a big solid fence during a day's hunting.

Horses are measured at the shoulder from the highest point of the withers. They are traditionally measured in hands (that is, 4 in./10.16 cm), but metric measurements are now being used in some places. In most instances, animals of 15 hh (hands high), that is 60 in. (152.4 cm) and under, are ponies.

If a specific height is required for a particular sport or classes you are interested in, be sure to get the animal properly measured so that you are sure it qualifies on the day. Remember that horses are usually not considered mature until they are six years old, and they have certainly been known to grow even after this age.

Getting to know your horse

Grooming time and during general mucking out are excellent times to gain confidence and get to know your horse, and they are discussed thoroughly in Chapter 2. When you groom a horse regularly, it will not be long before you know every square inch of the animal and will instantly be able to detect any changes or swellings in the legs or elsewhere. The horse will usually appreciate what you are doing. Tidbits are often given to the horse; while it is all right to occasionally give a treat, tidbits should never be given on a regular basis as the horse may then come to expect them. If they do not appear, the animal may become bad-tempered, bite or even kick in its frustration. Feed tidbits only in moderation and never on a regular basis.

Watch your horse's eyes and ears to assess the likely reaction to noises or frightening objects. Understanding these two revealing indicators will certainly help to make up for the fact that the horse cannot speak

When you become acquainted with your horse, you must learn how to lead it with a halter and rope and how to tie it up securely. Always approach the horse gently and quietly from the front or the side where it can see you. Talk to it in soft low tones as you get near, gently put the lead rope around its neck, then put on the halter by slipping it over the nose and placing the headpiece over the poll before securing.

Lead the horse from the left side, and keep its head up in front, while you are walking at its shoulder. Do not let the horse drag behind you where you cannot see it, or it may trip you up or knock you if it becomes frightened by anything.

Getting to know your horse may take a bit of time until he relaxes into unfamiliar surroundings and adjusts to his new way of life.

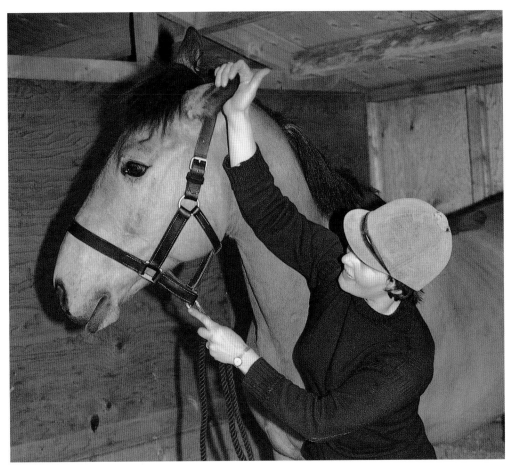

How to tie up a horse

Always follow the rule of "ring-string-rope." It is safest to have a piece of strong string fastened to the tie-up ring or post on which you intend to secure the horse. This is because, should the horse panic, the string will break rather than the halter. Occasionally a horse may learn to pull back and will do this for fun. Such a habit needs to be dealt with firmly before it becomes well-established and harder to break.

A safety quick-release knot is essential and must be used at all times when tying up a horse. This method of tying a knot must be learned before you tie up the horse for the first time.

Leave enough room above the knot so that, should the horse pull back and put pressure on the knot, it will not tighten up too close to the securing ring, which can sometimes make it difficult to release. To prevent the loop itself from becoming tight, loop the end through the first one loosely two or three times.

A safety quick-release knot

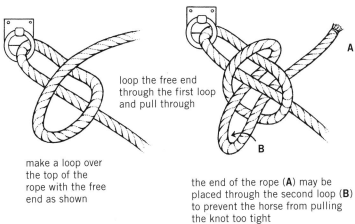

loop the free end through the first loop and pull through

make a loop over the top of the rope with the free end as shown

the end of the rope (**A**) may be placed through the second loop (**B**) to prevent the horse from pulling the knot too tight

One of the first lessons every rider must learn is how to put on a halter and lead the horse. The horse is usually led from the left side at the shoulder. On catching the horse, place the rope around its neck to deter him from moving away, and then quietly fit the halter over the nose and fasten the headpiece as shown. It is important to talk to the horse and approach him quietly. Horses will often come up to you when called, once they get to know you.

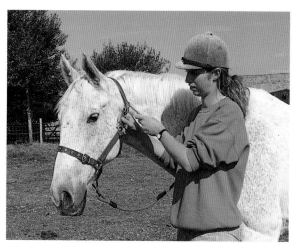

Tack

It is very important that the beginner learns early to understand how to tack up the horse and what the various items of tack are for and why they are used. Unfortunately many riding schools omit to teach this because it takes time. Very often the learner is presented with a fully tacked-up mount ready to ride and often becomes a quite proficient rider without ever having put on or taken off any of the animal's tack.

The bridle and saddle and their various accoutrements are shown below. The essentials are a snaffle bridle, a general purpose saddle with fitted irons of the correct size, leathers, and a suitable girth. If you intend to keep a horse and ride regularly, you will also need several other pieces of equipment, although exactly what you need very much depends on the amount of riding you intend to do and whether or not your horse will be permanently out at grass or stabled. These items are covered in a later chapter.

Tacking up

The horse should first be tied up in a halter and the required tack brought to the stable. The martingale, if used, is placed over the head first. The saddle cloth is then placed on the horse's back, at first well forward and then slid back into position, going with the lay of the coat and pulling the mane free over the withers. (A saddle pad, if used, should already be fitted under the saddle.) The saddle with the stirrup irons run up on the leathers and the girth already attached is

Tacking up

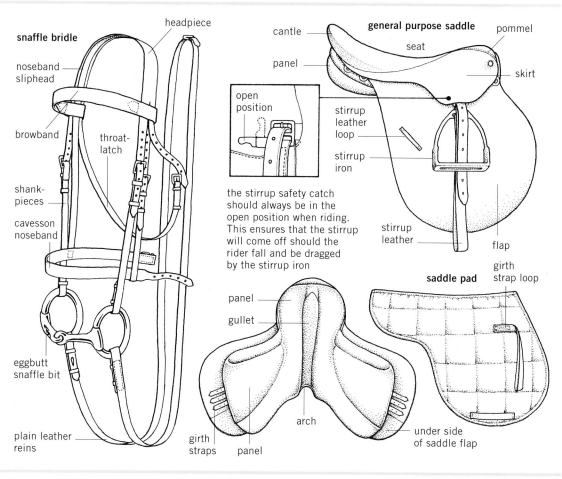

Always bring all the equipment you need to the horse when you are ready to tack up. The horse should have been brushed first so that it is clean and ready to go straight out when tacked up.

snaffle bridle
headpiece
noseband sliphead
browband
throat-latch
shank-pieces
cavesson noseband
eggbutt snaffle bit
plain leather reins

open position

the stirrup safety catch should always be in the open position when riding. This ensures that the stirrup will come off should the rider fall and be dragged by the stirrup iron

general purpose saddle
cantle
pommel
seat
panel
skirt
stirrup leather loop
stirrup iron
stirrup leather
flap

panel
gullet
arch
girth straps
panel

saddle pad
girth strap loop
under side of saddle flap

positioned on top, and the girth gently let down on the far side so that it does not knock the horse's legs.

Martingales Placing the neck strap of the martingale over the horse's head, check that everything is straight and untwisted before putting the martingale loop through the girth and fastening securely.

Do not tighten the girth too much at first, but be sure it is secure enough to hold the saddle in place without pinching the skin. Take the bridle and untie the throatlatch and noseband and place the reins over the horse's head. Take the bridle in your right hand, and draw it gently up the horse's head until the bit is near the mouth.

Hold the bit with your left hand, feeling between the horse's lips with your fingers to find the gap between the teeth at the side of the mouth. Draw up the bridle until the bit is taken into the horse's mouth, then ease the bridle first over one ear and then the other.

Ease out the mane and forelock; then straighten the browband and noseband if necessary. Do up the throatlatch, then the noseband, which is always placed inside the cheekpieces, being sure to push all the ends securely through the keepers. The throatlatch should allow for the full width of the hand

Above: a correctly fitted English saddle pad

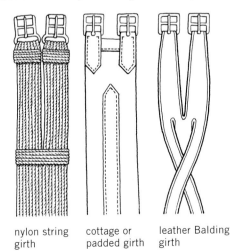

nylon string girth   cottage or padded girth   leather Balding girth

between it and the jaw bone. The noseband should allow for approximately two fingers to fit between it when tightened. Drop nosebands are placed below the bit, taking care to make sure that they do not get too low (or tight) to interfere with the horse's breathing.

The running martingale should be adjusted so that the rings reach just to the throat to make it the right length. The bridle reins are threaded through its rings without any twists. Rein stops, to prevent the rings from catching on the buckles or billets near the bit, must *always* be used.

The standing martingale should be attached to the cavesson noseband, after adjusting the length so that the end reaches to the top of the withers before attaching to the noseband.

Check that all is in order before leading the horse out by taking the reins over its head Lead from the left side with the reins held approximately 6 in. (15 cm) behind the bit with the slack in your left hand. Always check and tighten girths before mounting and again once you are on the horse and after your warm-up period.

To untack

Once you have dismounted, first run up the stirrup irons and loosen the girth. There are no particular rules about whether saddle or bridle comes off first, but generally the saddle is taken off first and the horse allowed roll and relax before being groomed.

To unsaddle Lift the saddle flap on the left side and undo the girths, letting them go gently so that they do not bang the legs. If used, unloop the martingale from the girth. With one hand under the front arch and the other on the cantle, lift the saddle up and slide it off toward you onto your arm, taking hold of the girths as they come over the back. Place the saddle gently on the stable door or a fence.

To take off the bridle, work from the bottom up. Undo the noseband and then the throatlatch. Undo the reins and slip off the running martingale rings, if necessary. With the reins and headpiece in your right hand, gently ease the bridle over one ear and then the other, giving the horse time to open its mouth to release the bit. Put your left hand on its nose as the bridle is eased off to stop it from throwing its head up and hurting its mouth before the bit is out. If this happens it might be headshy about the bridle next time. Slip the martingale over the head and tie the horse up or leave it to relax and roll.

Take the saddle and bridle to the tack-room, and put them up on a saddle rack and hook ready for cleaning. Rinsing the bit immediately will save a lot of soaking later.

Cleaning tack

All tack requires regular care and inspection if it is to remain in good condition and last well.

Equipment required:
- Sponge or rough rag (toweling) for cleaning
- Small sponge for soap
- Saddle soap
- Metal polish
- Leather polish and brushes
- Soft dry cloth
- Bucket of warm, soapy water

How to clean the bridle
- Having taken the bridle apart, thoroughly clean all parts with a dampened rag or sponge and wipe dry with a towel.
- Apply saddle soap on as dry a sponge as possible on both sides of the leather and particularly in any creases. Take care not to apply too much, as it will make the leather feel sticky. Show bridles may need a coating of leather polish to restore their color and shine.
- Thoroughly dry all metal parts and, if necessary, use metal polish on the bit rings only and rub off. Never apply metal polish to the bit.
- Put the bridle back together and hang it on the bridle peg with the reins fitted through the throatlatch and the noseband wrapped around the outside of the bridle.

How to clean the saddle
- Once the girths, pads, stirrup irons, and leathers have been removed, the saddle needs a good wipe all over with a damp cloth to remove the dirt and sweat.
- While you are doing this, the irons can be soaking in warm water.
- Saddle-soap all parts of the saddle thoroughly, including the girth straps, underneath the saddle flap, and on the underside.
- Polish the irons, removing the rubber treads to clean and dry them before replacing.
- Once a week all tack should be thoroughly cleaned, soaped, and oiled with neatsfoot oil or leather dressing.
- Leather girths require a good clean and soaping. Webbing needs brushing with a stiff brush.
- Saddle pads and cloths should be brushed or washed in mild detergent.
- Regularly check all tack not in use, and keep it covered up in a dry place.

Mounting (English saddle)

First check your girths and tighten if necessary, making sure that both stirrup irons are down with the leathers approximately at the right length. If you are a beginner, it is essential to have someone with you until you have mastered this none-too-easy first step in riding. Standing on the left side, take the stick and reins in your left hand, held short enough to prevent the horse from moving forward, with your hand resting on the withers. Face to the rear standing close to the horse's shoulder and place your left foot in the stirrup. With the right hand, turn the stirrup toward you and guide it over the foot. As you pivot around, avoid digging your toe into the horse's side. Place your right hand on the seat of the saddle and swing your body up, straighten the knees and swing your right leg over the saddle, taking care not to kick the horse on the rump. Ease gently down into the saddle and quietly organize yourself, putting your right foot in the stirrup; check that your stirrup leathers are the correct length and are equal before taking the reins in both hands and moving off. Check your girths once more after a quiet warm-up period.

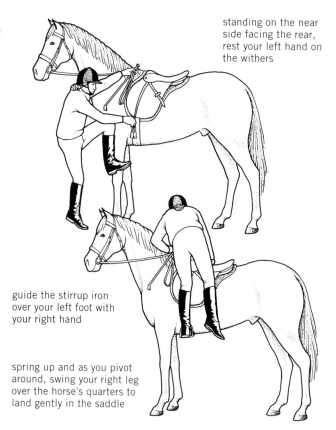

standing on the near side facing the rear, rest your left hand on the withers

guide the stirrup iron over your left foot with your right hand

spring up and as you pivot around, swing your right leg over the horse's quarters to land gently in the saddle

Mounting is not the easiest of maneuvers and may need quite a bit of practise, especially by beginners. The mounting block makes it a much easier exercise and also saves putting pressure on the horse's spine, as does having a leg up (see below center) if you have an expert helper at hand.

the rider faces the saddle and then springs up as the helper lifts her into the saddle

Mounting block The use of a block makes getting on a horse much easier, and it also puts much less strain on a horse's back as well as on the saddle and stirrup leathers. It is always worth alternating the stirrup leathers to avoid the left side one getting stretched with wear. Take the horse to the block close enough that it can be climbed with ease and proceed as before. The horse may need to learn to stand still beside the mounting block for the first few times, and a helper talking quietly may be needed. Make the horse stand still for a short while once you have mounted.

Having a leg up To give a rider a leg up, first check the girths and see that the stirrups are down. The rider should have the reins short and the whip in the left hand, with the right hand on and facing the seat of the saddle. The helper works out a system with the rider on exactly when to spring up, such as "one, two, three, up." The rider bends the left leg as a pivot, and the helper holds the leg at the knee and ankle. At the agreed signal the rider springs up off the right foot and is lifted up high enough to put the right leg over the saddle and then eases gently into the saddle as the helper lets go of the other leg.

To tighten the girths when mounted Once mounted, tighten the girths immediately before moving off. Take the reins in one hand just lightly enough to keep the horse still. Place your left leg forward of the saddle flap, with your foot still in the stirrup, and lift up the saddle flap, feeling for the girth straps. If these are not sufficiently tight, ease up the girth one hole at a time, making sure both straps are even. Pull down the girth guards and put the flap back into position. Put your legs back in place before moving. When the horse has warmed up, tighten the girths once more.

The correct position

the shoulders should be square and relaxed with the head up and looking forward

Ideally it should be possible to draw an imaginary line straight from the top of your head down through the hip to the ankle. The rider's weight should follow through this line.

there should be a straight line from the elbow through the wrist to the bit

the balls of the feet should rest in the stirrups with the heel positioned lower than the toe

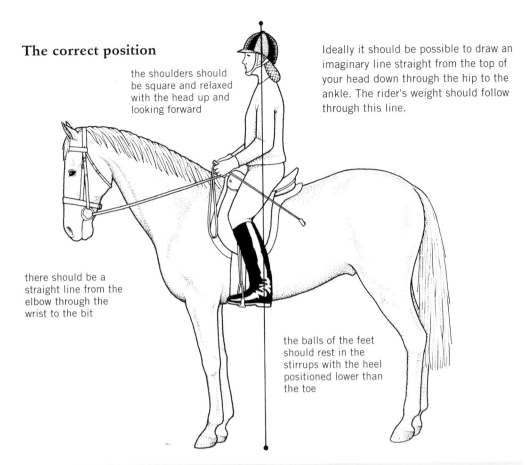

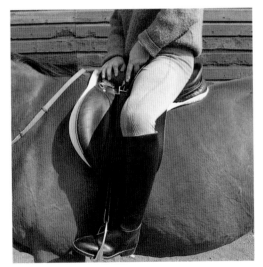

To alter the stirrup length when mounted Take both reins in one hand and, keeping both feet lightly in the stirrups, take hold of the end of one of the leathers and ease it upward. Once free of the stirrup bar, the buckle can be shifted to ease out the tongue into a shorter or longer hole. Pull the buckle back up to the top of the bar. Repeat the process with the other stirrup. Gently stand up in the stirrups to center your weight again before moving off.

Running up stirrup irons Once the stirrups have been run up, loop the leathers back through the stirrup iron to secure.

To dismount

First put the reins and stick in your left hand, and remove both feet from the stirrups. Place your left hand on the pommel of the saddle, then lean forward, and in one quiet but quick movement, swing your right leg back up over the saddle, taking care to make sure you do not kick the horse on the back. Slip off the horse and be prepared to land gently on both feet with bent knees. Pat your horse, run up your stirrup irons, take hold of the reins, and slip them over the horse's head ready for leading.

Mounting and dismounting generally takes place from the left side, but it should be possible to do it from either side (see Riding responsibly, p. 43).

running up stirrup irons

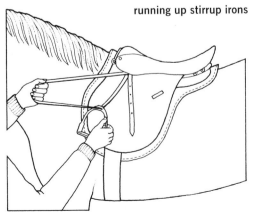

The rider's position

The rider's position will influence all the horse's movements, so it is vital that the way the rider sits on the saddle and the positioning of the body is correct from the start. The most important part of the body is the seat, which should always be central, relaxed and deep in the saddle. If you are not centered, you cannot use the rest of your body properly and stay balanced. The rider must be able to feel both seat bones evenly in the saddle and the body should be upright but relaxed, with the shoulders square but supple and the head up and looking forward. The arms should hang naturally and bend at the elbows, with the hands placed just above and on each side of the withers, with the thumbs uppermost. The legs should also hang naturally, allowing the hips, thighs, and knees to relax and with the balls of the feet resting (not standing) in the stirrups with a supple ankle and the heel lower than the toe.

The whole picture should be one of suppleness and balance, and this is most important once the horse starts to move. You must allow your body to relax and remain at one with the horse. It should be possible to draw an imaginary line straight from the top of your head down through the hip to the ankle. The rider's weight should follow through this line, from the head, down the spine, through the seat to the heels.

Control

The rider must be confident that he or she can control the horse. Although the degree of control depends largely on the horse's training, the idea that the rider can stop or move off at will makes for confidence.

In order to look at each part of the rider's body in detail, it is first necessary to discuss the rider's contact with the horse's mouth and how to hold the reins.

Holding the reins

The rider should be able to feel the horse with his hands through contact with the bit. There should be a straight line from the elbow through the wrist to the bit. The beginner should keep his hands low to start

with until his balance improves, and they should always be as still as possible.

The rein is held between the third and little finger, coming out over the palm between the thumb and index finger. The fingers should remain relaxed; a feel of the reins should be retained, but it must never be tight or stiff.

It is difficult but vital to learn to use the correct length of rein to maintain a light contact at all times without interfering with the horse's mouth.

The rider also has to learn to shorten or lengthen the reins without losing contact in the process, and to learn to ride always with an even length on both reins; otherwise, the horse will have to go forward crookedly.

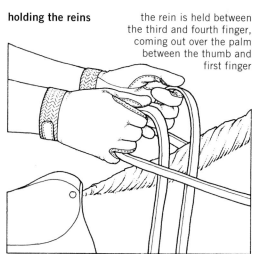

holding the reins

the rein is held between the third and fourth finger, coming out over the palm between the thumb and first finger

The aids

The aids are the rider's indications to the horse through the use of the hands, legs, seat, back, and voice, collectively known as the natural aids. Additional artificial aids include the whip and spurs (see p. 122) which supplement the rider's natural aids .

With the advanced rider, the aids become a subtle chain of messages which are clearly indicated to the horse, even though they are almost invisible to the untrained eye of the onlooker. Any shouting, pulling, kicking, and tugging is not acceptable and is certainly not the way to get the best out of your horse.

The hands

The hands are the most basic aid for controlling and steering the horse by controlling the direction of the head through the reins. A gentle resistance from the hand will tell the horse to slow down or stop. It is important for the beginner to understand that he should not tug the reins to the left, right, or backwards, even though this will probably give the desired result. The horse's mouth is very sensitive; just a small amount of pressure from the rider's third finger is enough to get the message across.

Using the legs in conjunction with the hands will create the correct balance and impulsion to enable the desired movements to take place easily. At all times the rider must indicate a give-and-take motion through the fingers. This allows for the upper and lower arm to be relaxed and in the correct position at all times. Even on a strong pulling horse, the arm muscles must never be set against the horse's mouth and neck. If the horse refuses to respond to your hands, use your legs, and, but only if necessary, use the stick to make it take notice.

A continuous pull on the reins will inflict pain and discomfort and create tension and

The rider in this photograph has managed to get her pony going very effectively by creating the right amount of impulsion with her legs. The pony is being controlled by a even contact on the reins. The rider has a strong seat and a good leg position with the weight going down through her heel. She is looking up and forward in the correct manner. The pony's frame has been shortened to create a good outline at collected trot, showing higher steps than would be the case with a working or a medium trot. However, the horse is slightly behind the bit. This could be corrected by a softer contact on the reins to avoid blocking the forward movement.

stiffness in the horse's mouth, jaw, and neck.

The hands are greatly influenced by the suppleness to be found in the shoulders, elbow, arm, wrist, and fingers. Above all they must be relaxed and still, with the fingers ready and able to "play" with the reins. On a bend, the inside hand indicates direction, while the outside hand controls the degree of bend, speed, and regulates the pace. With the more advanced rider, the hands may influence the position of the horse's head and neck.

The legs

The rider's legs control the horse's quarters, create impulsion, bend, and balance, and can be used independently of one another or together. The position of the legs is most important and is crucial to all types of riding.

The hips, knees, and ankle joints should be relaxed; this is essential if the horse is to receive the correct information from the rider. Stiffness in these joints will mask the effect of the aid. Used together, the legs keep the horse in balance. Used independently, the inside leg creates more bend and can also create greater energy when needed. The outer leg controls the quarters, preventing them from falling out, and holds them in the position required for certain movements. It also gives the command to canter, with a momentary squeeze and release as the horse responds.

Any kicking or excessive use of the heel is unacceptable as an aid and must be discouraged from the outset. Not only is it incorrect, but it allows the toes to point outward in an unsightly manner.

Using the aids

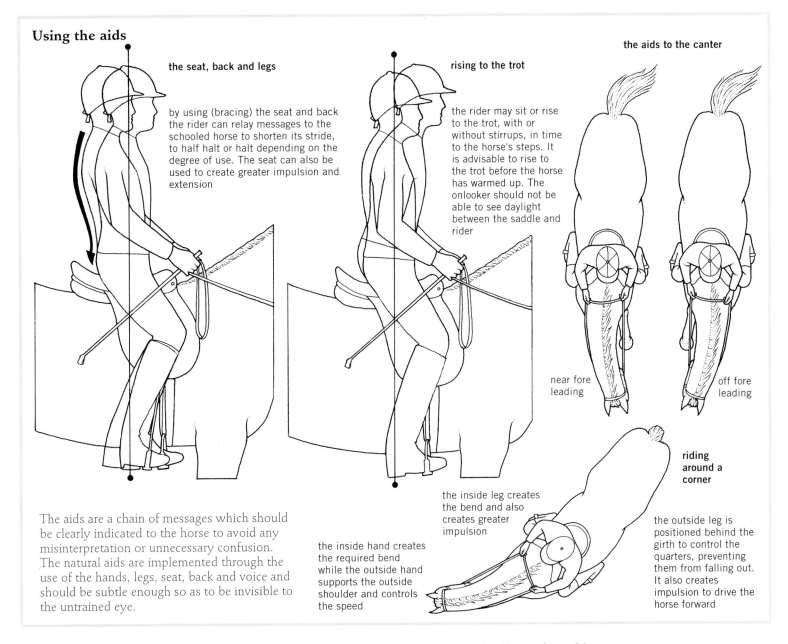

the seat, back and legs

by using (bracing) the seat and back the rider can relay messages to the schooled horse to shorten its stride, to half halt or halt depending on the degree of use. The seat can also be used to create greater impulsion and extension

rising to the trot

the rider may sit or rise to the trot, with or without stirrups, in time to the horse's steps. It is advisable to rise to the trot before the horse has warmed up. The onlooker should not be able to see daylight between the saddle and rider

the aids to the canter

near fore leading

off fore leading

riding around a corner

the inside leg creates the bend and also creates greater impulsion

the inside hand creates the required bend while the outside hand supports the outside shoulder and controls the speed

the outside leg is positioned behind the girth to control the quarters, preventing them from falling out. It also creates impulsion to drive the horse forward

The aids are a chain of messages which should be clearly indicated to the horse to avoid any misinterpretation or unnecessary confusion. The natural aids are implemented through the use of the hands, legs, seat, back and voice and should be subtle enough so as to be invisible to the untrained eye.

The seat and back

The seat should be deep and relaxed in the saddle, so that the rider becomes part of the horse. To achieve this successfully, it is essential to relax the hips. The seat, together with the back, influence the degree of impulsion, and the more schooled the horse, the more effective these aids can be. Balance is essential; allowing the weight to come too far forward or go too far back will greatly affect the horse's ability to move correctly.

The back must relax with the horse's movement. Any stiffness will quickly be relayed to the horse, creating a tenseness and shortening of the stride or even a signal to halt. The rider must remain supple and upright without straining, with the shoulders relaxed and head held up and looking forward. Here it is as well to note that the position of the rider's head can considerably affect the horse as it is the heaviest part of the human body and any tilting will affect the rider's weight distribution, thereby affecting the horse's balance and any aids given.

The voice

The voice can be used in a number of useful ways, for instance to issue commands, to control, to encourage, soothe, and reward the horse.

If in its early training the horse has learned to obey words such as "whoa," "walk on," "trot" and "canter," other aids will be used mainly to complement the voice. It is the tone of the voice that is important to the horse. Whether soothing, encouraging or sharp, it must be consistent.

The whip

Used with discretion, this is an extremely useful artificial aid. It can be seen as an extension of the natural aids, to reach the parts of the horse which the natural aids cannot (for example, the quarters), and a gentle tickle with the stick can regain the horse's attention. It is carried in the inside hand, unless it is specifically needed to reinforce an outside leg aid.

Its use can create extra impulsion and is used for schooling and special training. The whip should be used only rarely as a form of punishment; here, the voice should suffice.

All young horses should be schooled or ridden with a whip. Like all tack, the whip should become an everyday item of equipment, but its presence should never evoke fear in the young horse.

The paces of the horse

The horse has four natural basic paces: walk, trot, canter, and gallop.

The walk is a marching pace in which there are four beats to one stride as each foot hits the ground in turn, and it should be possible to count "one," "two," "three," "four," evenly as the horse moves. There are four main types of walk: free, working or medium, collected, and extended.

The sequence of the footfalls in walk are near hind, near fore, off hind, off fore. There will always be two feet on the ground at any one time. Occasionally some horses get out of sequence and put an opposite front with a near foot, causing the horse to "pace."

At the walk the horse uses its head and neck, and it is important that these are not in any way restricted by the rider; otherwise, the horse will tense up or shorten its stride.

The trot is a two-time pace in which the horse moves his legs in diagonal pairs. The sequence in trot is near hind and off foreleg, then off hind and near foreleg.

The horse's neck will shorten slightly, and the head should be steady. The steps should always be even and regular with good elevation, and it should be easy to count "one," "two," "one," "two," when trotting. There are four main trots: working, collected, medium, and extended.

The canter is a three-beat pace, and it should be possible to count "one," "two," "three," "pause," "one," "two," "three," "pause." Three beats take place, followed by a moment of suspension when all four feet are off the ground before the next stride.

If the horse is balanced, the canter should be light and controlled with some movement of the horse's head as it takes each stride. The sequence of footfalls in canter will depend which foreleg it is leading with. If the horse is leading with the near foreleg, the foot sequence will be: off hind, off fore and near hind together, then near fore, followed by a moment of suspension.

Occasionally the horse becomes unbalanced and disunited, whereby the leading hindleg is on the same side as the leading foreleg. The animal may also be doing a false or counter lead, in which case it is going to the right with the near fore leading or to the left with the off fore leading.

The gallop is the fastest pace, in "four time." In a gallop, the horse really lengthens its stride and stretches over the maximum amount of ground. The sequence with the off foreleg leading is: near hind, off hind, near fore, off fore, followed by a period of suspension. With the near foreleg leading, it is: off hind, near hind, off fore, near fore, with a moment of suspension.

the walk

the trot momentary suspension

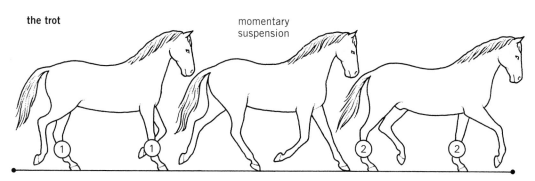

the canter – with the near fore leading (3) moment of suspension

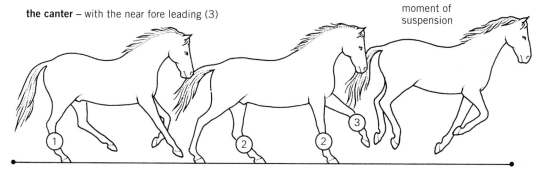

the gallop – with the off fore leading (4) moment of suspension

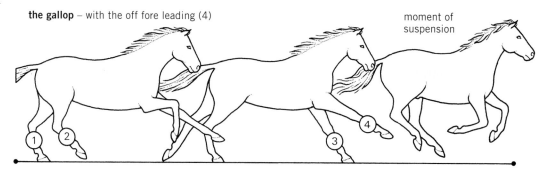

A transition

A transition is the change of pace or speed from one to another. It should be done as smoothly as possible and will only be achieved after proper preparation on the part of the rider and obedience on the part of the horse. Each transition should flow and not cause any change of rhythm or balance. A transition will only be really successful if the horse is going well in its existing pace. Transitions become increasingly important as the horse becomes more advanced in its work, as within the pace a clear difference is required to demonstrate the change from a collected to a medium or to an extended movement. Transitions from one pace to another need to be very well executed and call for the utmost obedience.

Work on the lunge

Whatever level of ability, the rider can derive tremendous benefit from being lunged on the horse. When lunging, you can concentrate totally on yourself rather than worrying about the horse. The instructor will control the horse and keep it at the right rhythm and pace so that you only need to think about what you are doing.

It can be an excellent exercise to gain an independent seat, that is, a balanced seat without the use of the reins and stirrups as means of support.

Once you have mastered the basics of mounting, walking, and trotting, and can manage these without any help, and can also stop, start, and steer your horse in a well-balanced manner, you will very likely benefit from a few lunge lessons.

Safety is of paramount importance, so a steady, sensible horse is necessary. A young or nervous animal would not be suitable. When doing exercises when the horse is standing still, the instructor should always stand at the horse's head to make sure it does not move at a critical moment.

Lungeing exercises will help to loosen up the rider, improve balance, coordination and confidence, and get the horse and rider more "together." The reins should be knotted up to prevent them from flapping if an exercise is to be performed without them. The stirrups should either be removed or the buckle pulled away from the stirrup bar and then crossed over in front of the saddle out of the way. The rider should always be encouraged to breathe normally throughout the exercise.

Exercises at the halt

These are designed to relax and loosen the rider; children usually find them quite easy, but adults tend to be stiffer and so find them more difficult. The horse must be held when all these exercises, except the first one, are performed.

Leaning forward to touch your toes First raise the right hand slowly above your head and bend over to touch the right foot; next do the same with the left hand, then sit up straight again. When you have mastered this, you can progress one stage further. Lift the right hand above your head and lean over to touch the left foot without either leg swinging back as you bend over, then sit up straight again. Repeat once or twice and then do the same on the other side. This exercise helps balance and suppleness.

Hugging the knees The legs are drawn up slowly as high as possible, and the knees hugged before being slowly returned to position. Alternatively the knees can be drawn up and the ankles clasped. Repeat

Work on the lunge is invaluable to help improve the rider's position, balance, and coordination.

once or twice. This exercise helps to keep the knees and thighs supple.

Exercises on the move

The following exercises can be done standing still, but if done at the walk or trot they will be particularly useful in helping balance and coordination as well as suppleness.

Raising the arms above the head and counting "one," "two," "three," in time to the rhythm of the horse before bringing them down and repeating the words once more. Do this two or three times to start with. The next step is to put the arms forward and counting, and then sideways. The complete sequence might end up something like "up and one, two, three, down, out and one, two, three, down and forward and one, two, three, relax."

Swinging the arms is another exercise which helps to loosen the waist and improve balance. Start by lifting both hands out sideways; then slowly twist the body and arms around in one direction as far as possible. Relax, then repeat twisting the other way. This exercise is best started in walk; only if the rider is proficient and has good balance should it be done in trot.

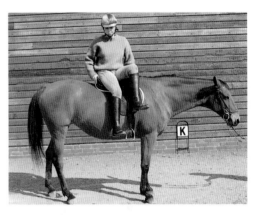

Round the world This is a children's favorite. Draw the legs up and over the horse's quarters and swing around in the saddle to face backwards, then continue around to return to the original position. This exercise is good for balance and coordination. For safety the stirrup irons should have been crossed over in front of the saddle.

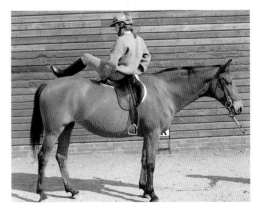

Riding without stirrups

This is the best way to improve your riding, to concentrate on your position in the saddle, and to learn balance on the horse at all paces. Depending on the ability of the rider, riding without stirrups can be undertaken in walk, trot, or canter, with the rider making particular efforts to make a smooth transition from one pace to another. This exercise should never be attempted until the rider has a fully independent seat and does not hang onto the reins for security.

Seen without stirrups, a rider's faults are more noticeable. The instructor can see more clearly the balance of the rider and how he or she reacts to a slowing or quickening of pace. The leg position is normally a problem area, and the rider often finds it difficult to relax the hips enough to remain low and central in the saddle, with the leg held long and relaxed, the toes up and in, and the heels deep.

Being lunged or riding without stirrups are both excellent ways to practice concentrating on your position and balance. This is true at all stages in your riding career, and you are just as likely to see Olympic riders as beginners practicing without stirrups.

It cannot be over-emphasised how important safety is when working in this way, particularly for an inexperienced rider. A quiet environment, an enclosed area, a suitable horse, and good instructor are vital. For the unfit or inexperienced, work without stirrups can be very strenuous and should not be overdone.

riding without stirrups

Riding in a manège or school

One of the best ways to improve riding skills is to work in an arena. In an enclosed space it is possible to concentrate more easily on specific points and to work toward doing things at a particular time. It will help with balance and coordination as well as control and confidence.

There are two sizes of arena. The usual size is 65 x 131 ft. (20 m x 40 m) and the larger 65 x 196 ft. (20 m x 60 m). They are both used for training, schooling, and dressage tests worldwide. An arena is marked with letters at different points along the sides and, when competing, you have to imagine additional markers down the center line.

Schooling areas may be larger than these two standard arenas, but it is worth getting used to their shape and lettering if you want to venture into dressage or eventing. Once you are confident and have mastered various exercises on the horse in an enclosed area, you will find riding out in the open much more enjoyable and relaxing.

Simple schooling exercises

Simple exercises which the rider needs to master include the following:

Riding in a straight line For this it is essential that you can make the horse go forward. An even contact on the reins and a strong leg, keeping the horse moving energetically, will help to keep the animal straight. This may be relatively easy along the sides of the arena, but try going across the center or quarter lines and see how much more difficult it is without the side walls to guide you.

It is also possible that your horse will hug the wall with its shoulder, giving the illusion of going straight as its forehand is narrower than its quarters. This will without doubt mean that it is going crookedly. A little more inside leg will correct this.

Circles Going around in circles requires a horse to go forward well if the rhythm is to be maintained and the circle is to be uniform. The curve in the horse's body should correspond to the circle being ridden.

It is most important that the rider sits up straight and in the center of the saddle and does not collapse the hip bones or lean to the inside of the circle. The rider's shoulders must also be straight, following the line of the circle. The horse must be bent slightly to the inside to achieve this.

The rider should just be able to see the inside eye of the horse. This can be achieved by releasing a little contact on the outside rein and taking up a little on the inside rein. A bend of the head or quarters to the outside is incorrect.

The size of the circles that riders are normally asked to execute vary, the largest being 65 ft. (20 m) and the smallest 32 ft. (10 m).

Serpentines are movements whereby the horse executes a series of loops, changing direction and bend on crossing the center of the arena. As the serpentine becomes more advanced, requiring more turns, the degree of change of bend will become more exaggerated. There should not be too much neck bend. As when riding circles, there is a danger of the rider, having achieved the correct neck bend, to assume the horse has taken up the correct position. This is not so unless the quarters follow through on the bend as well. This can be controlled by the use of a stronger outside hand to prevent the horse from bending its neck to the inside too much, and a strong outside leg to avoid the quarters swinging outward. Serpentines can be performed at walk, trot, and canter, with "simple changes" over the center line to change leg.

Half circles off the track require the rider to ease the horse off the long side of the track, performing half of a 65 ft. (20 m)-circle before reaching the opposite side, for example

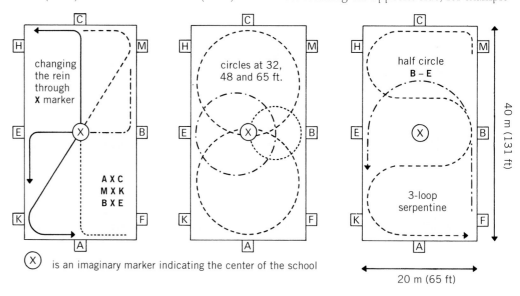

X is an imaginary marker indicating the center of the school

from the B to the E marker. The art is to perform all these exercises without any change of pace or rhythm.

The halt requires the horse to stop and stand quite still and balanced without stepping forward or backward. The horse should stand four-square, and its halt should not be abrupt.To achieve a good halt the rider should ask the horse to slow down with a sensitive give-and-take on the reins combined with a deep seat and stiffened back (see half halt p.112) with both legs on, keeping the horse moving forward up "into the bridle" to keep it off its forehand. Sit quite still and relaxed until you want to move off again.

The rein back is really a progression from the halt. First establish a halt, keeping the horse steady. Ask for a forward movement by squeezing with both legs, but restrict the horse with your hands, thus blocking the forward movement so that it steps back instead. Keep asking with the legs, restricting forward movement until the desired amount of backward steps are achieved. Start with one or two steps until you have mastered the technique of stepping backward in a straight line, with even, rhythmic steps. The horse should never be pulled or forced but "asked" to step back slowly.

Unlike the forward walk, the rein back is executed with diagonal pairs of legs, the near hind and off fore being moved together and then the off hind and near foreleg. It is an excellent exercise for getting the horse's hocks underneath him, and why show jumpers often execute a rein back before starting to jump a round. Only three or four steps backward should be attempted; otherwise, the horse's hocks will be so far underneath it is likely to lose balance.

These are straightforward movements which should be mastered early. It is worth practicing them in all paces, although the serpentine in canter is an advanced movement which will be covered under dressage.

Riding faults

Poking the head forward This is extremely common. Unfortunately, it influences the whole of the rider's position. The head is extremely heavy and must be kept upright. If it is too far forward, it upsets the balance. Always sit up and face forward.

Rounding back and stiff arms The back must be kept straight but not stiff. If the head pokes forward, the back will inevitably round slightly, so sit up. Draw the shoulders up and back before relaxing into a supple, erect position. Once the back is straight, let the arms hang naturally, then softly bend them at the elbows, keeping the wrists and fingers supple. Stiff arms will always affect the horse's going.

Gripping upward with thighs and knees This is a common fault, particularly with beginners who have not learned to relax and lengthen their leg properly into the movement of the horse. Riders have to "open the hip joints" so that they get low enough into the center of the saddle. They then have to stay relaxed enough to make sure there is no daylight visible between them and their horses in trot and canter. If the hips are relaxed, the rest of the leg will be less inclined to shorten. Do not grip with the knees; this tends to push you up out of the saddle.

The knees should be supple with a light contact on the saddle, the thighs relaxed and the tip of the toe directly below the point of the knee. With the seat, knee, and thigh in position, the lower leg is free to move and exert pressure as needed.

Toes down – heels up This is actually the opposite of what is required and will certainly tend to happen if the rider is riding with a shortened leg. First master the correct leg position, then with the stirrup positioned across the widest part of the foot, sink the heel down with a supple ankle joint. It is vital for your whole position that the leg is correctly placed and that the lower leg is free to move. This is impossible if the heel comes up. The toes should be pointing up and forward at all times.

Leaning forward With a very novice rider, leaning forward to help maintain balance is understandable, but as confidence grows, to be effective the rider must sit up straight and drive the horse forward. Unless the legs are firmly applied, the rider who leans forward will find the impulsion is having no effect, as his movement is encouraging the horse on to its forehand. Sit up and get your leg position correct and be sure to keep your head up.

Leaning back This causes stiffness and a dead seat, and will probably make the horse shorten its stride, for when leaning back the rider tends to push down hard into the saddle, making it uncomfortable for the horse on that part of its back. The legs cannot be properly effective if the rider leans back, as his knees will be raised, the thigh muscles will tighten, and balance will be affected. Sit relaxed in the saddle, and keep the line from shoulder to hip to ankle joint straight.

Hanging over on one side This is a very bad fault. The rider must sit centrally in the saddle, positioned square on the horse's shoulders. Check regularly that you have an even feel in both stirrups – first make sure they are an even length – and that you can feel both your seat bones evenly in the saddle. Do not collapse the inside of your hip as you use your inside leg on a circle, causing your body weight to fall to the outside. This will cause the horse's shoulder to run in on the circle to support your body weight and force it to move out of track.

If you still have difficulty sitting centrally, check that your saddle sits correctly on the horse; it may need restuffing.

A picture of a typical beginner, who will need to be taught how to sit up straight, relax the arms and legs, and get down into the center of the saddle and hold his head up. He is rounding his back, poking his head forward and his arms are stiff.

Riding out and hacking

Once the rider is competent enough, one of the most pleasurable activities is to go out for a ride in the countryside to gain confidence and cope with situations as they arise.

Learning to deal with different terrains, riding safely on the roads, stopping, starting and turning, and opening gates, among other things, will all become necessary at one time or another, and soon, without realizing it, you will have coped with all manner of situations which you probably would have felt were out of the question when you first started to ride a horse.

Riding on the road

This is best restricted to quiet country roads, if possible. Generally riders should ride single file down narrow lanes or on busy roads, and always on the right-hand side following the flow of the traffic. However if there is a young horse or a young or fairly inexperienced rider, he or she should ride on the inside next to a more experienced rider. If the road is wide enough, it is acceptable to ride in pairs, side by side. The greater overall bulk makes you both more visible to oncoming traffic.

Care must always be taken on the roads to obey the traffic laws and to be considerate to pedestrians and other road users. Remember that the same rules, signs, and traffic lights apply to a horse whether it is ridden or in harness. You must use hand signals to indicate when you wish to stop, turn left or right, or pass stationary traffic.

Check frequently that there are no cars behind you. Look over your shoulder regularly. The clip-clop of your horse's shoes may easily mask the sound of approaching traffic, especially on a windy day. Always thank people who slow down for you, and wave them on if appropriate. Never use your stick to wave or indicate.

Never go too close to stationary cars in case you hit them with your stirrup irons; try to anticipate the opening of car doors, and take care when riding over white road markings or drains in case your horse might shy or spook into the road. If you think the horse is looking at an approaching hazard, either ask for a lead past it or wait at a safe distance until traffic has gone by.

Always use strong leg aids to prevent the spooked horse's quarters from swinging into oncoming traffic.

Be very careful in icy weather as the horse could slip badly. If you must go on the road in such conditions, keep near the edge where the ground is a bit more rough, and the animal will have a better grip. Ask your

Riding up and down hills

To do this correctly, you must keep yourself in balance with your horse. Lean forward when going uphill and keep your weight out of the saddle, freeing the horse's back and hocks to allow them to work extra hard to push you both up the hill. Riding uphill can greatly benefit your horse's fitness program.

Lean back and adopt a vertical position when coming down hills, with your lower leg braced forward a bit. Leaning backwards takes some of the strain off the horse's forehand and foreleg as it picks its way downhill. Do not hang onto the horse's mouth to balance yourself. The horse will need a free head and neck for balance and to be able to descend safely. Do not go down very steep hills until you feel you can keep the horse under control by using your legs to keep the balance and your hands to measure the control. An experienced horse can usually control itself if left alone as long as you stay in balance, so if you are coming down steep hills, let the horse pick its own path and also choose its own speed and line of descent.

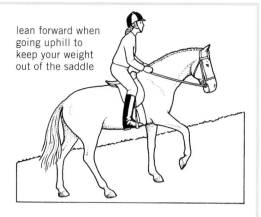

lean forward when going uphill to keep your weight out of the saddle

lean back to adopt a vertical position when coming down hills

blacksmith to use frost nails or borium on the shoes to give extra grip in such conditions. Try to ride late in the day in winter, when the temperature will have risen a bit. If the snow is deep, rub oil into the feet to stop the snow from becoming impacted in the hoof. If you cannot avoid riding in these conditions, always put knee pads on your horse to avoid injury if it slips.

Riding at night

This can be extremely dangerous, so avoid it if you possibly can. If you must ride at night, make every effort to be seen by wearing light-colored clothing and reflective armbands and a vest, and put reflective leg bandages on the horse. Fluorescent vests are

only effective during the daytime, as they have no reflective qualities, so make sure you get one with additional reflecting stripes. A stirrup light, showing white to the front and red at the rear, should be worn on the outside foot. Research has proved that when you ride at night, best visibility is achieved by attaching reflective boots to the horse's fore and hindlegs. The movement of the legs attracts car drivers' attention quickly. Try to plan your ride so that you return home before it gets too dark. If there is a gray horse in your group, place it at the outside rear as it will stand out more clearly than a dark-colored horse.

Remember that while you may be able to see fairly well, car drivers behind a windshield may not necessarily be able to see you, especially if there is another car approaching with headlights on. At dusk when the sun is setting, a car driver may be temporarily blinded. Always ride to be seen. Pony clubs and riding schools sometimes provide training and facilities for taking a road safety test. Some places have a municipal safety officer who can devise a test for all aspects of riding on the road in traffic, a must for anyone who wishes to take up a career with horses.

Opening a gate

At some time you will have to open and shut a gate. This should not be too difficult. First ride up so that you are standing parallel with the gate. Put both reins and your stick in your outside hand and bend over to unfasten the gate. Push or pull open, using your legs to guide your horse in the correct direction (see leg yielding, p.113). It is to be hoped that the gate will stay open, allowing you to ride through. Repeat the process to close the gate. An experienced horse and rider should be able to open and walk through a gate by executing a turn on the forehand (see p.113) before closing the gate in the usual manner. It is important that the horse should learn to

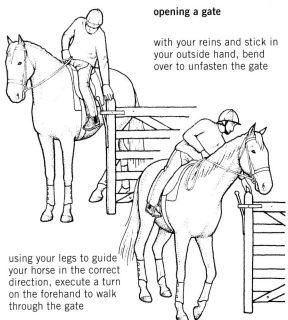

opening a gate

with your reins and stick in your outside hand, bend over to unfasten the gate

using your legs to guide your horse in the correct direction, execute a turn on the forehand to walk through the gate

stand still during such maneuvers before moving away. Never rush the process of opening a gate or the horse may get impatient or confused – make it wait until you are ready to move off. If the gate is difficult or your horse becomes too impatient, it is best to dismount. Run up

your stirrups so that they do not catch on the gatepost or hook, and lead the horse through, shutting the gate before re-mounting. A hunting crop can be very useful as you can use it to push or pull at the gate and to prevent it from slamming in front of another rider.

Riding responsibly

This is very important. You must never forget that you are in charge of an animal with thoughts of its own and which may not always react in a totally predictable way. Sadly, other people do not always appreciate this and do not allow for the unexpected to happen. Often, they seem unaware that certain happenings might easily frighten a horse, however bombproof it may appear to be. The following points are to remind you how to avoid unnecessary pitfalls.
• Always wear a hard hat with a harness and the correct footwear that will not slip or get caught in the stirrups.
• Always make sure that your tack is safe, clean, and comfortable and that the stirrup irons are the correct size. The girths must be tight and the horse comfortable.
• Make sure the horse is well shod and not likely to slip on the pavement or cast a shoe.
• Always use a bridle with a suitable bit whenever riding or leading another horse – a halter is not enough to guarantee sufficient control. When you lead another horse while mounted, the horse should be led on the inside to protect it from traffic. If you are leading a horse on foot, put yourself between the horse and the traffic,

leading the horse from the off side.
• Know the rules of the road. Obey all signs and signal your intentions in time and clearly. Always look over your shoulder and all around you before signaling or starting any maneuvers.
• Try to anticipate potential hazards such as loose dogs, blind corners, old papers and trash blowing around.
• Never ride on the sidewalk or grass shoulder. The latter may have hidden hazards such as broken bottles or drains.
• Always keep to the far right, even at a traffic circle.
• When crossing a junction, always go straight over as quickly as possible and not at an angle.
• If you have to get off and lead your horse, run up your stirrups correctly. Running martingales should be unfastened from the reins and tied safely before the reins are taken over the horse's head.
• Practice mounting and dismounting from the wrong side, as you may need to do both at some time or other.
• Respect the countryside and ride responsibly. If you are allowed to ride on somebody's land, give it considerable thought beforehand. Treat gates with care

and always shut them.
• Always walk past all livestock, and keep as far away as possible from other animals to avoid disturbance.
• Take extra care in wet weather to avoid damage to fields, crops, and paths.
• Make every effort to learn about crops. Always ride around the very edge of fields and avoid them, if possible, from seed time to harvest.
• Respect other users of the same paths, especially pedestrians, and do not get too close or ride past them at speed. Hikers and cyclists may be frightened by a horse and will not appreciate being splashed. Above all, be courteous and respect others. Always consider how you would want others to treat you and your own land or property and respect other people's wishes accordingly.
• If you are in any doubt about the law or your rights as a rider, contact your local police station, the appropriate equestrian group, or the municipality.
• Make sure you have minimum third-party insurance to cover yourself in the event of injury to others – preferably have full cover. After any damage has been done, it will be too late.

An introduction to jumping

Trotting poles and cavalletti help to teach the rider balance, timing, coordination, and rhythm and to develop an eye for the fence. For the horse they help to teach obedience, balance, and rhythm and to gain suppleness and a good stride.

Trotting poles

These can be used in various different ways, but to start with the rider should get used to riding over them placed at random, in order to get the feel of a horse trotting over them. Some horses will have a more exaggerated stride over the poles than others.

The next stage is to trot over a line of poles. They should be set approximately 4½ ft. (1.3 m) apart for the average horse's stride, but the width may need adjusting to suit a horse with a shorter or longer stride. Poles can also be set at 9 ft. (2.7 m) apart, which allows for a full stride between each pole, and should be spaced this way for cantering.

The secret of riding over poles, and later for jumping, is to look up and ahead. Looking down is the rider's worst fault, for this not only unbalances the rider but also the horse, causing all sorts of problems.

Acquiring a sense of rhythm over the poles may be hard for some riders, who may

Trotting poles are a most useful way of introducing the horse to jumping, and they will also help to improve its rythmn and balance on the flat. When you are quite certain your horse is confident over poles, you can then gradually introduce it to small jumps. There are all sorts of exercises that will help supple the horse which can be done by going around and through as well as over poles. Raised poles or cavalletti off the ground require more effort and suppleness from the horse. The rider must remain in balance throughout during these exercises.

find it helpful to count "one," "two," "three," "four," over the closer poles and "one and two and . . . " (etc.) over the more widely-spaced ones. With firm use of the legs, the rider learns to ride the horse over the poles so that this rhythm is maintained and he does not miscalculate his stride, having to put in an extra short step to make the distance. If the horse starts to hurry, take it around in a small circle in front of the poles until it settles down. This should solve the problem.

The horse and rider have to aim for the center of the poles so that they learn to ride straight at fences. This is most important. Cutting corners or wiggling toward the poles will not be helpful later on. (See Chapter 4 for further jump training.)

Cavalletti

These were once used in all training work. They have a tendency to roll and cause accidents, but the basic principle is excellent. Cavalletti consist of a pole set in a cross at each end which can be rolled over to give three different heights from the ground. Jumps made by placing wooden cavalletti on top of each other have proved very dangerous, and cavalletti should never be used like this. (Safer plastic "block" style cavalletti are now generally used.)

A line of cavalletti set at the lowest level, about 3 in. (7.6 cm) off the ground, will make the horse work a little harder, having to lift its legs that bit higher, yet still maintaining the regular rhythm of its stride. The cavalletti can then be used at the next height up, about 6 in. (15.2 cm) higher. At their highest level 9 in. to 1 ft. (22.8 to 30.4 cm), some horses will jump rather than trot over them.

Finally, set the first three or four poles at trotting distance of 4½ ft. (1.3 m) on the lowest level with the last pole at 9 ft. (2.7 m) at its highest. Make the horse trot over the first three or four, followed by a small jump out over the last. This last exercise can be the rider's first introduction to using the jumping position.

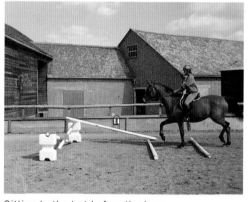

Sitting to the trot before the jump

The takeoff over plastic block-style cavalletti

The rider's position when jumping

The rider has to stay balanced right through the horse's jump; this needs some practice, for he has to take up a change of position over the fence if the horse is not to be interfered with when jumping.

For maximum security, the stirrups are shortened for jumping to allow the rider to fold into the jumping position, taking the weight off the horse's back and quarters. The rider must keep his weight over the horse's center of gravity at all times, never getting in front of or behind the movement. If the stirrups are too long, the lower leg will swing and it will be impossible to fold out of the saddle. If they are too short, the legs will become ineffective, and the rider will tend to slide to the back of the saddle, showing too much daylight between saddle and seat.

The lower leg is most important and must remain in the same position throughout the jump; it must be secure and strong to support the rest of the body. For utmost security the stirrup iron should be under the widest part of the foot, and the rider must feel that his weight is being pushed down into the feet with each stride. The heels must never be allowed to come up. Shorten the stirrups to the length you find most suitable to achieve this position comfortably.

The rider's body should fold forward from the hip, but the back must remain straight. The shoulders must relax, and the seat should be pushed up and back to maintain the balance, showing little daylight between the saddle and the rider's seat. The arms should stretch forward along and down the neck, giving as much rein as the horse requires during the jump. Always look ahead between the horse's ears.

The lower leg must remain in the same position throughout the jump with the weight deep into the heel. The leg must remain close to the horse at all times to ensure full control and balance. This can be practiced while trotting or cantering around the school at a steady pace before attempting a jump. Once the rider can maintain this position, all that is necessary is to master the art of positioning the horse at the jump and timing the takeoff.

The rider's position is vital as it affects the horse's jump. Horse and rider are dependent on one another if an obstacle is to be jumped successfully. See p.41 for Common jumping faults and how to how to correct them.

The jumping position

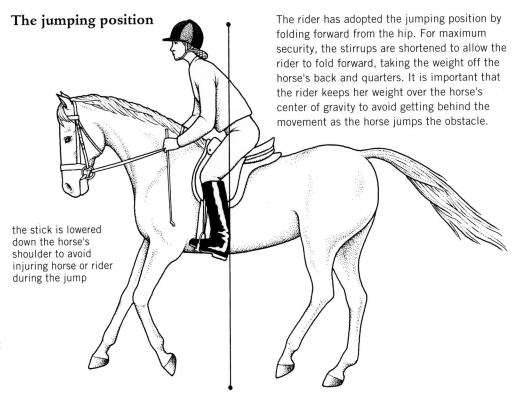

the stick is lowered down the horse's shoulder to avoid injuring horse or rider during the jump

The rider has adopted the jumping position by folding forward from the hip. For maximum security, the stirrups are shortened to allow the rider to fold forward, taking the weight off the horse's back and quarters. It is important that the rider keeps her weight over the horse's center of gravity to avoid getting behind the movement as the horse jumps the obstacle.

How the horse jumps

A successful jump depends very much on the correct speed, pace, balance, and position of the horse and rider for the size and type of jump to be negotiated.

The jump can be divided into five different phases:

On the approach, the horse gauges the fence ahead and at the last stride lowers its head to allow its hocks to come further underneath ready for the spring. At this point the rider should be sitting in an upright, central position, with legs on, with a slight give in the rein to allow the horse to lower its head, maintaining a light contact throughout.

The takeoff At this stage the horse readjusts its balance by shortening its neck and engaging its hocks beneath it. The animal will lift its forehand, fold up its forelegs and spring into the air from its hocks. Only when the horse begins to rise into the air does the rider adopt the jumping position. This split-second timing is crucial and probably one of the most difficult exercises to master. Adopting the jumping position too soon will throw all the weight forward onto the horse's lowered forehand, causing a loss of balance. Adopting the jumping position too late will leave the rider behind the movement catching the horse in the mouth (see p. 41).

phases of the jump

flight

takeoff

landing

The moment of suspension (flight) Once in the air, the horse will stretch out its head and neck and round its back over the jump. Its withers should be its highest point as it goes over the top of the fence, and its legs will, fleetingly, be well tucked up under its body before beginning the descent. At this point the rider must allow the horse total freedom. Any tension or resistance in the rein will prevent the horse from stretching its head and neck. The stretching of the neck releases the shoulders, allowing the forelegs to be fully bent and tucked under.

The landing At this point the horse will stretch out its front legs ready to land, usually with one foot placed ahead of the other. The horse will raise its head to readjust its balance and to allow the

hindlegs to come down ready for recovery. The rider remains in the jumping position, giving the horse a free rein.

The recovery At this stage, the horse has to pick itself up and prepare for the next stride, so it must quickly shift the weight back from its forehand to its hocks to be ready for another fence. During the landing and recovery phase, the rider must stay in the jumping position and not land with a bump on the horse's back. At the same time as the horse's hindlegs and hocks engage underneath, the rider sits upright, takes up the contact on the reins, and rides on with both legs. Never let your horse get the habit of stopping after it has completed a jump. Ride on in a controlled manner before halting.

Improving your jumping

Once you feel confident about jumping over cavalletti or small single fences of up to 12 in. (30 cm) you should then be ready to attempt the various types of fences, including doubles (two fences within one or two strides), trebles (three fences within two or three strides), and grids (a sequence of fences used for schooling).

At this stage you must learn each of the different types of fences which may be encountered and whether they fall into the upright (vertical), spread, or combination category.

Uprights or verticals are single fences which require a degree of collection and accuracy to jump cleanly. It is most important that the horse is presented to the fence at a sensible pace to be able to jump clear. Verticals are probably the hardest fences for the horse to jump accurately. It is difficult to judge the distance, though a ground pole always helps. The horse will need to get a little closer than with spread fences, making more of a vertical jump than the gentle rounded type of jump required by the spread.

Upright fences include gates, planks, walls, stiles, and single poles in numerous different varieties.

Spread fences are made up of two or three parts consisting of a front and back rail to the fence, usually with a filler pole or brush in between. As these are wide fences, clearing them requires a lot of effort on the part of the horse, so the rider must generate the extra impulsion needed to clear the fence. Spread fences can vary in design, ranging from sloping rails such as those with triple bars to the true parallel where both front and back rail are at the same height. The sloping, curved spreads are seen to be the most inviting jump for the horse, though true

parallels are very difficult as they combine the worst aspect of the vertical and the spread fence. Spread fences include hog's backs, triples, oxers, and water jumps.

Combination fences include the following: Doubles, where there are one or two non-jumping strides in between the two fences. These can be two verticals, or spreads, or a combination of both. Trebles consist of three fences, usually with one or two non-jumping strides in between. They may also consist of spreads or uprights. Bounces consist of fences without a stride in between. They are not often used in show-jumping classes, but may often be found on cross-country courses. Usually made of two single fences, bounces require a balanced, controlled approach if they are to be negotiated safely. They are excellent schooling fences as they teach the horse to sit back on its hocks and balance itself. The riders must learn to be in the right position with perfect timing.

upright or vertical fences

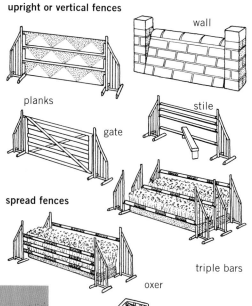

wall

planks

gate

stile

spread fences

triple bars

oxer

hog's back

water jump

Jumping a grid with ground poles in between each jump.

Jumping combinations

In order to jump a double with two strides in between, the distance between the fences when low will probably be around 30-33 ft. (9-10 m) or approximately ten to eleven normal walking strides. (Once the fences are up to 3 ft. 3 in. (1 m) or above, this would tend to increase to 33-36 ft. (10-11 m) – eleven to twelve walking strides. The best way to feel the number of strides taken is to jump the fence, saying "jump" as you take off and then "one," "two," as you make the two non-jumping strides before the next fence. It may take a lot of practice to get your timing right, but it will soon fall into place if you work on it with your instructor.

Some people find it easier to tackle a combination with one non-jumping stride in between the elements, so that they take the jump saying, "jump – stride – jump."

Trebles are really just a longer version of the double, with a third fence added to create a treble.

Grids often have poles on the ground in between the combinations to help with the striding.

Learn to sit up over the poles and fold your weight forward over the fences. The poles help to balance the horse and make it take off, jump, and land with its feet square.

Grids can also be positioned with the jumps side by side. Horse and rider then work in a figure of eight to practice bending and changes of leg after a jump and meeting the next jump squarely.

The different types of fences

Practice makes perfect, and it will be necessary to keep on practicing until you have mastered the art of approaching a fence correctly and at the right speed.

The ease with which you can do this varies according to the horse you are riding. The youngster will need to be taught the correct pace and how to lengthen and shorten its stride as part of its training, but a real schoolmaster of a horse will make it seem quite easy as it will regulate its own stride and do it the way it wants, whatever instructions you try to give from the top!

It is important to maintain a consistent and rhythmic approach. You must keep the horse moving forward up into its bridle so

jumping a combination at canter

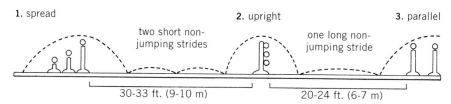

1. spread

two short non-jumping strides

2. upright

one long non-jumping stride

3. parallel

30-33 ft. (9-10 m)

20-24 ft. (6-7 m)

Common jumping faults and how to correct them

Inevitably you will pick up some bad habits. The sooner you know what they are, the sooner you can set about correcting them. The following are the most common.

Insecure leg position This is usually caused by the stirrups being too long for jumping, or the weight not being pushed down into the heel to provide proper security. Shorten the stirrups, if necessary, to give a broader base for support. Check that the knees are soft and supple, with the lower leg placed securely against the horse's sides and the weight well down into the heel.

Catching the horse in the mouth This is generally caused by lack of balance at some stage during the jump. In this case, the rider usually gets left behind as the horse either takes off unexpectedly, or the rider fails to follow the horse's movement throughout the jump and hangs onto the reins for security.

At all times the rider has to be sympathetic to the horse's needs when jumping over the fence. Freedom over the jump is vital for the horse if he is to jump correctly.

Practice over small fences until your confidence is restored, and allow your arms to go forward along the neck.

Make sure you are folding forward from the waist as you go over the jump. Stiffness in the back will result in loss of balance. Practice sliding the reins forward up the horse's neck, and keep your arms soft and pliable.

Fixed hands This will mean the horse will not have enough freedom on the approach, nor over the jump, to use its head and neck. The animal will start to flatten its outline and rush at the fence in its efforts to pull the reins out of your hands, or it will feel so restricted and frustrated that it stops dead.

Soften the hands and play with the reins on the approach using a supple give-and-take motion and really "give" the hands forward over the fence. It will take time for the horse to settle into this new routine if the fault has become a long-standing habit.

Dropping the horse in front of the fence is a common fault where the rider literally drops or loses contact at the very last stride in front of the fence. It will completely unbalance the horse which may lose confidence. The horse may also think you have changed your mind and do not want to jump. Your contact with the horse must remain light but constant throughout the jump.

"Fiddling" in front of the fence is one of the worst faults. In this case the rider will be pulling or pushing the horse all the way to the fence, totally muddling it and losing any sort of approach. Sit still and keep the horse in balance by playing it lightly with the reins, and allow it to come to the fence undisturbed. Above all, sit quiet. Even the most inexperienced horse can judge its stride. Never interfere with this. Only the top-class professional showjumpers can ask for another stride successfully. As a rider, concentrate on getting the correct pace and impulsion for the jump; let the horse choose its own stride and above all try to keep a rhythm.

The rider may sit up too quickly at the end of the jump causing the horse to hollow its back.

The rider may swing to one side or the other over the fence, making the horse jump to one side or the other to compensate and thus becoming unbalanced on landing.

Regular instruction, with emphasis placed on the rider's position, will ensure that bad habits do not get out of hand. Once the rider rides correctly and well, the horse will be able to jump to the best of its ability and experience.

The approach and the takeoff greatly affect how horse and rider cope with a fence. In the pictures on the left, the horse has started his jump too far away, so that the rider is being left behind and catching the horse in the mouth. Although the jump is clear, the landing is uncomfortable, which will not give the horse confidence for its next fence.

that it is off his forehand and able to take the jump easily. This applies to all fences. Keep the balance by riding forward, and control the impulsion with your seat and legs, and your approach, by playing with your hands to keep the horse soft and responsive.

When jumping spread fences, keep the same balance and forward going approach, but make sure you have enough bounce in your stride to negotiate the extra width. If you feel the horse is having to stretch, then you probably need a little more push and a longer stride. If it feels easy, then all is likely to be going well. Your instructor will be able to tell you about anything that might be going wrong. Remember that a bad mistake will have knock-on effect at the next fence, often in the form of a refusal as the horse anticipates the discomfort it felt the previous time. If you have made a mistake, ride on to the next fence positively to give the horse confidence and reassurance.

Jumping a course of fences

The next stage is to put together three or four fences and jump them as a course. Remember to give the horse room at each fence to get the best approach. Do not cut corners. Aim straight at each jump. Keep up a consistent, forward-going pace.

As soon as you have jumped one fence, look ahead immediately for the next one and work out how to negotiate it. Gradually build up a course of up to eight or ten fences, with changes of direction and including an upright, a spread, and a double. Try to make the best use of the arena and of riding out of your turns so that you make it as easy as possible for the horse to negotiate each obstacle. Include as many different types of fence as possible, such as gates, walls, and different colored poles. Keep the jumps small until you can guide your horse around the course with confidence. Then they can gradually get a little larger.

First events

Once the rider feels confident enough to join in the activities in the riding school, he or she will find there are many things to do.

Pony Clubs For a child, joining a pony club will open up a whole new world and will mean regular instruction and training in everything ranging from games to polo, show jumping to eventing, general riding to road safety.

Riding clubs For adults riding clubs cater for a number of different disciplines; they also arrange outings and shows for members. Joining a national equestrian body is always worthwhile. As a member you will be able to keep up to date with everything that is going on in your locality as well as further afield, and you have the chance to become more involved. In the United Kingdom there is the British Horse Society and in the United States the American Horse Shows Association. Wherever you live in the world, there will be an equestrian governing body which will provide you with relevant information and membership, and there are usually advantages such as special rates for insurance and discounts at certain stores.

Hunting Joining a local hunt will provide excellent opportunities to ride cross-country and meet new friends, as well as learning about how hounds work. Be aware of the manners and dress required.

Sponsored rides are enormously popular and are often run for charity. There may be optional jumps which cater for all standards. This is a great way to gain confidence and enjoy the countryside.

Novice shows and training clinics are designed for both inexperienced riders and horses so that they can gain confidence at the different disciplines. The more shows you can go to, the better, and if all goes well at the first two or three, you can enter for the next standard.

Extra equipment for the rider

For competitions you will be expected to dress according to the rules for the particular type of event. During your training, your equipment may get somewhat battered and need replacing. It is a good idea to set aside special show clothes and equipment which you never use on a day-to-day basis.

For children there are often flourishing secondhand clothes and equipment sections at pony clubs, and many saddlers also have secondhand items. Always check that everything is safe, clean, and in good condition. If you intend doing a lot of cross-country riding, it is always wise to wear a back protector. Moves are being made to make these obligatory for all cross-country events and competitions.

Preparation

Before going to an event, a certain amount of planning is necessary beforehand, and it is worth looking at each item in turn.

The horsebox or trailer Check this is in good condition and ready to be driven, with oil, water, and fuel for the journey. Check the tires. Check that the map and directions are inside.

Prepare tack Thoroughly clean and polish everything. Check each item required and put out ready.

Prepare the hay, feed, and water Take two buckets, one for water and one for washing

the horse down after the competition, as well as a haynet and feed container.

Prepare the horse The animal must be clean and neat, so an extra special grooming should be done the day before. Wash the mane, tail, and legs, and the whole horse if is hot and/or dirty, but take care not to give it a chill if the weather is cold.

The horse should already be clipped and its mane and tail pulled and trimmed in advance, but these may need extra attention just before an outing. Try to think ahead so that things are not left to the last moment.

On the day

Feed before loading, according to the time you are traveling. It is always worth checking before the actual day of departure that your horse is happy to be loaded into a horsebox or trailer, especially if you have a new vehicle or have not traveled with the horse before. Be sure that all doors or partitions are fully open and secure before fetching the horse. Put a halter and rope, as well as any protective clothing or blankets needed, on the horse; then lead it purposefully toward and straight up the ramp before turning the animal into position, if necessary. Get a helper to close the partitions and put up the ramp, or do this yourself as soon as you have secured the horse.

If there are any difficulties, try a bowl of food. Some horses need a little time; others need a smart slap on the rump and a bit of firmness. If these methods fail, get a lunge rein, and with one person on each side, place the rein below the horse's buttocks and above the hocks and pull it forward strongly up the ramp. It helps to lift a foreleg and place it on the ramp. Be firm but calm. Take the lunge rein with you if there is likely to be a problem on the way home. Make a fuss of the horse when it is in the horsebox.

Setting off

Check all the tack and equipment is loaded and that you have all your own equipment as well – plus a picnic.

Remember to take the tickets and rule book, if necessary. When you are ready, set off, allowing plenty of time to get to your destination. Drive carefully around corners, making sure you give the horse as smooth a ride as possible. Allow extra time when braking and accelerating. Above all, enjoy yourself when you get there!

a leather poll guard, fitted onto a halter

When traveling, a specially-designed poll guard is invaluable for vulnerable heads liable to knocks. Alternatively, improvising with some foam padding, as shown on this tall horse ready to load, will help. Note that it is wearing traveling boots and a tail guard for extra protection. Never pull on the lead rope when loading as this makes the horse put its head up.

Accidents and how to cope

Riding is a high risk sport, and accidents inevitably happen. You should always be prepared in case of an emergency.

Falling off This can be a rather nerve-racking experience, but it may be comforting to know that all riders, however experienced, fall off their horses and that it tends to happen quite frequently. A child is usually told of the need to fall off at least a hundred times before being able to ride properly. The art of falling is to stay relaxed and to learn always to roll away from the horse if at all possible. Hang onto the reins if you can do so safely, but if not let go. Always get up as soon as possible, gently, and assess any damage. Lying brooding will not make the aches any better, and it is usually pride that is far more hurt than anything else! Jump back on the horse as soon as possible without dwelling on the incident. Bear in mind that the horse will be just as shocked as you are and may need time to settle.

It is wise to carry a small emergency pack with you at all times when riding, to serve for both horse and rider. Always remember the golden rules:
• Keep calm.
• Assess the situation.

• Deal with priorities first.

Action in an emergency. Always think of the rider first and then the horse. It may be necessary to leave the rider to summon help.
• If the rider is lying, still ask "Can you hear me?" If the rider can speak, ask where it hurts and act accordingly.
• If the rider is unconscious, always place him or her in the recovery position and check that they are breathing properly. Stay with the rider if at all possible.
• Do not remove the hard hat.
• If there is severe bleeding, apply a pad and firm bandage to the area.
• Do not move the rider if there are suspected breaks. Call an ambulance, and keep the rider as warm and comfortable as you can until help arrives.
• Catch the loose horse only after you are satisfied that the rider is unharmed or being looked after. If the horse is injured, call a vet.

First aid. Every rider should have a sound knowledge of first aid, and reminders of emergency care should be regularly discussed and written notices displayed prominently in the stables. First aid kits should be kept in the tack room.

If the horse is cut badly, apply a bandage or tourniquet (see p. 75). Sudden lameness may be caused by a stone in the foot or a lost shoe. Check for this. Stiffness of the muscles usually indicates a strain or Azoturia. In this case, do not move the horse, but keep it warm and bring the trailer as near the horse as possible. If necessary, call the vet. (See p. 75 for dealing with injuries.)

Emergency pack

My emergency pack, which has served me well for many years, consists of the following items:
• 2½ in. (5.5 cm) bandage
• Multipurpose penknife (pushed down inside the bandage).
• Money for the telephone.
• A piece of string.
• Nonadhesive dressing and medical wipes.
• Ballpoint pen and paper, preferably with the phone number of your vet unless you know it by heart.
• Three large safety pins.

I keep these items in a money belt which I wear all the time, and which is no trouble to carry. Decide for yourself, on the basis of my list, what you think should be the essentials for your emergency kit, and always remember to replenish it when necessary.

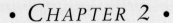

CHAPTER 2

STABLE MANAGEMENT

'A little neglect may breed mischief . . .
for want of a nail, the shoe was lost; for want
of a shoe the horse was lost; and for want of a
horse the rider was lost.'

Benjamin Franklin, *Poor Richard's Almanack* (1758)

The management and day-to-day care of the domesticated horse is important in its development and for the role for which it is being prepared. A thorough knowledge and understanding of the horse and how it thinks and reacts to events will help make sure that it receives the very best care. It is vital that horse owners fully understand all the work involved in owning a horse, particularly if it is to be stabled. Horses are usually stabled, with the exception of children's ponies, which may be able to live out all year round if a suitable area is available.

Natural habitat and instincts

The horse is a herd animal and, in the wild, would roam in large numbers, constantly nibbling the vegetation available, especially in early morning and late evening when the grass is moist. The horse will graze for up to 20 out of the 24 hours of the day. Its natural diet is a mixture of grasses, herbs, leaves, and bark. In the wild, the horse rarely lies down. Resting while standing, it seldom sleeps as we know it but takes a series of "cat naps."

If danger arose, the animals would be ready to react with "fright and flight." To overcome this very strong instinct, the horse has to learn to trust its human handler, and the approach must be to build up the horse's confidence throughout its training and handling.

A great advantage for the handler is that the horse, having an inbuilt herding instinct, will usually fare better in a busy stable with other horses than on its own.

Consistency and patience are two of the most important qualities required by horse owners. A horse's temperament may be quite complex, and while some animals may be extremely easy to handle and may quickly learn to do whatever is demanded of them, others may be much harder to deal with.

The gelding

The domesticated male horse, unless kept specifically for breeding, is generally gelded. Gelding is a minor operation performed under local anesthetic, usually in spring or fall, in which the horse is castrated. Once gelded, the horse becomes much more gregarious and manageable. The colt is usually castrated before it becomes sexually mature, that is, sometime between 18 months and 2 years old. Some owners prefer to defer gelding for as long as possible as this means the horse is able to develop a stallion's stature with a thick, well-muscled neck and a prominent crest. (For the stallion and mare, see p. 81.)

Routine

The horse is very much a creature of habit and learns best through repetition. Therefore a routine plays an important part in its training program. If it is possible to do the same things at the same time and place each day, this will mean that learning is mastered quickly. Once mutual trust has been built up between the horse and its owner, it will be surprising how soon the animal will adapt to new circumstances if a long-term routine becomes impractical or difficult to manage and changes have to take place. Once the horse learns something, it won't forget very easily. It goes without saying that the horse must be taught and rewarded for the right things from the start, because it is very difficult to get rid of bad habits already learned!

A tranquil scene of mares and foals grazing. The young animals will get a good start on this excellent pasture with slightly sloping ground.

Grooming

One of the best ways to get to know your horse is during grooming, for the groomer soon gets to know every square inch of the horse. Grooming is necessary to keep the horse clean and the coat in good condition; it also stimulates the circulation as it is a form of massage and makes the horse both comfortable and presentable. The process may take from 10 to 45 minutes if it is done thoroughly. It leaves the horse feeling relaxed and refreshed. Grooming is best done after exercise, when the pores are still open.

How to groom

Put on the halter and tie up the horse, and, if covered up, fold the blanket back over the horse halfway if cold, or remove if warm.
The hoof pick Pick out the feet, starting at the heel, and work toward the point of the frog. You may need a bucket of water and a brush to clean them thoroughly both inside and out. Clean out the feet into a bowl.
The dandy brush is used to remove heavy dirt and mud, especially on a grass-kept horse. Brush the horse thoroughly, starting on the near side on the neck and working backwards, at all times following the natural line of the hair, without using too much pressure around sensitive areas. The dandy brush should not be used on the head or on clipped or sensitive-skinned horses.

The body brush, which is softer, should then be used and the horse brushed all over, still working from front to back and each side in turn, with firm strokes, not forgetting the areas under the mane, around the elbows and up between the legs. You may need to rub around these areas with the palm of the hand to help shift sweat and get into the folds of the skin. Care in these areas is important; soreness can occur if they are not attended to regularly. The head should be brushed carefully and gently, especially around the ears and under the throat.
The curry comb, which is usually made of metal, is used to clean the body brush, pulling across it with short, sharp strokes. Knock this against a hard surface to shift dust and dirt. Rubber and plastic ones may be used directly on the horse to rub off mud or dirt and to help shift the winter coat. A curry comb must never be used on the mane or tail. When grooming the near side of the horse, the body brush should be held in the left hand, with the curry comb in the right

Start your grooming routine by picking out and inspecting the hooves and checking the shoes.

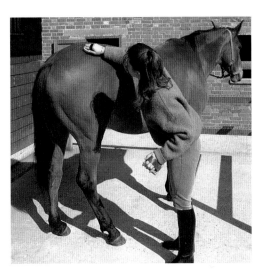

The body brush should be used from head to tail in the direction of the coat.

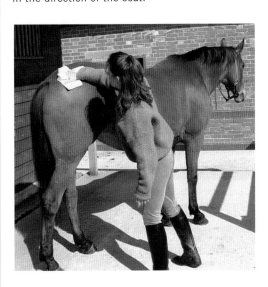

The final polish with the stable rubber will remove any particles of dust or grease.

Grooming kit required

Hoof pick for picking out the hooves.
Dandy brush to remove heavy dirt and mud, especially on a grass-kept horse.
Body brush used for general grooming throughout, together with a curry comb.
Curry comb usually made of metal and designed for cleaning the body brush.
Two sponges one for sponging the eyes and nose, the other for sponging the dock area.
Mane and tail comb to keep the mane and tail neat and tidy.
Stable rubber a soft linen cloth used for rubbing over the horse and for giving a

final dust and shine to the coat.
Hoof oil used to promote growth and keep the horn healthy. It also makes the hoof presentable and is a must for the show ring.
Water brush for washing the feet and for damping and laying the mane and tail.
Sweat scraper These come in several shapes and sizes and are used after the horse has been washed or washed down after exercise to remove excess water from the coat.
Massage pad used for strapping and stimulating the horse's muscles.

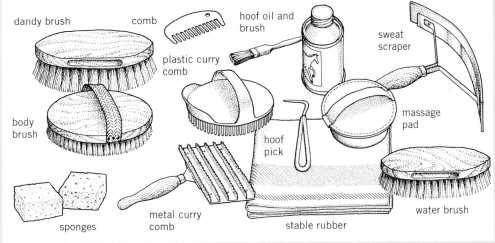

dandy brush
comb
hoof oil and brush
sweat scraper
plastic curry comb
body brush
hoof pick
massage pad
sponges
metal curry comb
stable rubber
water brush

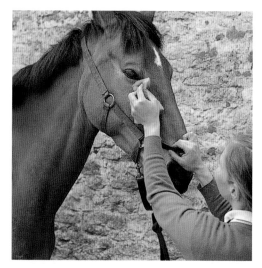

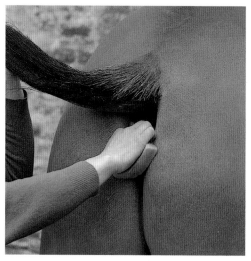

Above: Sponging around the eyes, nose, and dock not only cleans the area, but is very refreshing for the horse. Do not neglect the muzzle or lips.

hand – the opposite for grooming the other side. If you keep and ride a horse, you have to learn to be ambidextrous!

Sponging Always have two sponges. Use a soft damp one to wipe the eyes, ears, nose, and face, and rinse it out frequently so as not to spread infection. Some horses are very head-shy, so sponging has to be done with care and patience. Using the second sponge, wipe down the dock area and inside leg, if necessary. In the wild, the horse will take great care not to stale or defecate on itself, standing still while performing with the legs wide apart. In the confined space of a stable or even during exercise, this is not always possible.

The stable rubber is a soft linen cloth; it is rubbed in the direction of the hair to remove dust and give the coat a final polish.

The mane and tail comb The mane should always be encouraged to lie on the same side of the neck. The natural lay of the hair dictates a particular side, but the offside is generally considered correct for showing and competitions. Stubborn hair should be encouraged to the desired side by plaiting the section after grooming. The weight of the plait will encourage the hair to fall to the side desired. Do not brush the tail too much, and then only with a soft brush; brushing too often will gradually thin the tail, spoiling its looks and effectiveness as a fly swatter. Hay and straw can be picked out by hand when necessary.

Hoof oil Finally, the feet can be oiled both inside and out with hoof oil or hoof dressing. This promotes growth and keeps the horn healthy. If the feet are brittle, they should be oiled daily; if they are healthy, two or three times a week will be enough. Hoof oil adds the finishing touch to a beautifully turned-out horse and is a must for the show ring.

The grooming kit should be kept in a suitable container and should be washed regularly with a mild disinfectant.

Strapping or whisping Strapping is a type of massage designed to develop and harden muscles and improve the blood supply to the skin or coat through increased stimulation. Although not as popular as it once was, strapping can help to improve the condition and muscle tone of the horse – particularly if it is doing hard or competition work. Strapping should be built up gradually.

Massage pad A leather pad is used by banging it down on the coat, particularly along the muscles of the neck, quarters, and thighs. Gradually build up the number of strokes each time, starting with five and working up to ten, working up evenly on both sides. For this to be really effective, the muscles should be given time to contract and relax in between strokes. Avoid all bony or sensitive areas. Strapping is usually done two or three times a week on competition horses.

A sweat scraper is used to remove excess water after washing. Some are made with rubber on one side for sensitive areas and metal on the other for general scraping.

Automatic grooming machines are popular in big stables and can be used to clean the horse thoroughly with good effect. Because of the way they work – rather like a vacuum cleaner – it is best to have an assistant until the horse is used to the noise and feeling of these machines; they are generally used once or twice a week rather than every day, but this is a matter of personal preference. Care must be taken to make sure that electric cables are kept away from the horse.

Grooming the grass-kept horse

The horse kept at grass relies on the skin's natural oils to keep it warm and waterproof, so its grooming need not be as thorough as that of the stabled horse. What is needed is more of a general neatening-up.

The dandy brush is the most effective way of removing dried mud. If the horse is still in work, take care to remove any sweat around the elbows and girth area and inspect regularly in cases of soreness. Otherwise girth galls may appear, especially if there is a thick winter coat, or the horse has not been ridden for some time and has a grass belly.

To help prevent girth galls, fit the saddle,

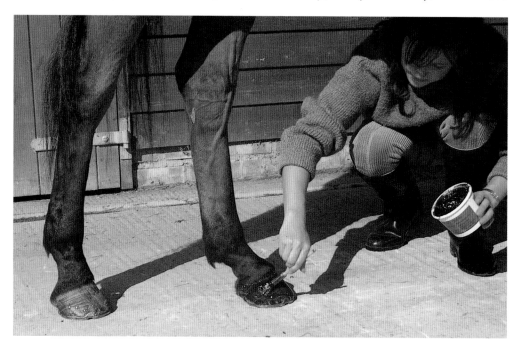

Finish by painting on a hoof oil or dressing. Do the insides and the outsides as necessary. Keep the coronary band moist by regular dressing.

Applying a tail bandage

After combing the mane and tail, for added neatness the mane can be brushed and damped and the tail can then be laid with a water brush.

A tail bandage applied for a short interval daily after grooming will make a good tail shape, especially if the tail is kept neat and pulled at regular intervals. However, it may be left natural if preferred (see Pulling and plaiting, p. 131).

Starting well up under the tail, bandage firmly and evenly down to the end of the dock and back with a slightly elasticized bandage. Tie the tapes firmly but not too tightly, or fasten with velcro and fold up.

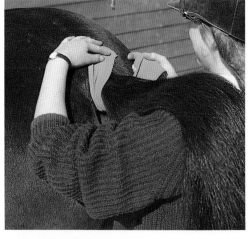 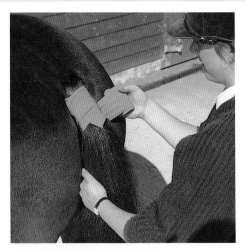

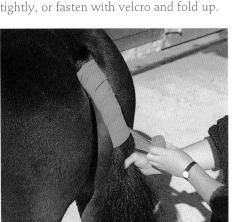 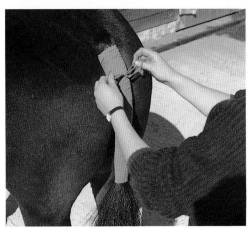 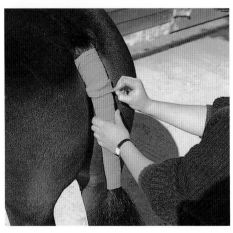

then tighten the girths gradually to avoid any puckering of the skin. To help harden the skin around the saddle and girth, rub rubbing alcohol into the area, but never use it on broken or tender skin.

Check the horse's legs, paying particular attention to the heel areas to make sure there are no cracks, crusting, or soreness, especially in wet weather. You may need to trim the hair around the heels in these conditions to allow the area to dry more easily. Pick out the feet and check that the shoes are in good condition, with clenches in position (see Raised clenches, p. 68).

Finally, groom the mane and tail, removing any grass or anything else caught up in them. Oil the feet, especially in dry weather, to keep them in good condition. Generally the feet of a horse kept at grass are in prime condition, unlike those of the stabled horse who inevitably has to stand on soiled bedding at some time during the day.

Grass-kept horses build up grease in their coats for warmth, so only remove excess dirt to make them neat. Check and dress their feet regularly.

Food and feeding

The art of good feeding can only be learned from experience. The need to treat each animal as an individual is important when deciding on your horse's diet.

In the wild a horse picks at grass intermittently throughout the day and night, as its very small stomach (approximately the size of a football when empty) is not designed to digest large amounts of food at any one time. The first rule in feeding the stabled horse is "little and often." Remember this to ensure good health, and also bear in mind that any changes in diet should be introduced gradually.

How and when to feed

Grass is the natural food for horses and ponies, but the domesticated animal requires additional feeding to keep it in condition to perform its expected role. It is impossible to get a horse truly fit on a solely grass diet. There are various things to take into account when deciding what to feed.

The type of horse or pony Brood mares, for example, need additional food to prevent them from losing condition. A stallion at stud will need a high-energy, but low-fat diet to prevent obesity.

The horse's temperament and how it responds to hard feed. Some horses find hard food more heating than others.

The age and condition of the horse Youngsters require more feeding while they develop. Milk pellets are a good source of extra calcium for bone growth. Old horses may feel the cold and so need extra food to maintain condition. Sick or convalescing horses may be on a special diet recommended by the vet. They will be on food high in nutrition, but without the high energy and heating qualities of some concentrates, such as bran mash.

The weather and time of year The horse needs more food in cold weather to compensate for the amount used up keeping warm. Grass has more nutritional value during the spring and early fall, but extra food will be required during the summer and winter months.

The work the horse is required to do The balance of bulk food (hay) and hard food high in protein (oats) changes according to the type of work. The horse's food might have to be adjusted to cope with a break in routine while traveling.

Some of the grasses most commonly used to make hay. From the left: (1) meadow fescue, (2) timothy grass, (3) perennial rye, (4) and (5) highly prized bluegrasses, and clover.

Types of feed

Hay is a substitute for grass and provides the main bulk food in the stabled horse's diet. Good quality hay is essential, as moldy and dusty hay can cause a number of respiratory problems.

To help a horse with respiratory illness, allergy, or cough, feed dampened hay. Put the hay in a large bin, pour over a couple of buckets of water, weight down and leave for at least 12 hours. Drain and place in haynet.

Poor quality hay has little food value and does not provide the necessary goodness.

Hay should always be weighed accurately according to the feed program. Never rely on pulling out sections of hay, as some bales are packed considerably more tightly than others.

Hay should be stored in a damp- and rodent-free area, and stacked to allow air to circulate. Hay which is less than six months old should not be fed as it may be indigestible. Good quality hay is said to have a good "nose"; it smells sweet and is fresh and dust-free.

Types of hay

Seed hay is generally accepted as the choicest type. It consists of a variety of grasses such as rye, timothy, bluegrass, redtop, and clover, and comes from reseeded land usually put to pasture for a year or two. Good-quality seed hay should be sweet to smell, crisp, and fairly hard to the touch, with a pale greenish-brown color. It has a high nutritional value.

Meadow hay is much softer than seed hay as it comes from permanent pasture. It contains a variety of grasses, but its nutritional value varies considerably depending on what these are. It is usually greener in color. Many horses prefer it to the coarser grasses of seed hay.

Alfalfa or lucerne hay is the highest in protein and is generally used only by the racing industry.

Haylage and horsage are vacuum-packed hay similar to silage, cut when it is at its nutritional peak and baled in air-tight bags when half dry (that is, 36 hours after cutting) Because of its high protein value, it is fed in small amounts and is useful for horses with allergy problems. Once a bag has been opened, the contents will deteriorate quickly as it begins to ferment and so should be used up within three days.

Chaff is a mixture of straw and good quality hay chopped by a machine called a chaff-cutter or "choppy." Chaff can be used mixed with hard food, adding bulk to encourage the horse to chew his food rather than bolt it. Brands of chaff coated with molasses are a popular addition to the diet, and they are very palatable for the sick or convalescing horse.

Silage is becoming popular as a horse feed. It must be introduced very gradually, but once accepted horses appear to thrive on it. Advice

Meadow grasses used to make hay

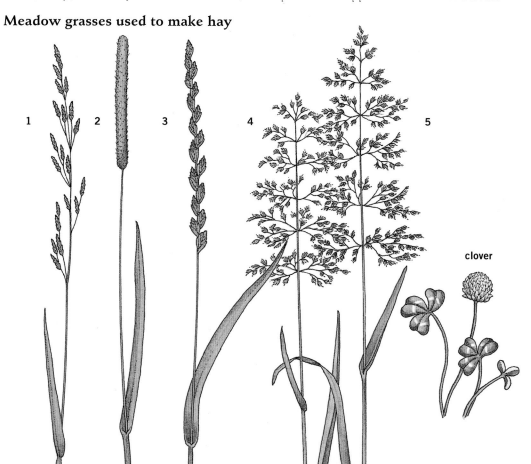

1 2 3 4 5

clover

How to make a bran mash

Put one to one and-a-half scoops of bran in a bucket. Add salt or Epsom salts for added laxative effect, and pour over enough boiling water to make a damp, crumbly mixture. A handful of oats, barley, or coarse mix, and some chaff and succulents such as carrots may be added and the food left to cool covered with a cloth. Feed while still warm in cold weather. Wet mashes have a laxative effect. Bran fed dry has a constipating effect and benefits the horse with loose droppings. Bran mashes are usually given the day before a rest day to ensure there is

no build-up of food in the system. A bran mash is very digestible and therefore ideal for the horse after a day's hard work and before a day off.

on how to feed horses on silage is best obtained from your veterinary surgeon.

Other low-protein bulk foods

Bran, that is broad wheat bran, should be fed in small amounts as a bulk food. Give a bran mash once or twice a week when the horse is off work. It is usually mixed with chaff.

Dried sugarbeet pulp is a high energy source and a useful addition to the diet to help maintain weight. The pulp must always be soaked in cold water for 12 hours before

being fed, by which time it will have swollen to at least three or four times its original size. (If fed dry, it could cause acute colic, choking, and death.) It is vital that it is stored in a sealed container so that there is no danger that the horse could get to it should it get loose. It may also come in cube form, which should be soaked in exactly the same way. Because of the fermentation process, the pulp should be used up within twenty-four hours. Some horses react to its fairly high laxative qualities.

The ten rules of feeding

The following generally accepted rules on feeding should help make sure that no bad mistakes happen.

• **Feed little and often** This is perhaps the most important rule. To feed more, feed more often.

• **Introduce all new foods or changes gradually** The horse is very sensitive to change and might develop colic if care is not taken to prevent it.

• **Feed according to the amount of work being done** Make sure that concentrates are reduced if the horse is not working hard. After hard exercise (for example, a day's hunting) the horse will need a bran mash which is easily digestible or a small nutritious feed.

• **Keep to a feeding routine** Feed at the same time each day.

• **Feed top quality food only** Horses tend to be rather fussy eaters; musty or poor quality food may do damage and put it off its feed. Always store food in metal or rodent-free containers to avoid the spread of disease.

• **Keep fresh water freely available** Always make sure the horse has had access to water before feeding. Remember that excess drinking after feeding will wash the food out of the stomach and through the system too quickly. No nutritional value whatever will be gained.

• **Do not work the horse immediately before or after feeding** Allow one hour either side of feeding. When the stomach is full, it rests on the diaphragm and lungs. This might affect the breathing mechanism and could cause colic.

• **Allow the stabled horse to have some green food,** that is, freshly cut grass, root vegetables, or other succulent regularly. This is to help make up for the lack of natural food in the stabled horse's diet.

• **Feed at least 40 percent roughage (bulk food).**

• **Assess the horse as an individual.** Note its preferences, check its ability to chew and digest its food properly.

A selection of the common foods used for feeding horses today: (1) good quality hay, (2) micronized barley, (3) soaked sugarbeet pulp, (4) bran, (5) cubes, (6) flaked corn, (7) whole oats, (8) chaff coated with molasses, and (9) whole barley. Coarse and sweet mixes are becoming increasingly popular.

Concentrates

Oats have traditionally been the choice food for horses with their high nutritional value, rich in protein and energy. The grains should be large, hard, and not dusty. Oats are either whole or, in their more easily digested form, bruised or cracked, rolled or crimped (crushed). Once treated like this, they should be fed within a month as they soon lose their nutritional value. Oats tend to be heating and may have the effect of "hotting up" some horses; for this reason they are rarely fed to ponies. Oats can be cooked and given as a light gruel.

Barley is similar in nutritional value to oats, but is generally considered to be less heating. However, it is more fattening and has a higher energy content. Barley must be fed rolled, bruised, or micronized, and is an excellent substitute for oats. It can also be fed as a boiled food, which is excellent for fattening and following hard exercise. (Whole grain barley should be soaked overnight, boiled, then simmered for approximately four to six hours until the grains split, forming a gelatin). Too much barley may cause colic.

Linseed The seed of flax, it is rich in oil and protein. Useful for the out-of-condition, underweight horse, it is the best food for improving the coat as it adds gloss and condition. Linseed must be soaked overnight and then boiled for several hours until the grains split and begin to form a gelatin. It should be mixed with hard food or bran mash and fed within 12 hours as it does not keep. One double-handful is normally given daily.

Nuts or cubes are available in several types, formulated in such a way as to cater for the various needs of the horse. They are a convenient food for the busy horse owner. Each variety is designed to cater for different requirements, and they range from the low-protein horse and pony cube of approximately 9 to 11 percent protein to the competition, stud, and racehorse cube of approximately 16 to 22 percent protein. The ingredients may form a balanced ration and may include essential minerals and vitamins. Check carefully on the label whether the cubes are classified as a complete food or are considered only part of the diet. Make sure that your horse or pony is fed the cube with the correct protein level for its type and the standard of work being done, and the right amount for its weight and size. Supplementary foods such as apples and root vegetables chopped up with the cubes will stop the horse from getting bored with this type of food.

Coarse and sweet mixes are becoming increasingly popular and are generally formulated to give a completely balanced ration. They consist of a variety of foods including grains, peas, beans, dried grasses, and molasses, and are extremely palatable. The protein content determines the type of work each brand is suited for, so it is important to change formula if the horse's workload alters significantly.

Flaked corn is a very fattening food and good for increasing condition. It can cause the blood to overheat and so should be used with discretion.

Supplements

Most complete feeds such as coarse mixes and cubes contain the essential minerals and vitamins which are necessary to the horse's wellbeing and health. Care must be taken not to unbalance the diet by giving extra supplements unnecessarily. Discuss any shortcomings with your veterinary surgeon. If your horse is having just the traditional feeds of bran, chaff, and corn, by all means choose a good supplement to ensure the animal receives the necessary minerals and vitamins to keep it in good health. For example, cod liver oil added to the feed is a rich source of vitamins A and D and helps to give a shine to the coat. It is particularly valuable during the winter months. In racing stables horses are fed large quantities of oats; supplementary foods such as glucose, eggs, and molasses are added to encourage horses to eat.

Salt or mineral licks or blocks should always be made freely available to the horse, especially one that is kept on poor pasture or is permanently stabled.
This picture shows one of the most basic ways of providing a salt or mineral block – as a lump placed straight on the ground. This is a wasteful method, however, and if the block is kept in a container (some are specially designed for specific brands), it will last very much longer. Stabled horses can have a block placed in their feed bin or in a container fastened on the stable wall where they can lick it as and when they wish.
It is important to remember that extra salt and electrolytes will always be required by the horse when the weather is particularly hot, or after a great deal of exertion.

Molasses is a highly nutritious by-product of sugar. It comes either in liquid form which can be diluted or as a meal to spread over the feed. It may be mixed with chaff, which makes for a very useful addition of nutritious roughage.

Salt is essential for the horse's health. It can either be given in the feed, 1-2 oz. (25-50 g) per day, or provided as a salt lick on the wall or in the manger. Remember, though, that salt is included in prepared mixes.

Milk powder (pellets) are good for building up condition as they are fattening. They also contain calcium.

Garlic and other herbs can help specific conditions. Garlic is particularly good for respiratory problems.

Electrolytes are fed to replace the body salts which are lost through sweating in very hot weather or following hard exercise. They may be given directly with the feed or in the water, but this method must be introduced slowly to get the horse used to the taste. In severe cases of dehydration, intravenous electrolyte injections will be given by the vet.

Succulents such as apples, carrots, and root vegetables are always chopped lengthwise so that they do not get stuck in the horse's throat.

Freshly cut grass can be fed at any time. Do not use lawn mowings unless they are less than half an hour old as grass ferments very quickly in hot weather. Avoid grass which has been treated with weedkiller or pesticide.

Containers

Most stables have metal or plastic feeding bowls which must be kept clean so that stale feed does not build up. Some stalls contain their own mangers which also have to be checked to make sure they are clean. Mild disinfectants may be used, but all food containers must be rinsed thoroughly before they are used again as the mildest whiff of disinfectant will put a shy feeder right off his food.

Storing Store food in a dry, verminproof container in a damp-free feed room. Check that foods are used within the dates specified on the bags and that the food bin is empty before adding fresh supplies.

Feeding

Choose a feeding time which suits the stable routine and stick to it.

Mix all the feeds individually and thoroughly first and then give to all the horses in the yard at the same time so that those still waiting to be fed are less likely to get impatient and bang their doors.

Look at each horse carefully to make sure it is maintaining condition, and increase or decrease food as necessary, remembering to keep the balance between roughage and bulk and concentrate according to the work being done. A chart recording all the horses' feeds hung in the feed room is a valuable aid.

The horse or pony doing light work will need more bulk and less concentrates, whereas those undertaking heavier work will require less bulk and more concentrates. The ratio should never fall below 40 percent roughage and 60 percent concentrates.

"Feed only the horse"

The importance of regular worming cannot be over-emphasized, as no amount of good food will benefit the worm-infested horse. Likewise, the horse with teeth which have not been attended to regularly will fail to thrive. These things must always be borne in mind when assessing the horse's eating habits and condition. They are covered under Veterinary care on p. 74 and p. 77.

Feeding should take place at regular times. Note the solid feed bins with verminproof lids. The mangers should be rinsed out after every feed.

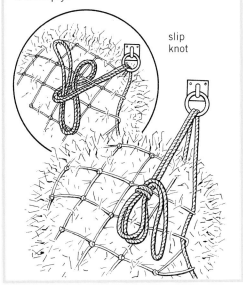

How to tie up a haynet

Pull the net up high through the ring and fasten to the net with a slip knot. Place the net with the knot facing the wall. The ring must always be high enough that the horse cannot get its legs caught in the net when it is empty.

slip knot

Water

Water is essential to life, and the horse should always have a fresh and constant supply available. If water is not provided, the horse will quickly become dehydrated, especially in hot weather, and lose condition. Horses may drink anything from five to ten buckets of water a day. Buckets in the stable or automatic systems are the usual methods of providing water; care must be taken to make sure the latter are working correctly, especially in freezing weather.

Buckets tend to get knocked over, so they should be tied or clipped to the wall. Place in a corner with the handle facing the wall where they are less likely to get in the way. If you use buckets, you can keep an eye on the amounts drunk. If the horse has been without water for some time, for example when competing, allow it to have only half a bucket at first, then further half buckets every 15 minutes until satisfied. In very cold weather it is advisable to take the chill off the water. The horse should be discouraged from drinking large amounts before and after hard work to avoid colic.

Automatic systems are not ideal as the amount the horse drinks cannot be monitored; however, they are becoming more and more popular because of their labor-saving qualities. It is essential to check that the horse is happy to drink from these as they can be too noisy for the timid horse. They must be checked and cleaned daily.

Keeping the horse at grass

The grass-kept horse has certain needs which have to be taken into account when planning how best to keep it in a fit and healthy state all year round.

The area has to be adequate; this will depend on the type of land, its position, the drainage, and the number of horses using it. The minimum size for one horse is one to one and half acres.

Watering For the grass-kept horse, a water trough should be provided in the field, which should be checked daily to make sure that it is safe and free from dangerous projecting metalwork on which the horse might injure itself, and to see that it is working properly. In freezing weather special care is needed to break the ice. The ball cock must be safely protected from the horse with a secure cover. It is always best to stand the trough on a firm surface such as concrete so that the surrounding ground will not turn into a muddy bog.

If the field has natural water, make sure that it is fresh and moving and that the approach is safe. Stagnant ponds won't do. Remember to check that your natural water supply does not dry up in hot weather.

Types of fencing

Fencing has to be safe and secure to ensure there is no possibility that the horse might injure itself. There are various types of fencing suitable for horses.

Natural hedges are ideal, so long as they are consistently secure and surround the entire area. Check them carefully to make sure there are no weak spots. Reinforce with post and rails, if necessary. Hedges provide shade and shelter for horses throughout the year.

Post and rails, well erected, are an excellent means of security, so long as they have at least two rails and are high enough to prevent the horse from jumping out. A good height is 4 ft. 6 in. (1.37 m). The rails must be strong, without projections or nails, and constructed of strong timber.

Straight wire strands, as long as they are kept taut, are effective, but the bottom strand should be at least 1 ft. (30.5 cm) off the ground to ensure the horse cannot put a foot over it and injure itself by pulling back. Likewise, wire with a post and rail on top can be useful and has the added advantage of being more easily seen.

Barbed wire is totally unsuitable for horses because of the risk of injury.

Electric fencing can be very effective, and horses soon learn to respect it. There have, however, been times when horses have been frightened, during thunderstorms for instance, when they start galloping and have

rushed straight through the fence, probably because they fail to see it.

Gates The security of any type of fence will be useless unless there is an effective gate which remains closed. It is vital that the gate has a secure latch. A padlock is also strongly recommended, particularly in fields that have gates leading onto public roads.

Shelter

The horse will need some form of shelter both in winter against the wind and rain and in summer against the heat and flies.

A good hedge line forms an effective shelter, especially if it is allowed to grow to a reasonable height, as it will serve as a wind-break. Large leafy trees provide shade from the sun and flies in summer, but if the

Electric tape makes a safe and effective fence as it is easily seen, and horses soon realize when it is working. Electric wire can cause problems as it is less visible and can frighten horses if they touch it without knowing it is there.

paddock has neither a good hedge nor trees, some sort of field shelter should be provided, preferably facing away from the prevailing wind. A firm base is important, if it is not to become very wet during the winter. It should also be as close as possible to the access so that daily checks and feed in the winter can be easily given. The shelter should be large enough to prevent overcrowding and the possibility of fights breaking out.

New Zealand rugs (see p. 60) are warm

and provide horses with excellent protection against cold and wet, allowing a clipped horse to be turned out in poor weather.

Extra feeding

Most ponies will require no extra feeding during the summer months, so long as the pasture is providing adequate food. If this is not so, hay should be fed to supplement the grass, and a mineral block can be placed in the field. A block should be available during the winter as well.

For working horses, brood mares and youngsters, and older horses, extra hard food will invariably be required and should be fed in individual feed bowls – well separated if there is more than one horse. Hay racks, placed on a firm base, will help to prevent wastage.

The amount of hard food given will depend on various factors (see p. 50) with usually one or two feeds per day, generally given both morning and evening.

Herbs Horses enjoy herbs, both fresh and dry. Spot planting of chicory, yarrow, burnet, mint, dandelion, and borage can be done in a selected area, preferably close to the fence or hedge.

General care and consideration of the grass-kept horse

Daily inspection out at grass is very important to ensure the horse is healthy and that nothing is amiss.

The overall well-being of the horse is very important. Does it look warm enough? Check to see if a blanket is necessary. The horse will use up energy reserves to keep warm in cold weather and will soon start to lose condition unless a blanket or extra feeding is provided. Usually, horses with a thick coat can withstand cold, but they do not tolerate wet, cold weather too well. Does the horse look generally well and in good condition? If not, assess the situation and act accordingly.

The state of a horse's feet and legs is very important. Check that there is no sign of injury, heat, or swelling in the legs and that the feet are kept trimmed and, if shod, that the shoes are in place. It is usual for the horse turned out to rest to have the hind shoes removed and grass tips on the front feet help wear and tear and to avoid grass cracks. If it is wet and muddy, shoes can easily be pulled off, and it is easy to miss that the feet are growing too long in such conditions. Mud fever can develop in damp conditions and should be treated as discussed under Veterinary care (see p. 78). Heel bug may develop in the summer, and with unshod horses, breaking of the feet

(grass cracks) may occur – particularly in dry conditions. It may be necessary for the horse to be shod or the wall of the hoof clipped if this becomes a serious problem. (Hoofcare is covered on p. 66-9.)

Infections and parasites Watch carefully for indications of sweet itch, founder, allergies, bot and warblefly infestation, etc., and treat as necessary. (See Veterinary care on p. 74.)

Worming has to be carried out regularly. This is generally done at least every six weeks, but if there are several horses in the paddock or if the land is rather horse-sick (see below), it should be done every four weeks. Consult your vet about the most suitable worming brands for the time of year.

Care of the paddock Make a regular check to ensure there are no poisonous trees or plants growing in the paddock and that no trash such as broken bottles has been thrown into the field. It is vital that this is done when first moving to new pasture.

The horse-sick field

This term is applied to a pasture which has been overgrazed and is of poor quality. It may contain undesirable weeds and plants which will have a detrimental effect on the horse, or it may be littered with worm-infested droppings. To return the pasture to good quality grazing land, the infested droppings must be removed manually or the land harrowed and laid to rest for at least a whole season.

Mixed grazing can be beneficial to pasture. Sheep are omnivorous eaters and will eat most things that horses, which are fussy eaters, will leave behind, including weeds. While sheep graze steadily in a continuous line, devouring everything in front of them before moving on, the horse picks only at the best grasses, avoiding areas which have been staled or are covered in droppings. Cattle and sheep are not hosts to the same worms and parasites as horses.

Poisonous trees and plants

Yew, found in northwestern areas, is poisonous all year round. Check that there is none growing around the hedgelines or nearby.

Privet is equally poisonous and should never be used as a hedge around a paddock.

Ragwort is perhaps the most dangerous of all plants for horses, in that the toxins cause the gradual destruction of the liver. It is not generally eaten in its growing state but is dangerous in dried form; for example, if found in hay. Any ragwort found in a field should be pulled up and removed.

Bracken, it is not always realized, is poisonous, and can be found at the edge of reseeded or improved pasture and on common land.

Buttercups are poisonous to horses when they are growing. However, they are harmless when dried. Spraying is the best means of eradication.

Nightshade is poisonous. All parts are toxic, particularly the berries and roots.

Other poisonous plants include those of the hemlock family, locoweed and some of its cousins, the vetches, foxglove, bluebells, laburnum, and rhododendrons. Maple, coniferous trees, and most trees with berries (like holly) are poisonous, and so are the decomposed leaves of the Black Cherry and acorns. It is wise to discourage the eating of bark, which kills the trees, although horses would normally eat it in the wild.

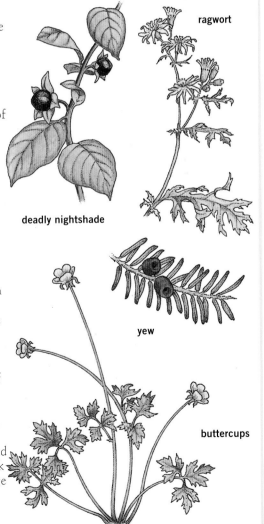

ragwort

deadly nightshade

yew

buttercups

The stable and yard layout

The design of a new stableyard should take into account, among other things, the siting of stables, drainage, water, access to food stores, tackroom, disposal of manure, access, and security. Usually, however, the yard and/or stables already exist.

The water faucet is important if the automatic drinking system is not used, as buckets of water are heavy. The faucet needs to be as close to the horses as possible; either place one at each end of a line of stalls or put one somewhere in the middle. The tackroom and the feedroom will also need water or at least be close to a faucet.

The feed store should be easily accessible to delivery trucks and not too far away from the stables themselves. The feed bins must be verminproof and, if food is to be stored, it should be kept off the floor on pallets to keep it dry.

Hay should be kept close to the stables, but not so close that it creates a fire hazard. If some horses are on vacuum-packed hay for allergy reasons, this should be stored separately, away from hay and straw, so that damaging spores do not contaminate the former.

The manure pile needs to be nearby so that the pushing of heavy wheelbarrows is reduced to a minimum. However it should be far enough away so that in the summer flies do not become too big a problem. It must also be accessible for removal.

Security

Security is most important, and the tackroom should be totally secure. Any windows should be barred or covered with a steel grill, and the door should be strong with secure hinges and locks. All tack should be properly marked. This can often be arranged through the police or a local security firm.

The stable area or barn should be secured at night – and at all times if it is adjacent to a public highway – and the gates should always be kept shut in case a horse should get loose.

A horse box or trailer should ideally be stored under cover in an easily accessible barn or shed. Never leave the keys inside.

The stables

While most stables are intended to be fairly basic, they can be made quite attractive to look at with the simple addition of some big, well-stocked flower tubs or other containers painted in bright colors. The horses, however, are frequently very partial to the floral contents of the containers, so be careful not to place them within reach of a hungry face! It goes without saying that a clean, neat yard always looks good, but this can only be achieved if it has an easily swept surface with good drainage or can be raked.

A stable with an overhanging roof (left) is typically British in design. The separate stalls help prevent the spread of infection, and the horses get plenty of fresh air and interest looking out.

Barn stables, like the one below, have always been popular in the U.S.A. and are becoming increasingly so in the U.K. It is very convenient to have everything under one roof, especially in winter. It also makes working conditions much more pleasant for everybody in cold and wet weather.

Types of stabling

There are basically three types of stabling.

Stalls were more popular during the nineteenth century when large numbers of horses were kept stabled in cities and towns where there was no room for box stalls. They are still in use today, their only disadvantage being a lack of space as the horses have to be tied up in rows, the ropes only slackened during feeding and in the evening to allow them to lie down. When horses are kept in stalls, frequent work and exercise are necessary to compensate for the lack of movement while stabled.

Individual blocks of stables, usually box stalls, which can be arranged in lines running parallel to one another, or in the form of an "L" shape, a square, or a single line. Ideally, stable blocks should face into the sunshine and away from any bitter winter winds.

The barn system, popular in the U.S., usually consists of two rows of box stalls enclosed within a large covered area. The wider the passage in between the boxes, the better. Care and stable management can be carried out under the same roof, but there may be a lack of ventilation, which adds to the danger of infections spreading. Encourage maximum circulation of air with open doors and windows wherever and whenever possible.

The stable

Various factors have to be taken into account when horses are kept stabled, especially if you are planning a stable from scratch. The site, the position of the buildings, and the choice of building materials all need careful thought. Many horses are stabled very adequately in a variety of stalls, sheds, or barns, but the following points apply to all stables.

Box stalls should be light, airy, well-ventilated, and of a suitable size for the height of the horse. Most boxes for horses are designed to be no smaller than 10 ft. (3 m) by 12 ft. (3.5 m) for horses and 10 ft. (3 m) by 10 ft. (3 m) for ponies. This size should be considered the very minimum for the horse which is to be stabled for an average of 22 to 23 hours a day.

Ventilation has to be carefully considered as the horse requires a constant supply of circulating fresh air, even in the winter months. Put on an extra blanket and keep top doors or windows open rather than restrict the air supply. Drafts should be avoided at all times.

Windows Most new buildings are designed with ventilation in the roof space, and it is preferable to have a window at the back as well as one in the front. Windows should always open outward so that they do not hurt the horse when opened; they should contain unbreakable glass or plastic glass and be installed high up with a metal grid so as not to cause injury.

Other methods of ventilation include the use of air bricks, extractor fans, and vents of different designs, as well as doors with special webbing fixtures so that they can be left open during the daytime.

Roof The height of the stall will play a big part in successful ventilation. Care should be taken to see that beams are high enough so that the horse does not hit its head, and any sharp edges should be covered with foam if they look likely to be a hazard.

Gutters must be efficient and kept clean and free flowing, with adequate downspouts to cope with the water from the roof. An overhang is now considered essential for protection in wet weather. Old stalls, however, rarely have this facility, particularly in the U.K.

The walls of the stable are usually made of concrete blocks, bricks, wood, or wooden partitions. Some may be constructed from wood with metal grids on top. The partition type are generally at least 7½ ft. (2.3 m) high.

Solid walls may tend to limit ventilation if there is insufficient circulating air, but will help to reduce the spread of infection.

All walls of whatever design must be strong and smooth with no projections. A kick from a horse will easily shatter anything but the strongest wood. It is always worth getting the very best materials available if they are to last. Most stables are lined with hard wood or wallboard to form a kicking board for extra protection and strength. These are essential if the walls are brick.

The floors of the stable are usually constructed with a concrete base at least 6 in. (15 cm) thick with a roughened surface so that it is not slippery. Old concrete floors can become very smooth and slippery so plenty of bedding is necessary.

Other floor surfaces include chalk which is fairly free draining, various composite floorings which are expensive but very adequate, and rubberized floors which are non-slip but quite difficult to muck out.

Stable doors should always open outward and ideally be in two halves. They should be strong and at least 4 ft. (1.25 m) wide, and the lower door approximately 4½ ft. (1.4 m) high, with a bolt on the outside low enough for the horse to be unable to open it. If he is apt to play, use one that has a safety catch.

As horses are notorious for chewing, it is suggested that the top few inches of the lower door should be covered with metal sheeting. The lower door should have a second kick release bolt at the bottom for strength and security. All doors should have a hook added to hold the independent section open as necessary.

Top doors have to fit properly and should always be held back securely when left open, and checked, especially at the beginning of the winter, in case they have warped or slipped during the summer, making it difficult to shut them when the cold weather arrives.

Sliding doors need special attention to keep runners clear of debris and straw, and to make sure that the stops remain in place.

Drainage is very important and must be a major consideration when designing new stables. Ideally, stalls should have individual drains with the floor sloping slightly either to the front or back and running into a shallow channel along the outside of the stable wall. Most drain toward the front, making it easy

The box stall

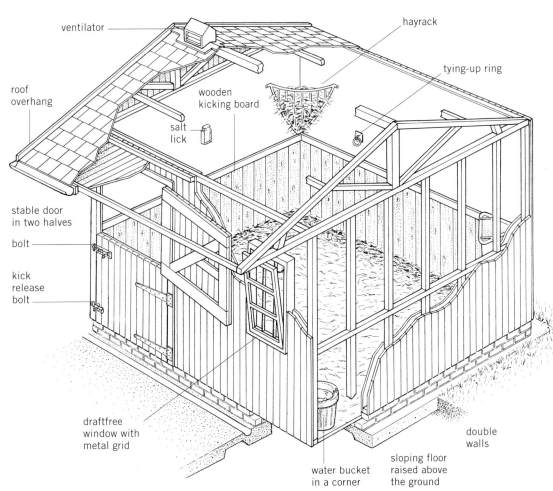

ventilator
hayrack
roof overhang
wooden kicking board
salt lick
tying-up ring
stable door in two halves
bolt
kick release bolt
draftfree window with metal grid
water bucket in a corner
sloping floor raised above the ground
double walls

to wash down boxes which can drain through doorways. Passageways should drain away from boxes, as should outdoor paving, to make sure no surface water runs back toward the stable. Three- or four-sided stables need careful thought if a central drain is to be installed.

The drains should be covered by a metal grill, flush with the ground and securely fitted. These covers should be strong enough to take the full weight of a horse if they are trodden on.

Electrical fixtures All electrical fixtures must be safe and sited so that they do not become a hazard to the horse. Electrical fires have caused numerous horrifying deaths in stables throughout the world, and a little fore-thought and sensible precautions might have prevented many of these. The following points should be noted.
• All wiring should be contained within a conduit unless well out of reach of the horse.
• All plugs and fixtures should be outside the stable and away from the horse.
• Electrical fixtures outside stables should be weatherproof.
• No hay or straw should be stored near electric cables.
• Any electrical fault should be thoroughly checked and all cables and fittings inspected regularly. Mice and rats are notorious for eating through cables, especially if food is kept nearby.

Stable routine

The stable routine can be arranged to suit your lifestyle within reason and should be worked out so that feed times change as little as possible. Some people prefer to ride or exercise early, so the horse has to be fed early, in which case breakfast later makes sense, whereas others (probably most people) will ride after breakfast or later in the day. The horse should always have at least an hour's peace and quiet after being fed before being taken out. It is a good idea to allow the horse at least two hours total quiet in the stable during the middle of the day or in the early afternoon.

Mucking out

This is probably about the least enjoyable, but most necessary part of owning a horse. How easy it is to do depends on your particular horse and how clean it is, the type of bedding used, how often you clean out its stable during the day and the thoroughness with which you do this job. A mature horse will defecate between 5-12 times a day and urinate 7-11 times a day, depending on the diet and its individual bodily functions.

Generally speaking, the horse should be

How to muck out

Start by fitting a halter and tying up the horse, preferably outside if the weather allows, and removing the haynet, water bucket, and feed bowl, if necessary.
• Bank all clean bedding up on one or two sides of the box; with the fork remove the wet and soiled bedding into the wheelbarrow, being as economical as possible with the clean bedding.
• Sweep the floor and the sides of the box which you have just cleared. Ideally, let the floor air and dry before replacing the bedding. If you are exercising the horse after mucking out and grooming, leave the bedding banked up until you return.
• Replace the haynet and water buckets and let the horse loose. Always sweep up thoroughly outside the stable, keeping it clean and neat at all times. Store all equipment well away from the horses to avoid accidents, and always check that you have removed all mucking-out tools from the stable.

A special fork can be used for wood chips, paper, or peat, whereby the droppings and wet patches are dug out daily and the whole bed thoroughly turned over and replaced with fresh bedding as necessary. It is important to keep shavings, paper, and peat as dry as possible.

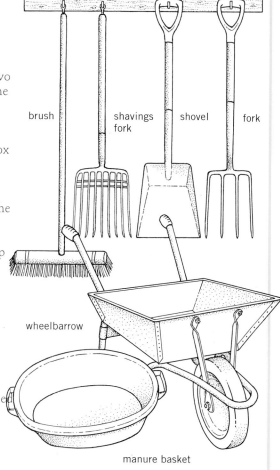

brush   shavings fork   shovel   fork

wheelbarrow

manure basket

thoroughly mucked out first thing in the morning and then droppings are removed in the manure basket during the day as necessary, especially at noon and in the early evening.

Bedding down Using the fork, spread the bedding evenly over the floor, adding fresh bedding as necessary. Spread this thoroughly and evenly over the whole floor, making sure there is enough to protect the horse from damage and that it is deep enough to encourage it to lie down and take the strain off its legs. Always bank some of the bedding up the sides for added protection in case the horse lies down and rolls or gets cast.

The deep litter system This can be used successfully with straw and can work fairly satisfactorily with wood chips; it is for a low maintenance stable and is particularly useful for the busy person who does not really have time to spend on the horse except perhaps at weekends. The horse is probably turned out by day and comes in at night. It is not recommended for the stabled horse for long periods, because the bedding can become warm from the buildup of manure which may cause thrush in the feet (see p. 79).

Usually the droppings are picked up and new straw is placed on top as required, with the stable being cleaned daily. Every few weeks or months, everything is cleared out completely. This can be quite a major undertaking, depending on the buildup. It is easiest in an open-fronted barn or stable with double doors where a tractor can be used.

Types of bedding

There are several different types of bedding, notably straw, wood chips, sawdust, peat, and paper. Which is the most suitable is a matter of personal preference, the horse's behavior, and in some cases availability.

Straw has been used traditionally as it is relatively cheap, warm, and comfortable and has excellent free-draining qualities. There are three types of straw, wheat straw being considered the best. This is springy, not particularly palatable, and provides good drainage. Barley straw is also good, so long as the ears have been removed, now usually the case with modern combining. If they have not been removed, the barley may be irritating to the horse and might cause choking. Barley straw is softer and more palatable, so there is a tendency for horses to eat this. Oat straw is rather porous; it becomes wet and soggy, so it is used very seldom.

Sawdust, if readily available, may be cheap and makes a good bed if kept dry. It tends to be a bit dusty if the weather is very dry, and

sometimes causes skin irritations, especially if it comes from pine trees. Because sawdust is so fine, it is important to make sure that the bed is kept deep enough to prevent the horse from injuring itself. The droppings and damp patches should be removed as soon as it becomes necessary. Because of its absorbency, the damp patches can become very heavy, making mucking out extremely hard work.

Wood chips are light and more absorbent than sawdust; otherwise they have much the same qualities and are used at the same time. They are not dusty once laid, but it is best to lay them when the horse is out of the stable. Sawdust and wood chips are commonly used for the horse which eats straw bedding; the only disadvantage is disposing of them as they do not make good manure unless mixed with a large quantity of straw and left for a long period.

Peat is light to handle and very absorbent, and is treated in much the same way as sawdust and wood chips. The damp patches should be dug out daily. It is the most expensive type of bedding.

Paper bedding has proved to be dustfree and is therefore the bedding choice for horses with breathing or dust allergy problems, and if you have your own paper-shredding machine, you will find it is very cheap! This type of bedding needs to be kept very dry; otherwise, it quickly becomes solid and congealed, and it is then extremely hard work to muck it out.

This horse, bedded on shavings, looks extremely relaxed and comfortable as it stretches out for an afternoon snooze in its deep, dry bed which is well banked at the sides.

The muck heap

It is as important to take as much care of the muck heap as of the stable itself. The art of stacking manure takes a lot of practice to make perfect, but large amounts can be neatly stored for some time if a good compacting system is adopted.

It is best to build straw heaps in sections, particularly if it is later to be used as fertilizer after a period of rotting down has taken place.

Be sure to build up your muck in an oblong or a particular shape, taking care to make square corners and a flat top. This requires time spent making the heap neat and even on top and at the sides. It should then be compacted by walking over it several times to press it down so that it can rot in its own, self-generated heat. Once the stack has built up to a certain size, it can either be removed, or a new stack started alongside it, giving the old one time to rot down properly before being spread on the land in the winter months. Other types of muck should be kept neatly contained, especially paper which tends to blow around. Any infected bedding used by a sick horse should be burned rather than put on the general muck heap to prevent any spread of infection.

Care and protection of the horse

There is a wide selection of clothing to protect the horse, enabling it to live out of doors in all weathers and at all seasons, as well as to compete and work in ever-varying disciplines and conditions throughout the year.

Blankets and their uses

The stabled horse will usually require one blanket or more at night for some of the year. (The added warmth of his stable will not have encouraged a dense, waterproof coat like the grass-kept horse.) How many and how warm these need to be will, of course, depend on the weather and whether or not the horse is clipped, is groomed regularly, and its general condition. The grass-kept horse will have a thick coat, which if ungroomed contains the thick buildup of natural grease and oil which helps to protect it from the elements.

There are numerous blanket designs on the market, as well as a huge variety of fabrics and linings suitable for all occasions and climates. The typical American version, which has crossover straps attached to the blanket, is designed to be relatively nonslip and to do away with the padded surcingle, which may sometimes cause soreness or chapping where it rubs or puts pressure on the back. The traditional English blanket and padded surcingle are, however, the only type used for "dressup" occasions and are also used when the crossover style does not suit the horse. It is essential that any blanket used fits correctly to avoid any flapping about, rubbing across the shoulders or hips, and that they stay in place.

Types of blanket

There are numerous different types of blankets, including the following:

Night blankets are used in the stable all the time for warmth and protection and come in a variety of materials, including polyester, nylon, jute, burlap, and the "comforter" type filled with lightweight mixtures. Night blankets should be hard-wearing and roomy, especially if in cold weather you intend to put another blanket underneath. They must be large enough to fit your horse — particularly across the chest and lengthwise.

Day blankets are generally kept for dress occasions such as traveling to and from competitions. They are usually made of wool blends; many people choose a special stable color and have their initials or logo on the rear corners to provide a distinguishing feature.

Pads are used for extra warmth and are placed under the blanket with the front corners folded up and then pulled back over the blanket. A roller is then needed to hold the pad in place and prevent it from slipping back. Generally made of wool or wool blends, pads are traditionally yellow with broad red, black, and blue stripes. Many people, however, use old house blankets on their horses.

The summer sheet not only acts as a stylish cover in hot weather, when it replaces the day blanket, but it protects the horse from flies and dust and is often used under the night blanket to protect it from dirt and grease as it is much easier to wash. Summer sheets are made of cotton, linen, or other light mixtures. Those made of toweling can be useful, especially at competitions or when the horse has been sweating or has just been washed, as they are light, very absorbent, warm, and easily washable. All sheets have to be fitted with fillet strings to prevent the back from blowing up and frightening the horse, and to help keep them in place along with a surcingle or crossover straps.

Coolers are designed to allow for evaporation to take place on hot and sweating horses. Usually made out of string, wool, or cotton mixtures with large holes or other similar design, they can be used alone

The New Zealand rug

The New Zealand rug has been a horse's best friend for years. Made of canvas or other lightweight waterproof material, it is designed to protect the horse from wind, rain, cold, and snow. In many cases it has enabled owners to keep horses out all year round, regardless of the weather. It is especially designed to be relatively non-slip and has special leg straps to help keep it in place and prevent rubbing. Take care when first using a New Zealand rug until the horse is used to the feel of it. The rug usually has a double fastening in front and is sufficiently deep and long to give extra protection. There are several designs on the market, based on the traditional canvas rug. Care must be taken that they are a good fit and not too heavy or too loose. It should be taken off daily and the horse checked to see that there are no rubs or chapped areas which need attention. The points of the shoulder and hips tend to be the most vulnerable to chapping, especially on fine skinned horses.

in warm weather until the horse dries off. A sheet or blanket placed over the top in cooler weather will prevent chilling. If the horse is liable to "break out," fit the outer blanket inside out so that the moisture is absorbed. When the horse has cooled and dried off, it can be reversed with the correct, dry side next to the horse's skin to keep it warm and dry.

Coolers are frequently made of cotton and are used to protect the horse from the sun. All-enveloping, they also provide protection against dust and flies.

The paddock sheet is used mostly in racing circles. It is a blanket without a front fastening, which is placed over the light racing saddle in the paddock and secured with a surcingle or roller. It is also used as an exercise sheet, fitted under the saddle with the front corners folded up under the saddle flap, and it is particularly useful for clipped horses doing slow work in cold weather.

Waterproofs are particularly useful at competitions when the horse is having to wait around for different classes or phases, and they keep the tack dry as well. There are a variety of designs, ranging from the blanket type to the all-enveloping kind which literally covers the horse from head to tail.

Surcingles are generally used to keep the blanket in place. They are usually made of leather or webbing. There are several different types, and care must be taken to protect the spinal area which can get rubbed or put under constant pressure if fitted too tightly, even though most of them are designed with a raised padded area to prevent this. Special wither pads or foam rubber used under the surcingle will help. Some horses tend to get cast in boxes when they roll or lie down too close to the wall, and a hooped anticast surcingle will prevent this.

Sheets and light blankets should always be covered by a surcingle to prevent them from blowing up in a breeze and frightening the horse. The elasticized surcingles on the market now are ideal, but they are not designed to hold a heavy blanket in place.

Hoods are now very much back in fashion, as new designs have appeared to help the overworked horse owner. Originally designed for warmth and made of wool, modern hoods are often made of lightweight stretchy material which can be pulled on over the horse's head all at once, leaving holes for the eyes and ears. They are now used as much to keep the horse clean in the field as for warmth. If put on with the mane carefully pushed over to the correct side, the stretchy hood acts as an excellent mane layer. In very cold weather, this protection is much healthier for the horse than shutting it in the stable.

The different types of blankets

Blankets come in all shapes, sizes, and designs to cater for the various needs of the different types of horses. Some have fastenings attached to keep them in place while others require a pad and surcingle to secure them. Blankets must be the right size for the horse and are generally measured from the front of the chest to the point of the buttock.

night blanket

day blanket and hood

fitted with a padded surcingle

summer sheet

fitted with a surcingle

paddock sheet

fitted with a breastplate and surcingle

fillet string

cooler

fitted with an elasticized surcingle

Clipping

A horse generally changes its coat twice a year; in the spring, there is a change to a thinner, summer coat and in the fall, there is another change to a thicker coat for the winter months.

A horse should be clipped according to its type, lifestyle, conditions, and the amount of work it has to perform. A horse with a thick coat will sweat if worked, which may well cause distress and loss of condition. The horse will also be prone to chilling while cooling off. Although a stabled horse's coat will never grow as thick as that of a horse kept at grass, clipping will make the horse more presentable, easier to groom, and less prone to chapped skin.

A horse should be clipped first in October when its winter coat is fully established, and every three weeks thereafter. The last clip should be no later than the end of January so as not to affect the summer coat, though competition horses will be clipped for as long as they are kept in work.

Clipping is usually done with electric clippers. There are two main types: the hand machine, and the heavy-duty machine, where the motor is suspended from the wall or a beam; with this type the clipper head is very light, but there is a long, flexible cord which can be a bit of a nuisance.

Hand clippers are most commonly used. The engine and clipper head are combined in one hand-held machine with a cable to the plug. They can be heavy, but are excellent for general use. There is also a smaller, very quiet model, excellent for trimming and clipping, which is useful for difficult horses.

How to clip

First prepare a suitable area, with very little or no bedding, which has a plug, or have an extension cord at hand. Prepare clippers, oil for the clippers, a cloth to wipe the blades, overalls, and some kind of headcovering to protect yourself from the hairs, suitable blankets or sheets for the horse, and a filled haynet as a distraction.

Groom the horse thoroughly; grease and dirt will quickly clog up the clipper blades and the machine will overheat. Check that the plug is in correct working order before plugging in and that the machine is oiled and the blades sharp. Check the tension by screwing the nut tightly, then releasing it by one-and-a-half turns; a high, fast rattle will indicate that it is too loose. If this is the case, adjust the nut to find the correct tension. The tension will need adjusting from time to time.

Check the blades regularly on the flat of your hand to see they are not overheating. Hot blades will irritate the horse, so switch off and allow to cool down. Oil and wipe the blades regularly during the clip. If the blades pull at the coat, they are probably blunt and should be replaced with a sharpened set.

Always clip against the lay of the coat, working along from the front to the rear, starting at the shoulder before attempting to clip the head and neck, so as not to upset the horse. Clip in long, sweeping strokes, slightly overlapping each strip so that you get a smooth area. Keep the angle of the clippers so that the blades run flat along the horse's coat. Clip in sections, and cover the clipped area with a blanket as soon as possible to prevent the horse from getting cold.

On difficult areas gently ease the skin over bony prominences and take care not to nick the horse where there are folds of skin. It may be necessary to have a helper to hold the horse if clipping around the head and inside the front and hind legs. In sensitive areas, make sure that the blades are not too

This horse is being trace-clipped so that it does not get too hot during exercise. With the clippers, start at the shoulder and work up the neck, working against the direction of the coat.

Types of clip

There are various types of clip that can be used.

The full clip means the coat is taken off completely, leaving just a small triangle above the tail.

The hunter clip means that all the coat is removed except for that on the legs and a saddle patch. This helps to prevent saddle sores and gives the horse extra leg protection; this clip is often done on hunters, competition horses, and horses in hard to medium work.

The blanket clip is done on horses and ponies in medium work which need extra warmth, but do not require a full or hunter clip as their winter coat is not thick enough to cause overheating. A blanket clip leaves the coat on the legs, but the head, neck, and lower body clipped.

The chaser clip useful for working horses in light work. The coat is left on the legs and from just behind the ears and along the top of the neck and back to the tail. This is useful for the horse which feels the cold or is out at grass during the daytime.

The trace clip means the coat is removed along the belly from the thigh and elbow up through the lower shoulder and underside of the neck. It is very useful for horses in light work or those out at grass in a New Zealand rug and for ponies which get very thick coats.

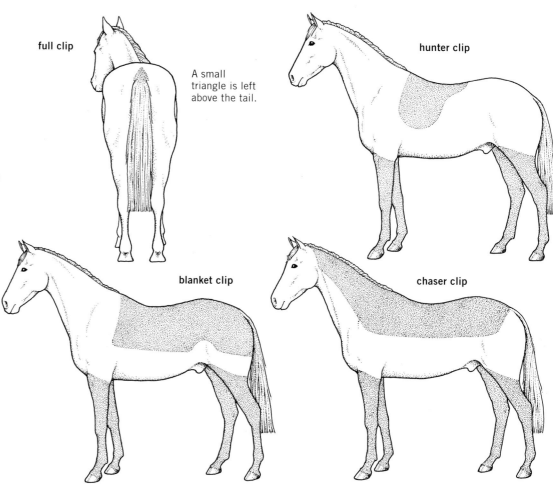

full clip

A small triangle is left above the tail.

hunter clip

blanket clip

chaser clip

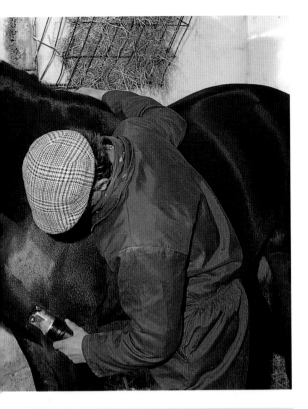

Full clip: a saddle patch gives extra protection

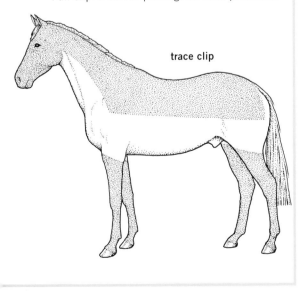

trace clip

hot. It may be best to do these areas after finishing work on the main part of the body. In some cases twitching may be required. If it is, put the twitch on when the horse is quiet; this way it will be much more effective than when the horse has got worked up about the clippers. Only ever apply the twitch to the upper lip and remove it as soon as possible and rub the horse's nose to restore full circulation.

The best way to learn to clip is to watch an experienced person before trying for yourself. It then requires practice to obtain the smoothness and evenness of a well-finished result.

Leg care and protection

The horse's legs are vulnerable to stress and injury, but a little thought and care will go a long way toward preventing unnecessary accidents. Study your horse's action by watching it run up in hand toward you and away from you. Handle the horse on a long rein so as not to impede his natural action. If possible, do this with your farrier as well so that he, too, is aware of any shortcomings which could perhaps be improved with careful shoeing.

Look to see if your horse moves very close in front or behind, and decide if it requires boots as protection when being worked. Study its legs and their shape, so that you can decide what type of boot might be best. If the horse has very large, round joints, the harder type of boot may well rub against them, so a more pliable design would be better suited. If the horse tends to knock itself a lot, then a stronger, padded type may be best to prevent bruising. There are numerous designs on the market, and it is best to discuss the horse with your saddler who should know the attributes of the various boots available. Keep all boots scrupulously clean and pliable, as a sore which develops through rubbing could cause long-term problems.

The legs should be inspected daily, preferably either first thing in the morning or last thing at night, so that any problem will be noticed immediately. Feel for any heat or swelling in the legs. Look for cuts, grazes, or lacerations.

The legs must be kept clean and free from scabs or dirt. A good wash with soap and water will help to keep them free of dirt and sweat, especially if the horse has been through deep mud. Care should be taken, however, not to remove all the natural oils protecting the skin, so a wash once or twice a week should be the maximum. In the winter the legs should be allowed to dry and the mud and sweat brushed off. Dry the

heels very carefully, rubbing in a little petroleum jelly to prevent dry cracks and sores forming, and treat any little nicks or abrasions with a cream, wound powder, or spray.

Types of boot and their uses

Brushing boots are designed to shield the horse's inside lower leg from rubs and knocks from the opposite leg. They protect the cannon bones, fetlock joints, and tendons of the lower leg, and are made of leather, foam or rubber-based materials, plastic, or felt.

The Yorkshire boot makes an effective hind joint protector. It is a simple rectangle of felt with a tape along the center. It is fastened on the outside above the fetlock joint with the top half folded down over the joint.

The rubber ring or sausage boot protects the area around the pastern, which is particularly liable to knocks and soreness with the jumping horse. It often works wonders on the horse, which gets very tense as it anticipates the pain from this type of knock. It is fastened around the coronet of the leg most prone to injury. The sausage boot is also used to prevent capped elbows, which are caused by pressure from the inner heel of the shoe on the elbow when a horse is lying down, usually on insufficient bedding (see Veterinary care, p. 68).

Bell boots are designed to protect the bulbs of the heels of the forelegs from overreaching. The jumping horse is particularly prone to accidents, especially in deep, heavy ground. These boots can be fastened around the pastern or if they are rubber they can be pulled on over the foot. They should be turned inside out to be pulled on and then turned back the right way, covering the heel and the coronet.

The well-padded bell boots used for polo.

Types of boots

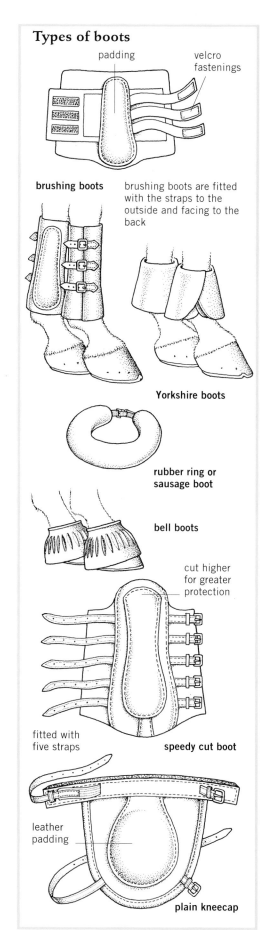

padding

velcro fastenings

brushing boots

brushing boots are fitted with the straps to the outside and facing to the back

Yorkshire boots

rubber ring or sausage boot

bell boots

cut higher for greater protection

fitted with five straps

speedy cut boot

leather padding

plain kneecap

This horse is well protected with open-fronted tendon boots, pull-on rubber bell boots, and a skeleton kneecap, which is probably protecting an old injury.

Competition boots come in a variety of designs to give protection to specific areas. They must have safe, secure fastenings, and be lightweight yet strong. Some such as the speedy cut boot are cut to fit higher on the inside of the leg for extra protection.

The event horse jumps stationary fences and goes through water and needs good, strong protection, but as weight plays a major part, it needs nonabsorbent boots. If they soak up the wet and mud, they rub and become uncomfortable.

Polo boots Because of the speed of the game, the polo pony needs extra protection, especially for the tendons running down the back of the legs. There are many types of boot, usually made of leather or felt.

Tendon boots are also available. They may be made of up to three thicknesses of leather or other padding to protect and support the tendons. They are usually fastened with four or five straps.

Traveling boots, although not as supportive as bandages, are good protection if they fit well. Some give protection over the knees and hocks, while others only protect the lower leg. They are easily applied and, if kept in good condition, work very successfully.

Fetlock or ankle boots are shaped leather pads which fit over the inside of the fetlock joint. The strap is therefore always fitted to the outside of the leg and in all cases is fastened to face backward.

Knee caps or hock boots are essential to protect these vulnerable joints if the horse is to travel, particularly in a box designed in such a way that the knees are up against the partitioning and the hocks are close to the back. The lower strap is always fastened very loosely to allow for joint movement.

Skeleton kneecaps are less bulky and can be used for exercise and during roadwork, especially if the ground is icy.

Tendon molds For exercise or competition work, there are various leg molds made of a variety of synthetic mixture which are lightweight and nonabsorbent and which can be bandaged in place.

Bandages

Bandages are often used instead of boots as they provide greater support and protect the legs equally well if used with a layer of wraps. They must be applied evenly and firmly, with equal pressure overall and without in any way restricting the circulation or the natural movements in the joints, especially during exercise. If bandages are used during competition or polo games, they need to remain secure. A strip of rubberized tape will add extra staying power, especially over the ties.

For bandages to be applied successfully, it is vital that they have been firmly and evenly rolled up with the velcro or tapes folded in on themselves so that these will be on the outside when used.

Wraps are used as padding under the bandage for protection when traveling, for warmth in the stable, and to keep dressings or poultices in place. Foam-filled felt mixtures and cotton wraps are also very good. The leg is covered from just below the knee or hock joint right down under the fetlock joints. If the legs are likely to get wet, for example when eventing, absorbent padding becomes uncomfortable and adds extra weight, so it must not be used.

Types of bandage

There are various kinds of bandages available, the most common being the woolen, cotton knit, or synthetic stretchy type generally used for traveling or as leg wraps in the stable to support the legs and to provide warmth.

The elasticized type is supportive and should be chosen carefully, as too much stretchiness when new may constrict circulation if put on too tightly. The medium-grade stretchy variety which expands without too much tension is best. The broader the bandage the better, so that tension is spread over a wide area.

For holding dressings in place and to support injured legs, the stretchy or crepe bandage is popular. There are also medical bandages with different properties, which stay cold, harden on application, or mold themselves to the shape of the leg, which may be useful in cases of injury.

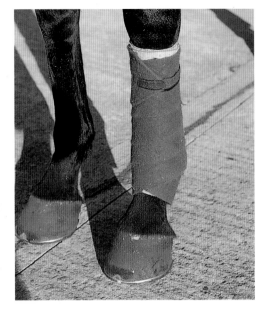

An injured leg has been dressed and is held in place by a stable bandage. When bandages are put on injured legs, the good leg should always be bandaged as well for support so that it does not take too much strain.

Fitting exercise bandages

Before bandaging, apply wraps, cotton padding, or foam-filled batting to the leg for protection. Start high up, leaving a corner uppermost, then roll the bandage evenly and firmly down the leg to the fetlock joint and back up again. The corner is then folded over and held in position by the last loop of bandage. The tapes are tied evenly and fastened on the outside of the leg.

Stable bandages can also be useful to soften and prevent swellings, especially on horses prone to windgalls, but should not be used too often so that they will be of greater benefit when there is a serious problem.

Fitting stable bandages

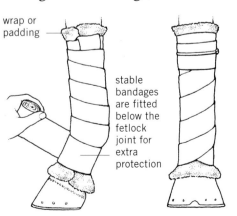

wrap or padding

stable bandages are fitted below the fetlock joint for extra protection

Hoofcare

The horse's feet require regular attention from you and also need to be looked at by the farrier every four to six weeks. Hooves should be picked out both morning and evening, before and after exercise on a daily basis, and oiled or dressed at least three to four times a week (daily in hot dry weather). Many people wash the feet out every day, and this certainly needs to be done in muddy conditions. Any signs of an unpleasant odor or oozing from the foot or frog needs immediate treatment. This may be thrush (see Veterinary care p. 79), which is caused by lack of proper foot care and damp, warm conditions underfoot.

If your horse has any specific problems, especially with his action, discuss the type of work it is doing with your farrier and consider the various shoeing alternatives which might help. Different types of shoe and how they are put on can quite dramatically improve the action of many horses, especially if they tend to knock themselves.

The shoe

Horseshoes are usually made of steel, although recently various other types such as plastic shoes, which are very expensive at the moment, have appeared on the market. Racing plates and those used for horses in the show ring are made of aluminum and are very light.

There are two types of shoeing – hot and cold.

The hot shoeing method is by far the most preferred. With this method the farrier is able to shape the shoe while it is red-hot, thus making the shoe to fit the horse. The red-hot shoe is used to burn an impression onto the trimmed hoof to ensure even contact all around. This will be repeated until the fit is correct. The shoe is then cooled in water and secured. Today farriers have portable forges, enabling them to hot shoe on site.

Cold shoeing only allows for very minor alterations to the shoe, and there is a tendency for the foot to be trimmed to fit the shoe, which can lead to many problems later unless great care is taken. However, given the correct size shoe and the expertise of a good farrier, this method can still be the equal of hot shoeing.

The shoe is measured by length, from the center of the toe to the heel, and by breadth, across its widest part. In a well-balanced foot, these two measurements are about the same. The shoe has clips to help keep it in place, one positioned centrally on the front feet and two, one on each side, on the hind feet. Front shoes often have two clips.

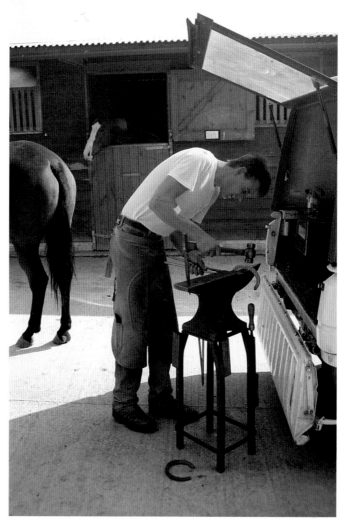

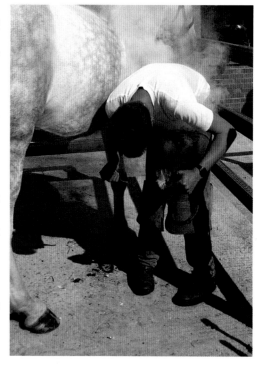

The anvil is the farrier's workbench and nowadays most farriers have portable anvils, which enable them to travel to their customers. In this series of pictures the farrier is working by the hot shoeing method using a portable forge. This gives a far more satisfactory result than the cold shoeing method. Left: The farrier is preparing the shoe to fit the horse by aligning it, making sure that it is flat and the correct size for the animal. In the picture below, the farrier is trimming the foot with the toeing knife. The three pictures on the opposite page show, from left to right, nailing on the shoe, preparing the clenches, and, finally, rasping around the finished foot. The foot is growing all the time and will require trimming approximately every four to six weeks whether or not the horse is shod. It cannot be overemphasized how vital it is to keep the feet in good condition and well shod if the horse is to stay sound and reach its maximum potential. The old saying "no foot, no horse" has proved true on countless occasions.

Types of shoe

There are various types of shoe available. If your horse has special needs, your vet and farrier might discuss the situation together and give advice jointly. Shoes should always be fitted in pairs: a matching pair for the front feet and a matching pair on the hind feet. Hind feet are always more pointed than the wider, more rounded front feet.

The fullered shoe Most horses doing ordinary riding and competitive work will use the hunter or fullered shoe, which can be made of different iron weights to suit the horse and the work being done. It is made of fullered or grooved iron to improve the grip, and may have penciled heels to help prevent overreaching from the hind foot. Clips help to keep the shoe in place and avoid twisting.

The grass-tipped shoe is occasionally fitted to horses out at grass to protect the toes from grass cracks. It consists of the front part of the shoe only, without a heel.

Corrective and surgical shoes are covered overleaf.

The farrier's tools

Every stable manager should be familiar with the farrier's tools and know what they are used for. In an emergency he should be able to remove a shoe that has become displaced and is likely to cause injury, or at least to pull out a loose nail. It does not take as much strength as people generally think.

The hammer, known as the driving hammer, has claws with which to pull out the nails once the clenches are raised and to twist off the points before knocking down the clenches.

The rasp is used for neatening and leveling the bearing surface of the foot. The serrated sides of the rasp can be used to cut into the hoof to prepare a bed for the clenches and for final trimming.

The drawing knife has a curved blade with a hook on the end. It is used for trimming the frog and lowering the wall.

The pincers are used to raise the branches and pull the nails when taking off the shoe. They can also be used for tightening the clenches.

The buffer has two ends. The blunt chisel end is used for knocking up the clenches before the shoe is removed. The other, more pointed end is used to loosen the heads of nails or remove broken ones.

The toeing knife is used with the hammer to remove overgrown parts of the wall of the foot.

Hoof cutters are rather like pincers, but have one sharp and one blunt jaw. They are used for lowering the wall of the hoof with the blunt jaw placed on the inside of the horn.

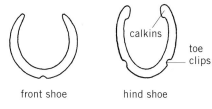

Parts of the fullered shoe

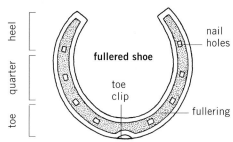

front shoe   hind shoe

calkins

toe clips

heel

quarter

toe

fullered shoe

nail holes

toe clip

fullering

Above: This fullered shoe has penciled heels.

The nails used to keep the shoe in place and to provide extra grip come in numbered sizes, the lower the number the smaller the shoe. The right-sized nail must be used when the shoe is fitted. Nails are designed so that they emerge through the wall of the foot when driven in at the correct angle. When asked how many nails should be used for shoeing, the answer must always be "as few as possible." Seven is the usual number, with four on the outside and three on the inside edge. This is because the foot is very slightly wider on the outer than on the inner edge. The wall of the hoof is also very slightly thinner on the inside and toward the back of the hoof.

Clenches are the points of the protruding nails which are hammered over and then downward to keep the shoe in place.

Calkins Some hind shoes are fitted with a wedge heel and calkin to improve grip, allowing for turning which is hindered if calkins are on both heels. The calkin on the outside provides the grip, while the wedge on the inside prevents damage to the opposite inside foot and keeps it more in balance.

The well-shod foot

It is essential that horses are provided with proper foot care if they are to stay sound. They should be shod at least every four to six weeks.

• The horse should be sound after shoeing.
• The shoe should be made to fit the horse.
• The front set and hind set of shoes should be in pairs, and it should be noted if the horse has odd-sized feet.
• The weight and type of shoe should be suitable for the work being done.
• There should be no rasping of the hoof other than in fitting clenches.
• There should be no dumping to make the shoe fit. This is sometimes unwisely done to avoid forging.
• The shoe should make maximum use of the bearing surface of the foot. There should be no gaps between foot and shoe.
• The nails should be evenly spaced with the clenches in a straight line, slightly higher at the toe than at the heel but not driven into old nail holes or cracks.
• Clenches and clips should be broad, flat, and well bedded in.
• The toe clip should be centered and aligned with the frog.
• There should be no excessive trimming of the sole and frog.
• The frog should be in contact with the ground to enable it to function properly.

Injuries relating to shoeing

Inevitably, injuries do occur with the shod horse which might not happen to the unshod animal. There may be a number of reasons for the injuries, such as poor conformation, weakness, laziness, lack of condition, the state of the ground, inferior shoeing, or it could be a combination of any or all of these factors.

Brushing is the most common injury, when one fore or hind foot knocks the opposite leg, causing bruising, a graze, or a cut. If this happens frequently, the horse may go lame. Some horses tend to brush badly or knock themselves with the opposite foot. In this case, some or all of the inside heel of the shoe is taken away to help prevent injury from brushing with the opposite foot.

The fitting of three-quarter shoes or feather edging may help, but the horse's legs should be given the additional protection provided by brushing boots, Yorkshire boots, or exercise bandages.

Over-reaching is quite common if the horse is doing fast work or jumping, or if it is ridden on its forehand. It is an injury caused by the toe of the hind foot catching the heel of the foreleg, resulting in a cut or a bruise. Rolled toes on the hind feet and bell boots on the front, and good protective boots or bandages help prevent this. The rider should also aim to get the horse going more off his forehand and should take care down hills or over drop fences.

Leg or tendon injuries The most common leg or tendon injury is when the toe becomes too long, putting a strain on the tendons by allowing the angle of the pastern to become misaligned. Horses ridden in this state are extremely vulnerable. Knocking the back of the tendon when galloping or jumping may also cause a severe bruise or cut to this area.

Dumping the toes excessively may create joint and tendon problems and a shortening of the stride, especially if the horse is very upright in front.

Forging and stumbling is caused by laziness or bad conformation, or by the toes growing too long, or the horse being allowed to work on its forehand. Rolled toes may help, but correct riding, pushing the horse up into its bridle into a more balanced outline, will be more effective. Young horses are often prone to forging and stumbling, but as they grow stronger and better balanced, they stop if properly schooled.

Corns may be caused by badly fitted shoes or bruising from a stone. They often appear on the heels of the foot due to pressure from the ends of the shoe. They may cause lameness and may become infected, and must be cut away before a new shoe is fitted.

Capped elbow can happen when the horse lies down and catches its elbow on the heels of the front shoes, causing a hard-skinned sore which may become infected. Plenty of bedding and possibly a three-quarter shoe may help (see sausage boots, p. 63 and 64).

Loose shoes and raised clenches may lead to cuts and injury, but they also indicate the need for shoeing. It is therefore essential that the horse be correctly and regularly shod.

Parts of the foot and their function

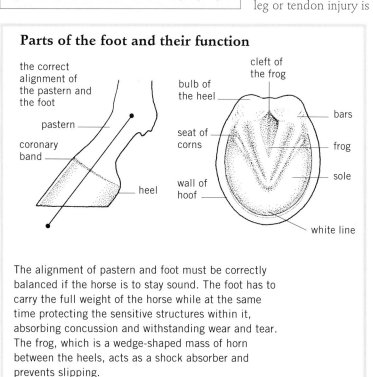

the correct alignment of the pastern and the foot

pastern

coronary band

heel

cleft of the frog

bulb of the heel

bars

seat of corns

frog

wall of hoof

sole

white line

The alignment of pastern and foot must be correctly balanced if the horse is to stay sound. The foot has to carry the full weight of the horse while at the same time protecting the sensitive structures within it, absorbing concussion and withstanding wear and tear. The frog, which is a wedge-shaped mass of horn between the heels, acts as a shock absorber and prevents slipping.

Corrective shoes

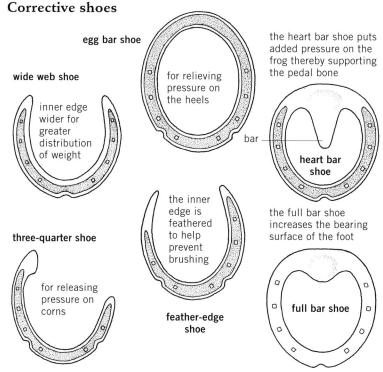

egg bar shoe

wide web shoe

inner edge wider for greater distribution of weight

for relieving pressure on the heels

the heart bar shoe puts added pressure on the frog thereby supporting the pedal bone

bar

heart bar shoe

three-quarter shoe

for releasing pressure on corns

the inner edge is feathered to help prevent brushing

the full bar shoe increases the bearing surface of the foot

feather-edge shoe

full bar shoe

Cleats

Cleats are removable screw-in grips, often used for competition work. They should only be used when they are needed and then removed so they do not cause damage to the horse. They may have a dramatic effect on the horse's grip in slippery ground. Because of this they are particularly useful if the animal lacks confidence. Usually, larger cleats are used in soft ground while small ones are preferred for hard going. Designs available range from square to round and wedge-shaped. The Mordax cleat, a permanent fixture, is a small, rounded cleat used for horses doing a lot of roadwork. It has a hard core which lasts well, provides a good grip, and is used on hunters. Cleat holes are cleaned out with a nail and the tap inserted to ensure the tread is clean. The cleat is then threaded into place.

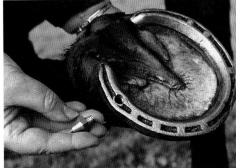

Concussion pads or cushions are generally made of plastic. They are fitted under the shoe where they protect the sole by acting as shock absorbers, providing a thin layer between foot and shoe. Care must be taken to ensure they do not cause further problems by putting pressure on the sole. They are useful for horses prone to sore shins, bruised sole, ringbone and sidebones.

Fitness and exercise

One of the most important aspects of good horsemanship is ensuring that the horse has adequate exercise to keep it fit and healthy. Whether it is being ridden, a growing youngster, an animal at rest, or one in peak fitness, no horse will really thrive or be mentally relaxed unless it has enough work or exercise to keep its mind and metabolism properly active.

The foal will be exercised by its mother who will move it around when it is very young, and it quickly becomes independent enough to dash around by itself. It is best for the foal to be outdoors as much as possible. If two or more mares and foals can be out together, so much the better for their development; like children, foals will amuse themselves for hours before falling asleep exhausted.

Once weaned, youngsters are probably best turned out in groups, if possible where they can play and exercise naturally. I prefer to keep them outside all the time for as long as I can, weather permitting. However the young need good food and regular feeds to grow strong and healthy and to reach their full size and potential; they do not do well if it is wet and cold, in which case they should be brought in and turned out daily for exercise, as conditions allow. In hot climates, shelter from sun and flies is very important.

Many people winter youngstock in large barns where they have the freedom to play. These are very convenient and make feeding much easier to manage, but adequate ventilation and exercise out-of-doors should also be arranged as often as possible.

Riding or lungeing

For the ridden horse, daily exercise is very important, especially if stabled all the time. This can be achieved by turning out for a period each day, lungeing, or being ridden.

If the horse is to be turned out, you must make sure that it actually does take some exercise. To wander around a paddock while gorging on grass can hardly be called exercise, and the animal has to be watched to determine whether extra work is needed. This in turn depends on what it is eating and what it is being used for.

Lungeing is a useful form of exercise in that the horse can be worked in a fairly controlled way with or without a rider. If a shod horse is being lunged, it is important that it wears brushing boots all around so it does not knock itself in the confined space.

Ridden exercise

Ideally, horses in regular work will be ridden daily and perhaps be turned out as well. All horses should be exercised for a minimum of one hour a day, if possible for much longer, but care has to be taken at first to gradually build up the workload and fitness according to what the horse is being trained for, and adjusting its feed accordingly. Every type of horse needs the same basic buildup of work before a fitness program can begin.

Roadwork Training should start with the horse walking either on the roads, if they are safe and convenient (see Riding on the road p. 36), or on consistently firm tracks or other prepared surfaces. When an animal is unfit, the tendons and muscles are soft and lacking in tone and are therefore prone to strain if the horse is ridden on soft, heavy, or irregular going. Gentle roadwork will help to harden the tendons. A minimum period of two weeks of walking is almost obligatory for any horse or pony coming into work, before a gradual program of walk and trot and then schooling is started.

Most horses undertaking any form of serious competition work will remain longer at this first, slow stage where half an hour's walking on the first day will be increased gradually to one and a half to two hours by the end of the third or fourth week. A further period of two to four weeks walking and trotting is then started, again with a gradual buildup. Start with short bouts of trotting and slowly increase the distance covered daily; work must be done at a slow pace so that the tendons and muscles are given time to extend fully and contract with each stride. This gives the tendons the best chance to attain the maximum tone and makes them less vulnerable to strain before any fast work is attempted.

Slow work A period of walking is always recommended before any exercise or schooling takes place. This will ensure that the horse loosens up well and that the circulatory system is fully stimulated.

Horse walkers are proving very popular in many stables nowadays where time is at a premium and staff are very busy. While they should never take the place of general exercise and schooling where the rider can carefully monitor the work done by each horse, a horse walker does at least mean that the horse has regular exercise at a controlled pace.

Care must be taken that the horse is introduced to the horse walker device sympathetically so that it is not frightened by it in any way. Usually, two or more horses use the walker at the same time and most quickly adapt to this method of exercise and seem to enjoy each other's company. It is most important that the horse walker is reversed halfway through the exercise period so that the horses walk in both directions for an equal length of time. Failure to do this might lead to a buildup of muscle on one side, which could eventually lead to weakness and lameness on the other. Make sure that the walking surface is kept in good condition and does not become slippery; most are sand-based.

Horse walkers are becoming popular as a labor-saving method of exercising horses. Outdoor designs such as this one give the horse interest during his exercise period. Once used to walkers, horses quickly adapt to their new lifestyle.

How to lunge

The horse should be tacked up before being taken to the lungeing area, preferably a school or corner of a field. If used, the side reins should be attached fairly loosely to start with, to allow the horse some freedom to play for a few minutes, before shortening the reins a little to insist on some collection and outline.

Side reins If fitted loosely to the snaffle bridle, side reins are useful as they encourage the horse to take hold of the bit correctly without interference from the rider's hands. The horse soon learns that if it stops pulling on the bit and side reins, the pressure is eased. By adjusting the length of the side reins, a correct head carriage can be encouraged without upsetting the horse and interfering with the mouth. Care must be taken with the young, unbalanced horse, which will always need more freedom in the head and neck to maintain its balance. Always walk with loose side reins at the end of the session as a reward and for relaxation before returning to the stable.

A lot of training can be done on the lunge in skilled hands to improve the horse's paces, transitions, and rhythm; it also allows the trainer an excellent opportunity to see from the ground how the animal is progressing. For general exercise, the horse must start by walking the circle, then be asked to trot on well so that all the muscles are used.

The handler The animal should be controlled by the voice with firm commands used to encourage a faster pace and

quiet, slow words or sounds to calm or slow down. When working on the left rein, the handler must always carry the lunge rein in the left hand and the stick in the right, and vice versa when working on the right rein. Any excess rein should be looped neatly and held in the outer hand with the stick. The rein should never be allowed to form a slack loop and must always maintain a light contact with the cavesson. The stick should be used behind the horse to get him to walk forward, or to his side to push him outward into a larger circle. It should not be necessary to touch the horse with the stick, a gesture is

The horse in the picture above is correctly tacked up for lungeing with a saddle and bridle, with reins and stirrups secured. It is working in side reins and protected all around with brushing boots.

usually sufficient. The horse should be encouraged to work on the circle around the handler, who remains in the center, turning on the spot. When lungeing a horse, it is advisable to stand facing its shoulder, with the lunge rein and stick forming a triangle for it to work inside. This will stop the horse from bolting forward or ducking behind on the circle.

Fitting the lunge rein The front lunge ring is the most severe and gives the handler most control when lungeing a new or difficult horse; otherwise, it is best to work off the side rings, changing sides with every change of rein. Be careful not to pull the horse on the lunge rein too much as this may cause crookedness and a loss of balance. Lunge on both reins in the circle in walk, trot, and canter if the horse is balanced and well-behaved enough to cope with this.

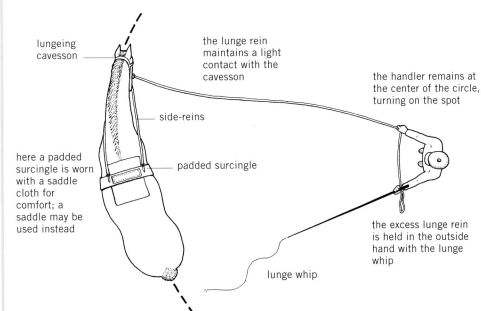

lungeing cavesson

the lunge rein maintains a light contact with the cavesson

side-reins

here a padded surcingle is worn with a saddle cloth for comfort; a saddle may be used instead

padded surcingle

the handler remains at the center of the circle, turning on the spot

the excess lunge rein is held in the outside hand with the lunge whip

lunge whip

Warning Work the unfit or young horse in as large a circle as possible for very short periods, working on each rein equally for five to ten minutes. It is very hard work even for the fit, athletic horse to be schooled in a small circle for long periods.

Fitness program

Once the horse has been through the road work stage, the rider will want to start proper training. If the horse is to arrive at its competition fully prepared, whether long-distance riding, show jumping, western riding, sidesaddle or in a show class, specific aspects of training will need to be worked on really thoroughly.

Hillwork

This is particularly useful when fittening horses, and going up hills can make an enormous difference for the horse being prepared for competitive work.

Uphill work stimulates all parts of the body, especially the muscles in the back and hindquarters, and makes the lungs and respiratory system work hard without resorting to a gallop. Cantering up hills will provide the horse with an energetic workout, especially if it is a long, gradual hill. The horse would need to cover three times the equivalent distance on the flat to give the same degree of work.

Downhill work The horse should always be worked at a slower pace, preferably a walk, as the horse and rider's weight is on the forehand. With the young horse, the front legs are being used as props as the horse picks its way downhill, but with schooling and improved balance it will soon learn to cope at faster paces.

Warning Care must be taken not to overdo hillwork until the horse has reached a fair degree of fitness, as it should not get overstressed; used sensibly, however, hillwork provides an invaluable aid to fitness and conditioning.

Interval training

Interval training is a method originally designed for athletes and swimmers to increase their aerobic level of fitness by delaying the point when the anerobic threshold takes over. American team trainer Jack Le Goff adapted this system to train his Combined Training team.

The horse is asked to do a specific amount of work and then allowed a short rest period to recover partially before working again. There are normally three work periods, with two rest periods of walking in between. The work periods increase in time and speed, while the rest periods become shorter. Each program should be worked out to suit the individual horse and the work expected of it.

Interval training should not be started until the horse has had at least six weeks'

conditioning work and is generally carried out every four to six days thereafter. It is essential to monitor the horse's progress by taking its temperature, pulse, and respiration (TPR) levels during training, and particular note should be taken of the recovery levels after work. To get an accurate picture you need to know your horse's normal resting TPR, which should be taken when the horse is at rest in his stable before exercise.

It may be necessary to vary the interval training program until you find out what suits your particular horse best. You might vary the distance or speed of each work session and allow more or less time in the rest periods, or undertake more, but shorter work periods.

Early sessions can start in trot and a training program may be something like this:

440 yard trot	work
three minute walk	rest
440 yard trot	work

This might be increased to four or five work periods in trot before moving on to embark on a cantering program. Measured distances can be undertaken after the horse has had an initial warm-up in walk and trot. To begin with, the cantering program might start quite slowly, with the speed gradually being increased as follows:

Canter at 380 to 440 yards per minute	
440 yard canter	work
3 minutes walk	rest
440 yard canter	work
3 minutes walk	rest
440 yard canter, etc.	work

Increase this program as the horse achieves greater fitness.

Five workouts like this would probably mean that your horse is ready to take part in a one-day event at novice level. Always bear in mind, however, that the type of horse, the going, and the speed will all make a difference to what can be achieved, but if the recovery time is good after a workout, you are certainly well on the way to being ready for a competition.

Interval training is probably of most use to eventers and long-distance riding horses, where a long-term program to build up fitness slowly but gradually is needed to bring the horse to its goal of a three-day event or a 100 mile ride. This training system works particularly well with inexperienced riders.

Working at speed

As with anything where speed is involved, the risk of injury is increased, so control, a good ground, and a sensible fitness program for galloping safely is essential.

Galloping is necessary in certain sports, notably racing, while others such as eventing and polo also require the horse to gallop. No horse should gallop until it has had at least six to eight weeks' conditioning and fitness work to prepare it for fast work. Thereafter, galloping sessions should be controlled, and judged over a measured distance. The ideal is on flat or, better still, gently rising good ground. For the first couple of galloping sessions, the horse should not be asked to go at more than half to three-quarters speed, that is, roughly 500–650 yards (450–600 meters) per minute. However this will depend on your horse and its striding and all-round ability. The buildup of speed and distance covered must be gradual, and galloping should not be overdone. It may be best at first to gallop over a longer distance at a slower pace, with final half-mile bursts at faster speeds, and then to increase the speed/distance ratio as the horse gets fitter.

To start with, a horse may need to gallop every four to six days, but once competing these sessions can be cut back as the horse will have then reached its peak and will need only short, sharp bursts of galloping to keep its wind clear between competitions.

Control

To gallop properly, it is essential that the rider can fully control his horse, and suitable tack fitted correctly is vital if the horse is to gain maximum benefit from the work. Horses galloping out of control are particularly prone to injury, and nine times out of ten, the horse gets into trouble through tiredness or exhaustion. Riders should learn to sit against their horses with bridged reins, never fighting or pulling back, but allowing their horses to settle and relax into the pace required.

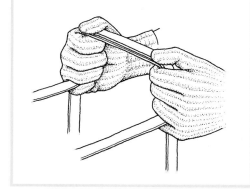

Veterinary care

Every horse needs a regular checkup by a veterinary surgeon and horse dentist. It is best to keep a stable book with details of each animal's treatments, including vaccinations and worming dates. If you are in any doubt about your horse's health, you should always call the vet.

The healthy horse

The horse in good condition should have a bright eye, an alert expression, a fine gloss on its coat, supple, loose skin, and be sound in limb with well-shaped and cared-for feet. Its body should be well covered but not fat, and the neck and quarters muscled and rounded. The appetite should be keen, and the droppings and urine a good color, according to diet. Droppings should be firm, breaking up on hitting the ground. The overall picture should be one of balance and good condition.

The sick horse

The sick horse will present a number of symptoms, depending on the particular problem, but a rise in the TPR rate will always mean that there is something wrong. The horse may also show signs of lethargy or loss of appetite; it may drink too much or too little water, and there could be a discharge from the eyes and nose. Shivering, colic (stomach pains), kicking and looking at its stomach, lameness, pawing at the ground, as well as general unrest and discomfort and tightness in the muscles are other symptoms. There may also be sweating and blowing and overall signs of distress. Droppings that are too dry or loose and foul-smelling urine are also signs that something is wrong.

Vaccinations

Tetanus and influenza vaccinations are now almost universally required among competition horses and are a sensible precaution for all horses and ponies. Certain states in the U.S. have extra health requirements, and if you are competing anywhere in the country, you should talk to your vet about these. If necessary, vaccinations must be given as and when required and entered in the horse's passport or vaccination record. African horse sickness and herpes vaccines are also available for horses competing in Europe.

To fulfil FEI and other equestrian society requirements, flu vaccinations take the form of two primary doses, followed by a booster which is given approximately six months later. Thereafter, annual boosters are necessary. It is most important that these are kept up to date.

Temperature, pulse and respiration (TPR)

The normal temperature, pulse, and respiration of a healthy horse should be:

Temperature:
100.5°F (38°C) for the adult horse;
101–101.5°F(38–38.6°C) for the foal.

Pulse (resting):
32 to 44 beats per minute for the adult horse;
50 to 100 beats in a foal.

Respiration:
8 to 16 per minute for the adult horse;
20 to 30 per minute for the young foal.

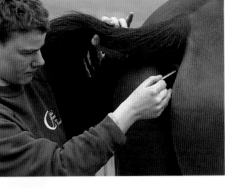

The horse's temperature, pulse, and respiration rates not only indicate its state of health, but are also a useful guide in its fitness training, enabling you to assess its condition. The pictures above and left show different methods of taking readings. For truly accurate assessments, readings should be taken at the same time and/or place each day, as should readings taken after exercise and during interval training.

How to take a horse's TPR

To take the temperature First read the thermometer and check that it has been shaken down until the mercury is below 99°F (37°C). Tie up the horse or, better still, have someone to hold and watch the animal as curling nostrils are a sure sign that a kick is to follow. Grease the bulb of the thermometer with petroleum jelly or, if none is available, a little spit. Talk to the horse, gently raise the tail, and insert the bulb end of the thermometer approximately two-thirds of the way into the rectum. Keep a firm hold on the thermometer, as it can be pulled forward, and hold in place for at least half a minute. Withdraw gently and read – a rise above 102.5°F (39°C) indicates the need to call the vet. Wipe the thermometer in disinfectant and shake it down ready for use another time.

Taking the pulse The normal resting pulse beats 36 to 42 times a minute; this will increase up to four to six times with hard exertion, but should return to normal within about 30 minutes in a fit horse. Feel the pulse with your fingers (not with your thumb) in one of three places. The first is under the top part of the lower jaw where the facial artery passes. Press gently and count the beats. This is the easiest method. The second is on the artery just above and behind the eye, and the third is on the inside of the foreleg, very slightly above the knee, where the artery crosses the bone. If you have a stethoscope, the heart itself can be heard best on the left-hand side, just in front of where the girth goes by the elbow. Count the beats for 30 seconds on your watch and then double this. Remember that a nervous horse may react to anything unusual, so give it a few moments to settle once you have found the pulse.

Respirations can be counted by watching the rib cage and the rise and fall of the flanks, the movements of which are counted as one. The nostrils are an easy place to feel the respiration; hold the back of your hand close to the nose. Again, do this when the horse is quiet and relaxed to get a normal reading. After exercise it is easy to see the flanks working. The normal respiration rate is between 8 to 16 breaths a minute in a resting horse. With youngsters, all readings may be slightly above those previously mentioned.

Care of the sick horse

Sickness can be caused by invaders, which are parasites such as worms and lice, by diseases, and by wounds or injuries.

Worms

Worming should be done every four to eight weeks. Your vet will advise you on the types and brands of wormers for treating the different kinds of worm, and how and when to administer them. The most common worms are the red worm, white worm, round worm, and lungworm. Most wormers are now produced in paste form in a syringe gun. This is placed high up in the horse's mouth and the required amount pushed in with the plunger.

Some horses do not show obvious signs of worm infestation; the problem may be diagnosed by a worm count of a feces sample. If you are in doubt about your horse or do not know how effectively it was wormed by the previous owner, it is as well to ask your vet's advice and put it on an intensive worming program, or take two or three sample of droppings to the vet for analysis.

The importance of keeping worms under control cannot be overemphasized. Any internal damage caused, especially by red worm, will affect the horse for life. Worm damage has caused the untimely death of many horses and ponies.

Other invaders

The bot fly lays its eggs on the grass and the horse's forelegs in the summer. The eggs hatch and the horse licks the larvae, which migrate to its stomach where they attach themselves to the lining of the stomach, causing general malaise and unthriftiness. The following spring, the larvae, now mature, are passed out in the horse's droppings. They then pass through the pupal stage, and three weeks later, the adult emerges and the cycle is complete. When the eggs are seen on the horse's legs, they should be scraped off with a knife or removed with a cloth soaked in kerosene.

The warble fly lays its eggs on the horse's coat, and the larvae burrow through the body, making their way to the surface in the spring and early summer where they cause "warbles," hard lumps or swellings in the saddle region. A warm poultice will encourage the maggots to emerge. Destroy all maggots caught in this process to prevent them from growing into adults and spreading further infection. Keep all pressure off the area until the maggots emerge.

The horsefly This is a fly with powerful wings. The female may reach 1 in. (2.5 cm) long. Horseflies breed and pupate in and around water or damp ground. Adults emerge in hot weather, when they bite host after host and can spread disease.

Bot flies and their larvae

Bot fly larvae are ingested by the horse and migrate to the lining of its stomach where their presence results in unthriftiness and general malaise. Top: Bot eggs on the forelegs of a horse. Below: Bot larvae in the stomach, where they cause pain and discomfort.

Diseases and infections

These are caused by bacteria and are usually contracted through an open wound or through a virus. Extreme cases should be reported to the U.S. Department of Agriculture.

Strangles is highly contagious and if left untreated, fatal. Caused by *Streptococcus equi* bacteria, the symptoms are swollen glands under the jaw where abcesses develop, a nasal discharge, high temperature, and cough. On diagnosis, the horse is quarantined and treated immediately.

Influenza is caused by a virus, of which there are numerous types. It is highly contagious, so vaccination is compulsory for many shows and competitions. As with a cold, the horse will show signs of fever and may shiver and be off its food. The vet may administer antibiotics for symptomatic relief. Further treatment involves keeping the horse warm in a closed stable with a vaporizer boiling at all times; eucalyptus oil can be added to aid breathing.

Tetanus or lockjaw is recognized by increased stiffness in moving, with the characteristic clamped jaw. The horse becomes very sensitive to light, noise, and touch, and takes up a stiff, outstretched stance in between the muscular spasms. Immediate veterinary treatment is vital if the horse is to survive. Vaccines are available and must be given regularly. Foals should have their first injection at three months.

Poll evil is caused when *Brucellus abortus* bacteria enter through a wound which may be caused by rubbing of tack or a knock on the head. Deep-seated abcesses develop, and there is danger of the infection reaching the brain, causing irreversible damage. Animals prone to knocking their heads should wear a poll guard when traveling or if kept in a stable with a low ceiling.

Fistulous withers is a similar condition affecting the withers, but injuries in this region can also be caused by badly fitting tack and heavy blankets. If they get infected, they are extremely difficult to cure.

African horse sickness is an extremely serious disease. Spread by infected mosquitoes, the afflicted horse soon develops a high fever with temperatures up to 105.8°F (41°C), a cough, and a yellow discharge from the nostrils. Horses suffering from the acute form of the disease lose condition rapidly and waste away and generally die within a matter of days.

These muddy ponies look contented, but they are vulnerable to worms and other infections if kept in overcrowded pastures.

Wounds and injuries

Thorough cleaning of all wounds is essential if they are to heal properly and not leave unsightly scars. Any serious cuts, punctures, or lacerations should be looked at by the vet, as these may require stitching and/or probing to determine the severity of the wound. At first, they should be gently hosed or bathed in a mild antiseptic solution. Do not spray or cover a wound with a grease preparation until it has been seen by the vet. Once cleaned, if necessary cover the area with a dry, nonadhesive dressing until the horse receives proper medical attention. Minor injuries should be thoroughly cleaned and sprayed with an antibiotic spray or powder, and if possible left open to dry, or poulticed for 24 to 48 hours to draw out any suspected dirt or pus before drying with a spray, powder, or a dry dressing.

Swellings and bruises Swellings caused by a knock require cold hosing and a cold poultice to constrict the blood vessels for the first 24 hours to reduce further swelling. Thereafter, hot poulticing will get rid of the bruising. This is usually applied in the form of a hot kaolin poultice or something similar for two or three days as necessary. Dry stable bandages applied for a time thereafter will ensure that the leg does not swell up. If the horse is prone to swollen legs after a hard day's work, it is best to put on dry bandages once the work is finished for 24 to 48 hours, and to assess its work program.

Cold hosing is the ideal first-aid treatment for all swellings and bruises, and should be done immediately or as soon as possible after the injury occurred. If a supply of crushed ice is available, this should be applied right away and renewed hourly. A bag of frozen peas makes a wonderful ice pack to help stop swelling. Thereafter, cold hosing three or four times a day for fifteen minutes will prove very helpful for the first 24 to 48 hours.

Strains of any sort may be serious, particularly if they involve the tendons, since strained tendons may put a horse out of action for up to a year. Any suspected strain which shows heat and possibly swelling in the tendon area should be treated with great care and the vet called as soon as possible. Apply a cold compress or ice to the area, or cold hose and then bandage firmly. Keep the horse quiet until seen by the vet.

Strains can happen at any time, but are particularly likely in deep or very hard ground if the horse is ridden at speed or over jumps. Careful preparation in the early fitness program and a gradual building up in the workload will help to prevent this type of injury.

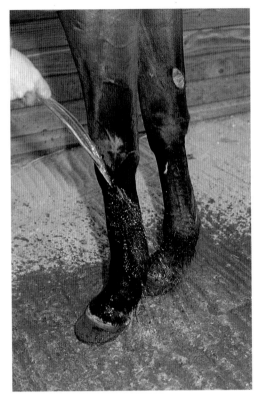

Cold hosing is very beneficial for all cases of bruising and is a useful first-aid measure for many leg injuries, ranging from open cuts to bruises and strains.

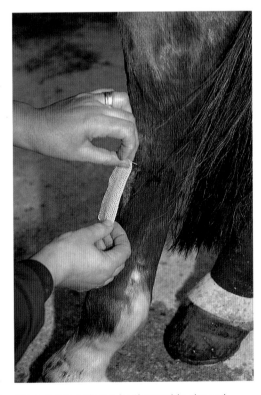

Wounds must always be thoroughly cleaned either with cold or tepid water and a mild disinfectant or some other cleansing agent. Severe wounds should be treated by the vet.

Bleeding from all wounds needs attention. Minor wounds will usually stop bleeding quite quickly when the blood clots, but if an artery is cut, quick action is needed to stem the flow. A large pad should be pressed over the wound and held firmly in place or, better still, bandaged. Arterial bleeding spurts out, whereas venous bleeding flows evenly. If the bleeding continues, even through a pad and bandage, put another one on top. A tourniquet to stop severe arterial bleeding can be applied between the wound and the heart. A pad or smooth stone is pressed over the affected artery and a very tight bandage applied to constrict the artery. The bandage must be loosened every ten minutes so that damage is not done to the circulation. Usually, if firm enough pressure is applied over the wound, this constriction will only be necessary for a short period to stem the bleeding, but it is vital to stop the flow of blood. The vet should be called as quickly as possible. Most wounds that bleed copiously to start with will have done a good self-cleaning job, so such injuries are best not disturbed once the bleeding has stopped except under veterinary supervision. While waiting for the vet, cover the wound with a nonadhesive dressing or clean lightly with mild hydrogen peroxide or other cleaning solution and dress as necessary.

Lameness The horse will often go lame when it has an injury or pain in a leg or foot. Lameness can also occur when there is pain in a joint or in the back, shoulder, or quarters, and this makes the exact location of the problem more difficult to diagnose. If there is no obvious injury such as a cut, check the legs to see if there is any heat or swelling anywhere and whether, if filled, these pit (leave an indentation) on pressure.

How to identify the lame leg

It is sometimes quite difficult to tell which leg is lame if you are not experienced; many is the time that the wrong leg has been examined!

Forelegs To determine the lame leg, have the horse walked away from you and back again and then trotted, if necessary, on a loose rein allowing free head movements. Don't look at the legs, but watch the horse's head at the poll, especially as it comes toward you. If the horse nods his head, it is lame in front. It will nod its head downward onto the sound leg to avoid putting weight on the lame side. Once you have determined the affected leg, trot the horse toward you again and watch how it moves. If it takes a short step but moves straight with the lame leg, the lameness is probably low down. If, however, it swings the leg and does not bend it too well,

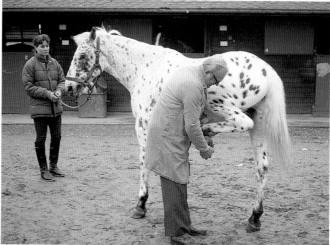

the chances are the injury is high up, perhaps in the shoulder.

Hind legs For lameness behind, watch the horse as it moves away from you, looking at the quarters. With lameness, one quarter will drop away more than the other. It will drop onto the good leg while the lame one will be lifted higher.

By watching how the horse lands on its foot on the lame side, you may be able to tell whether it is nursing the front or back of the leg. If it is putting its toe down first, this might indicate it is nursing the back of the leg; if the heel, lameness is most likely to be in the front.

If the lameness is anything other than an obvious and straightforward injury, or if there is a puncture wound, the vet should be called and the horse rested until the injury has been fully assessed.

Shoulder lameness is much more difficult to treat as the shoulder is made up of deep layers of muscle. Heat treatment is probably the most effective method as it increases the circulation to the injured area.

Identifying the lame leg can sometimes be difficult, but if there is no obvious injury, then always start at the foot. A thorough inspection may be necessary. The vet will use hoof testers to find any points of pressure or soreness. If this does not provide the solution, he will work up the leg and trot the horse away from and toward him for further clues. Tubbing the foot in a bowl of hot salty water before applying a poultice may help to draw out the inflammation if an abscess or bruising is found.

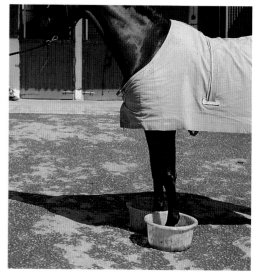

Foot injuries

Most injuries to the foot mean bruising or puncture wounds to the sole or heels of the horse. Check that no foreign body like a stone or nail has punctured the foot. Pick out the foot carefully as such injuries can be difficult to see, especially if the cleft of the frog is involved. Feel the hoof and sole to see if there is any difference in temperature; this will be difficult to tell if the horse has been worked immediately beforehand, but even so one foot may be hotter than the other, indicating bruising or an abscess developing. Having determined the problem – and, if it is a puncture wound, the vet must be called – the wounded area has to be thoroughly cleaned. This may best be done by soaking the foot in a bowl or rubber bucket to draw out any dirt. A mild antiseptic or salt in the water will help to clean the wound. A puncture can be cleaned out effectively with the use of a large syringe without the needle.

Heels may get very sore and be prone to bruising, particularly with a young or unschooled horse. Keep the horse on a flat surface and out of deep going until the wounds heal. The area must be kept clean, and sprayed or powdered to dry once it has healed up. Poulticing may be required for the first 24 hours.

If there is an abscess on the foot, the vet or blacksmith will need to make a drainage hole. The area will require soaking and then poulticing. The poultice can be kept in place with a foot bandage or with an equiboot of the right size and shape.

Mouth and teeth

A horse needs regular dental care and should see a vet or horse dentist at least once a year. With some horses a six-monthly visit may be necessary. The horse suffers if it has sharp teeth as they make it difficult for him to chew properly and they may also affect his way of going when ridden. Sharp hooks tend to develop on the sides of the teeth which do not get the wear of the eating surfaces, and it does not need very much of a sharp point to cause considerable discomfort to the cheek. This may lead to head tilting and mouthiness as well as one-sidedness. Horses seen dropping a lot of food out of their mouths or eating in an awkward manner are likely to have tooth problems. A stabled horse eating hard, dry food, such as hay or nuts, will wear its teeth more than a horse at grass. Old horses may be literally "long in the tooth." Sharp teeth need rasping. Surprising though it may seem, some horses enjoy this process, but others object strongly and need to be very firmly held.

Teeth need rasping once or twice a year to ensure no sharp hooks have developed which cause irritation.

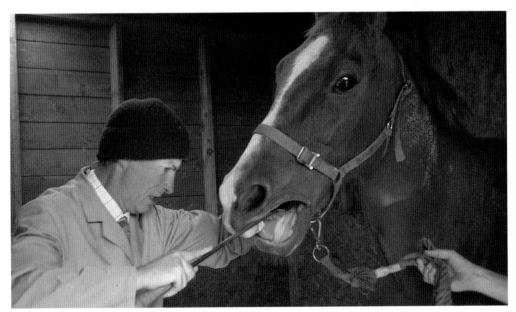

Common ailments and their treatment

Colic or pain in the stomach is perhaps one of the most common and worrying of horse ailments. There are a number of reasons why a horse might get colic, and the symptoms of pain are also varied, such as pawing at the ground, kicking at the stomach, rolling, a raised temperature and pulse rate, sweating, loss of bowel sounds and movement, and anxiety. There are three main types of colic – impacted, flatulent, and obstructive.

Impacted colic This is a blockage due to dry stomach and gut contents in the colon and/or cecum, causing a gradual onset of pain which may persist for a number of days. *Treatment* usually consists of lubricating the bowel and its contents with a liquid paraffin enema, known as back-raking. After two or three days the movements should be normal.

Flatulent colic The contents of the stomach ferment, causing the bowel to become distended with gas. Pain can be severe. Distention may cause rupturing of the nerves and blood vessels of the bowel, resulting in death in severe cases.

Obstructive colic is caused by a blockage, usually a twisted gut as a result of the horse rolling with the stomach pain caused by colic, which cuts off its own blood-nerve supply. Immediate surgery is needed to cut away the dead gut.

Other types of colic are biliary colic, caused by parasites blocking the bile duct; renal colic, due to abnormalities in the urethra; alimentary colic due to disturbance in the alimentary tract; spasmodic colic, caused by excess activity, such as diarrhea, and verminous colic, due to blood clots in the arteries leading to the intestines which cut off the blood supply to part of the gut.

Causes of colic

Colic is often caused by bad stable management or incorrect feeding, but it can also appear unexpectedly due to a poor worming program (sometimes dating back some years) or even stress. The most common causes however are:

• **Feeding** Sudden changes of diet, bad quality food, feeding cut grass or apples which have begun to ferment, irregular feeding habits, lack of water or a change to a different source, watering when hot or while still puffing after exertion.
• **Worms** This occurs particularly in young horses, but also in older ones where early damage to internal organs is beginning to take its toll.
• **Overwork** Leading to exhaustion and dehydration. This is quite common with unfit animals, or nervous and excitable horses.
• **Overeating** Either when the horse simply is given too much food to eat, or when the greedy horse gets out, finds an excess of food, and gorges himself.

Treatment The vet should be called immediately in all cases of colic. Keep the horse as quiet as possible and provide extra bedding banked up the walls to prevent injury. Remove all food and water and make sure that someone stays with the horse until the vet arrives, moving it only as much as necessary to prevent rolling. Walking the horse to reduce pain and with the idea of removing the problem altogether is not thought to be a good idea by most vets today.

Save any recent droppings for the vet to look at and note when and how often the horse may have passed dung and staled. Do not give colic drenches (which may have been in your medicine cabinet for years), as these can mask symptoms which would be helpful to your vet and can interfere with possible treatment. All colics are serious. Try to determine the cause and also check your stable management routine with your vet to see if there is anything which needs to be changed to prevent a future attack.

Azoturia, Setfast, or Tying up All these expressions relate to a condition of muscle cramps which may cause the horse considerable pain and usually affect the muscles of the back and the quarters. The horse goes into a state of muscle spasm and slows down as stiffness sets in. Sweating and obvious signs of pain follow. When passed, the urine is usually wine-colored due to an excess of pigment. This condition occurs after hard work during a rest period or day off, or at a competition, especially in hot conditions such as in the ten-minute box during a three-day event, or while out hunting when the horse has to stand in the cold after a long gallop.

Treatment Never try to move the horse, but get transportation back to your stable and call the vet at once. Keep the horse warm and reduce the feed, giving mashes and Epsom salts for a few days. Resume work gradually, instructed by your vet. Adjust the horse's feed to suit the workload.

Monday morning disease, Lymphangitis, or Big leg This is a hot and painful swelling, usually of the hind legs, due to inflammation of the lymphatic vessels. It normally occurs on a rest day after hard work (hence the name Monday morning disease), but it may also be due to an infection which causes abnormalities to the lymph channels.

Treatment Lameness will limit movement, but walking around will help reduce the swelling. Try to put the horse in the paddock on his next rest day and feed a laxative diet. Your vet will administer suitable drugs.

Disorders of the skin

Rain scald causes dry scabs on the back and quarters. Bacteria penetrate the skin when the coat has been soaked with rain over a continued period.

Treatment Kerosene will help make the skin waterproof.

Sweet itch is an allergic reaction caused by gnat bites. The back and quarters become inflamed and sore, and the mane and tail looked rubbed. Grass-kept ponies are particularly at risk during the spring and summer months.

Treatment Affected animals should be stabled at dawn and dusk and their coats cleaned and treated.

Ringworm is a contagious fungal infection which can be spread by a dirty grooming kit or dirty tack. The coat appears to have circles of raised hair, which later break off and leave bald patches.

Treatment The vet will provide drugs, and the horse should be isolated.

Mud fever is caused by irritation to the skin from chapping by mud and water, and occurs mostly on the lower limbs. It is particularly common in cold, wet weather and shows up as a hardened rash on the legs, the hair falls out, leaving the skin raw and inflamed, which in severe cases spreads across the belly.

Treatment Mild cases should clear up quite quickly if the legs are thoroughly washed with soap and water and poultices provided

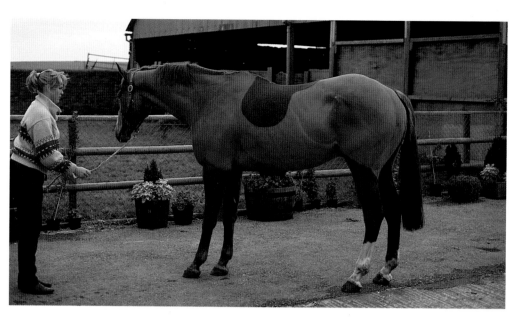

to draw out infection. Careful drying and an antibiotic spray should cure this condition.

Cracked heels also tend to occur in wet, cold weather if the heels are not kept dry and clean.

Treatment Wash the affected area thoroughly, dry and apply a good soft cream, either lanolin or petroleum jelly, to keep the area soft yet waterproof. Keep the horse away from mud or sand until the heels are better.

Heel bug may affect the heel and pastern of your horse. This is thought to be due to a fungal infection or an allergy caused by the harvest mite in the fall. It starts off looking like mud fever, but quickly spreads in a cluster of scabs.

Treatment The same treatment as for cracked heels usually works fairly well, but if not antibiotics may be necessary. All three conditions can be avoided if the legs are looked after properly and treatment given at the first sign of something going wrong.

Petroleum jelly helps to keep the legs and heels waterproof.

Disorders of the feet

Founder, or laminitis, is caused by inflammation of the sensitive laminae in the feet and is extremely painful as the hard foot cannot expand to allow for the inflammation. The foot is gorged with blood, thereby causing extreme pain and pressure. It usually occurs in the front feet, but in severe cases it affects all four.

The reasons for this disease are various, and new theories are still coming in. The most common reasons are: fat ponies which take insufficient exercise when turned out on lush pastures; too much protein in the stabled horses' diet; retained afterbirths, and allergies. The symptoms may appear as severe lameness and pain, with hot feet and coronets. The horse may try to relieve the weight on its front feet by taking it on its hind legs, leaning back with its head out in

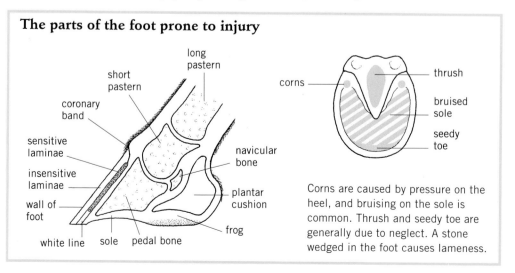

The parts of the foot prone to injury

long pastern
short pastern
coronary band
sensitive laminae
insensitive laminae
wall of foot
white line
sole
pedal bone
navicular bone
plantar cushion
frog

corns
thrush
bruised sole
seedy toe

Corns are caused by pressure on the heel, and bruising on the sole is common. Thrush and seedy toe are generally due to neglect. A stone wedged in the foot causes lameness.

The typical stance of a horse with founder; it is leaning backwards trying to ease the weight off its front feet, which are hot and inflamed.

front. In bad cases the damage to the bones of the foot causes a dropped sole, and ridges appear around the wall of the newly grown hoof.

Treatment Call the vet and/or farrier immediately, and keep the horse as comfortable as you can. Cold water bandages dripping on to the feet, or cold hosing three or four times a day may be very soothing for the animal. The farrier may pare away the sole of the foot until beads of blood appear; this process releases some of the pressure in the foot. A laxative diet of bran mashes and small amounts of hay should be provided, and the horse encouraged to walk again as soon as possible to help the cir-culation return to normal. Special shoes may be helpful by putting added pressure on the frog to draw excess blood away.

Thrush develops when the horse stands on soiled bedding or when the feet are not picked out regularly. The foot begins to rot and becomes very foul smelling.

Treatment The infected foot should be trimmed by the farrier and packed with an antiseptic dressing or Stockholm tar.

Seedy toe is caused by dirt entering the white line of the foot, causing a separation of the insensitive and sensitive laminae. If untreated, the infection spreads up to the coronary band which in turn oozes pus. In the early stages the complaint can be detected by tapping the hoof, which gives out a hollow sound in the affected area.

Treatment The farrier will cut away the outer wall of the hoof to let the abscess drain. The hoof can then be packed with a non-toxic filler which grows out with the hoof.

Navicular disease The arteries to the foot become increasingly blocked by clots due to decreased blood supply to the region, which causes degeneration of the navicular bone.

Treatment Anticoagulant drugs are very successful in improving the circulation and relieving the pain in many cases. In advanced cases, an operation to sever the nerves to the foot may be carried out. However this makes the horse legally unsound.

Sandcracks develop as the result of a blow to the coronary band, from where the new hoof grows from the periople. Splits appear in the wall of the hoof down from the coronary band.

Treatment The farrier may staple the hoof together to encourage the crack to close as the new hoof grows. Care must be taken not to get dirt in the cracks.

Stable vices

Certain stable vices should always be declared to a new owner if the horse is to be sold. Most such vices originate from boredom, though some appear to be hereditary. The most usual are:

Weaving is classed as unsoundness. The horse rocks from one foreleg to the other, often for very long periods and usually when looking out over the stable door. Some horses do this more when excited or at feed times, some do it continuously, while others only rarely engage in this pastime. This habit can be copied by other horses, so it is important to try to prevent it. Turn the horse out as much as possible, put up an antiweaving grill, and keep the horse busy.

Windsucking and cribbing. Both these habits are classed as unsoundness. The horse cribs by grabbing the door, fence, or manger, arching his neck and sucking in and swallowing air in the process. This unpleasant habit can cause indigestion and also wears the teeth down very quickly. Windsucking is the same sucking and gulping, but without the biting.
Remove all objects in the stable on which the horse may crib and put a grill on the door. If the horse still cribs, an anti-cribbing strap can be fitted tightly around the back of the ears and jaw which prevents it from arching its neck and swallowing. There are various sophisticated types of anticribbing straps, all of which may be quite effective. A surgical operation can also be performed, whereby two permanent holes are made in the horse's cheeks, which prevent it from

being able to hold in and swallow air. Try to keep the horse busy and do not let it get bored if at all possible. Turning out by day will help, but gates and fences may need creosoting to make sure it does not attack them.

Other vices include kicking and banging in boxes and on doors, tearing blankets, and chewing. Most such vices need to be firmly dealt with, bearing in mind that most of these unpleasant habits are caused by boredom. The more the horse can be turned out with company, the less likely these problems will arise. Horses are creatures of habit; once one horse starts something he will not forget, and others will quickly pick up the habit unless preventative measures are taken.

Stable vices generally develop through boredom, or the horse picks them up from watching others. As soon as they appear, try to nip them in the bud by changing your stable routine and feeding times. Weaving is particularly common, and the antiweaving grill, shown above, is very effective. Similar homemade versions can work equally well. Some horses become inveterate blanket chewers, and bibs on the halter can prevent them from chewing their own blankets. Never leave a blanket over the stable door if your horse is prone to chewing. Vices should always be declared when selling.

Breeding

A great many people would like to breed a foal, but very careful thought is needed before embarking on this project. Far too often there is indiscriminate breeding, with little thought of what will happen to the foal once it has been weaned.

Why breed?

It is important to be clear about what type of horse or pony you want to breed, as this will govern your choice of stallion. You will need to decide whether temperament, a certain type of ability, looks, movement, breed, or type need special emphasis to help correct a fault, or to bring out the special qualities already present in your mare. One of the most important aspects to remember is soundness. It is no good trying to breed if there is an inherent soundness problem. Here, a little investigation is worthwhile to check on any progeny of your possible stallion, bearing in mind any faults on the mare's side. It is not sensible to breed from a mare which has had to stop work because of serious lameness due to an inherited or genetic fault such as chronic navicular disease or pedal ostitis, or a degenerative condition. You have to be sure the lameness is due to poor stable management rather than genetic factors. Before breeding, it is always wise to get the mare checked by a vet or knowledgeable stud person.

Type

Decide what type of animal you want; it may be one for competition work, a child's pony, a future eventer, a general riding horse for the family, a hunter, a show horse, or a purebred to show in breed classes. Study your mare and work out what sort of stallion is needed to complement what you have and to produce what you want.

If you intend to breed for family use, bear in mind the length of time it takes for a horse to grow, be broken in, and become a reliable conveyance, especially if you are thinking of a pony for your child. A four-year-old pony,

The questions which must be asked are:
- What are you trying to breed, why, and for whom?
- How do you choose a suitable stallion?
- How will you care for the mare and foal?
- How will you cope with the foal when it is weaned and afterward?
- Have you sufficient grazing and stabling?
- Are you fully aware of the time and expense involved?

recently broken, may not be the ideal mount for your youngster longing to gallop around playing cowboys and Indians and horseback games. In addition, it will need at least a couple of years to mature, gaining experience, and you have to ask yourself if you can provide such training. When breeding ponies for children, the most important consideration is temperament.

Choosing the stallion

Once you have made up your mind exactly what you want to breed, it then becomes easier to start looking for the right stallion.

Conformation Think first about soundness. Weak hocks, poor feet, lack of bone, poor action, weak back, and straightness in the shoulder are all faults which should be carefully considered when choosing your stallion. (See Conformation, p. 22)

Temperament is an essential consideration if you are to get full enjoyment out of your foal. However perfect the stallion may be to look at, if it is difficult and intractable, it may well pass on these traits. More often than not, it is the excitable temperament which overrides the calm and sensible one. It has been said that two immature animals will produce an immature foal. Therefore a young mare or filly should always be put with a mature stallion, and vice versa. Usually, however, it is bad stable management and inadequate discipline when young which has brought about the undisciplined horse.

Ability is also a very important point when choosing a sire for your mare. If you want a good jumper, look for a horse which either jumps well itself or has progeny which jump well. The progeny are usually the best indicators of a stallion's potential. Most studs keep records of what successful offspring have achieved. With well-established breeds such as the Thoroughbred, it is easy to find out the breeding lines which produce the required attributes, though if you are trying to breed a competition horse, this may be a bit more difficult.

Go and look at the stallion you are considering and take into account the way he moves. Study his faults and his good points, and try to assess how these will mix with those of your mare. Remember, few animals are perfect, but if you like the stallion, his outlook, and what he is producing, book your mare into the stud.

Stud fees are normally arranged in one of three ways. Most common is "No foal, no fee," whereby the fee is returned by an agreed date. "No foal, free return" means that the mare can return to the stud free of charge.

The stallion chosen should be an excellent example of his particular type, possessing a temperament to match, good action, and correct conformation.

"No live foal, no fee" means no fee is paid if the foal does not survive more than 48 hours.

Color

Often a particular color influences the owner's choice of both mare and stallion. Unfortunately, this is an area which has proved unreliable, and at present extensive research is being carried out worldwide to overcome uncertainties. For example, crossing a gray mare with a gray stallion will in no way guarantee a gray foal. A gray foal will be born with a dark coat (unless it is an albino, in which case no color pigment is present), and only a few gray hairs around the eyes might give away its future coloring. Lipizzaner foals are classic examples; although gray is the dominant color in adults, all the foals are born with dark, almost black coats which gradually turn to gray as the foals mature. Crossing two Palominos will not necessarily produce a Palomino foal. Recent research suggests crossing a chestnut with an albino or cream offers the best chance of a Palomino, although it is no guarantee.

The stallion

Stallions require sensible handling, care, and attention. They are usually strong, so discipline from an early age is essential, with plenty of exercise to keep them fit, healthy and mentally alert.

As with all horses, the herding instinct is strong, but because of the stallion's powerful mating instinct and excitable nature, it will be necessary to keep him in a separate box or paddock out of sight of the mares. If he is kept in a paddock, the fencing must be strong and high enough to discourage the stallion from jumping out. It is advisable to have an empty field or paddock's distance between him and the other horses out at grass. In the height of the breeding season, a stallion might savagely attack any gelding or colt he came into contact with.

The stallion box This is usually larger than the average stable and can be up to 20 sq. ft. (1.8 sq. m) in size. Strong bars may be placed over the window, with the lower door a little higher than usual to stop him from jumping out, yet still allowing him to look over the top. Firm but quiet handling will ensure discipline, and the handler should keep the horse under control at all times. Stallions have a habit of nipping through high spirits or bad temper, so care must be taken when entering a stallion's box stall.

Food and exercise During the breeding season, which may run from February to August, the stallion will need to be fed a high protein diet, equivalent to that of a horse in competition work. A vitamin E supplement will promote the health and vigor necessary to sustain fertility.

Stallions should have plenty of exercise and, if at all possible, they should be exercised with other horses. If a stallion has been brought up with good discipline and stable management, he should be good-mannered enough to be ridden out in company by an experienced rider and will benefit from the companionship of other horses. It is necessary, of course, for him to avoid mares in season.

Performance Many stallions are used in competitions, whether showing, show jumping, or dressage, and with their added strength they do very well. Their performance is the best advertisement for their stud. Like other horses, they can be lunged or long-reined as part of a fitness program, but only when discipline and control allow for this.

The well-managed stallion will soon learn when he is going to do work and when he is expected to cover a mare and will react accordingly. He should be rewarded for his good manners.

The mare

The sexual cycle of the mare, known as the estrus cycle, is triggered off by the longer daylight hours and warm weather of spring, and continues throughout the summer. In racing stables, bright heat lamps are used in the stables from January onward to bring the mares into season artificially early.

A Thoroughbred horse's official birthday is on January 1 so an early foal has an age advantage over one born later in the year.

The mare covered in spring carries her foal for approximately 11 months, which means she will foal during the following spring when the new grass is at its best and high in nutritional value. This also means the foal will not be held back by cold weather conditions.

Before sending the mare to stud

Once you have decided on the stallion you want, book your mare into the stud. You may need to fill in a nomination form with relevant details about the mare, but many studs do not bother with all the paperwork until the mare arrives. It is important to make sure that your mare is in good general condition and has recently been wormed and vaccinated before she goes to stud; her hind shoes should be removed and she should be sent with a clearly labeled halter. If you know when she was last in season, it is best to send her to the stud a few days before she is next due to come into season; this will give her a little while to settle into her new surroundings and relax. Make arrangements with the stud about how and when they would like you to come and pick her up after covering. Most horses remain at stud until they have missed their next season, so they will stay for around four weeks, or even seven weeks to be on the safe side.

Estrus cycle of the mare

The fertile (estrus) period lasts for two to five days with a sexually inactive (diestrus) period of fifteen days before the whole cycle starts again. During estrus, the mare will accept the stallion, and she will be particularly sensitive to touch and smells and more excitable than usual. After this time (during the diestrus period), she will not accept the stallion. To ensure successful mating, the mare must be covered about 12 hours before ovulation, which is when the eggs are released from the ovary, and this usually occurs on the last day of the estrus cycle. Brood mares may be covered during their foal-heat, that is, approximately ten days after foaling, provided that there have not been any complications during the birth.

Generally mares come into season in the early spring as the weather gets warmer. The cycle usually stops during the winter.

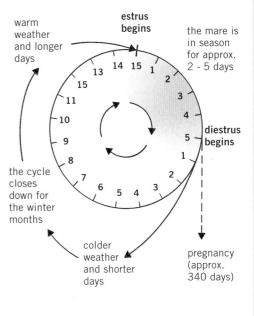

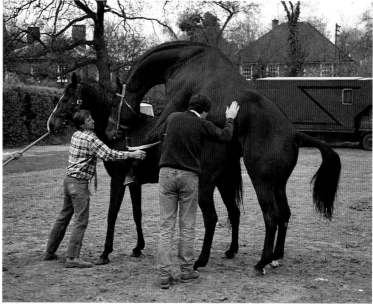

Teasing

To check whether a mare is in season she is usually presented to a teaser, while standing behind a kicking (teasing) board to escape injury if she rejects the stallion and kicks out. The teaser is usually a youngster or inferior stallion, though sometimes a rig is used. The teaser will be encouraged to sniff and nip the mare across the teasing board. If she accepts him, she will show willingness, winking her vulva and urinating; if she is not receptive, she will show extreme hostility, squealing and kicking out.

Covering the mare

Once the mare is receptive, she will be presented to the stallion. Before presentation, the mare's tail will be bandaged or tied neatly, and her dock and vulva may be washed. Covering boots are sometimes used on the hind feet to prevent injury to the stallion if she kicks out, although with an experienced mare this is generally unnecessary. The hind shoes are removed as a precaution.

Where the stud allows the stallion to run free with the mares, no extra care or facilities are required. This, however, is rarely the case as registered stallions and mares are very valuable. Some studs do allow their stallions to run with their mares at the end of the season during the fall.

It must be remembered that a two-year-old colt is capable of covering a mare, so precautions must be taken. Usually a stallion is put into full stud work at five years old, having been tested as a three- and four-year-old on inferior mature mares. In the wild a young stallion will quickly discover the wrath of the unreceptive mare. Having

received a few well-aimed kicks, he will soon learn to approach his mares with care and respect and will come toward a mare from the side to tease and sniff before deciding whether or not to mount her. At stud the stallion handler will have instilled the necessary discipline; the well-trained stallion will have learned to stand quietly and not rush his mare.

The mare in foal

The most reliable way of finding out if your mare is in foal is for her to undergo an ultrasound scan, which can be done from about nineteen days after service. Other methods are through a blood test, or a manual examination through the rectum. Neither of these latter methods is 100 percent reliable, so do not lose heart if at first your mare shows no signs of being in foal. When you pick up your mare, remember to ask for any relevant details such as the service certificate, the likely foaling date, and how you should register the foal with the appropriate body. It is becoming increasingly important to ensure that every animal is correctly registered. Only in this way can successful breeding lines be monitored and malpractices kept under control.

Foaling

There is nothing more wonderful than watching an animal being born, and foaling is no exception. Often a mare will foal during the night as she probably would have done in the wild. In their natural state, herds would roam during the day, but would rest at night to allow the mares to foal, the stallion taking on a protective role and keeping all inquisitive mares and youngsters

The mare will only stand for the stallion when she is in season. To determine when this is, studs have a teasing board over which the mare is tried until she is found to be receptive to the stallion or teaser. She shows willingness by urinating and winking her vulva.

at a distance while the actual foaling took place.

If the mare is to foal out in the field, make sure the paddock is flat and safe and that there is no chance that the foal might fall into a stream or some other undesirable place in the dark. If the mare is in at night and out by day, keep her stable clean and provide extra-deep bedding. The stable should be big enough for her to lie down comfortably and still have enough room for the foal, and there should be no sharp protrusions.

Early signs of labor

The mare's udder will be the first part of her body likely to show changes. It will probably have been enlarging slowly for some weeks, but as foaling time draws near, you may notice extra fullness, and some waxing on the teats generally appears approximately three to four days beforehand. The deposit peels off, and the teats become black and shiny and may run a little milk before waxing occurs again. At this stage, the muscles along the croup on each side of the tail relax; this is one of the best ways of telling that the foaling is likely within 24 hours. The mare will need watching very closely; take a look at her at least every hour or so if you hope to see the foal arrive, as mares have a habit of producing when least expected. As long as all is well, the mare is best left quietly alone.

Labor

Labor is divided into the three stages:

The first stage is when the body is preparing itself for the birth; this may take anything from two to twenty hours. The cervix, which has been tightly closed, has to open fully for the birth to take place. Contractions start and the foal is slowly pushed toward the cervix, which opens gradually under pressure.

The second stage The mare may now become quite restless and agitated and walk around, paw the ground, swish her tail, pass small amounts of droppings, urinate or strain, roll, hollow or arch her neck and back, sweating slightly. It may be hard to see when the waters break as this fluid is only a little darker than urine and is sometimes missed. After the waters break, the mare will usually have stronger contractions and may roll vigorously. The shiny amnion membrane which envelopes the foal will be the first outward sign of the birth at the vulva and will be followed by the appearance of first one foreleg and then the other. The soles of the foal's feet should be facing downward for delivery into the outside world. It often takes some time for the head and the shoulders in particular to appear, following some really strong contractions. Once the shoulders have been expelled, it does not take long for the rest of the foal's body to appear.

The amnion membrane may be eased away from the foal's nose, thus helping it to breathe, although this is not normally necessary for a healthy foal, who will break through its protective covering. Both mare and foal may need a rest at this stage, and they should be left well alone so that the mare can lick and smell her offspring, thus forming a bond. Under no circumstances should the umbilical cord be cut immediately after foaling. It will rupture of its own accord, but the longer it remains intact the better, because the foal will get the maximum benefit from the blood from the mare's placenta. Once the umbilical cord is broken, it can be used to tie up the amnion membrane, the weight encouraging the next stage of labor, when the placenta is discharged. It should be fastened high enough that the mare does not tread on it.

Eventually, both mother and foal will get up. It is often the foal that tries to stand up first, and it will make several attempts before it finally finds its feet and starts looking for the udder and its vital first drink.

The udder may be rather tender, especially if it is a first foal, and the mare may need holding if she keeps moving or kicking as the foal tries to suck. Some gentle assistance can help until the mare has settled. Usually, once the foal has made an initial few sucks at the udder, both mother and foal will manage best on their own.

It is crucial for the foal to drink this first milk, known as colostrum, to build up its strength, because this milk is very high in protein and contains vital antibodies necessary for the foal to develop its immune system. If for some reason the mare does not survive, she should be milked so that the foal can be bottle-fed with the colostrum.

The third stage takes place as the sucking action of the foal stimulates the uterus to contract and the placenta or afterbirth is expelled. This should happen within a few hours of the birth, and if it does not, the vet should be called. Never attempt to pull the afterbirth free yourself. It is important to check that all of the placenta and amnion membrane are expelled. It is always wise to have the vet or someone equally experienced to check that all is well if you are at all worried. Whether or not the horse is stabled, the placenta should be gathered up and disposed of to stop the mare or other animals from eating it.

The first few hours Careful but discreet observation of the mare and foal is important for the first few hours after the birth to ensure all is well and that mare and foal have accepted each other and are comfortable. If stabled, clear out and burn the soiled bedding, making sure there is plenty of new, clean bedding.

Mares may foal standing up or lying down. Usually the less interference from humans during the foaling the better, but if problems are indicated, the vet should be called immediately. This foal has arrived normally with head and front feet first and is being licked dry by its mother.

Caring for the mare and foal

Once mare and foal have rested for a few hours, if the weather allows, turn them out. Being able to move around freely will help to produce the necessary stimulation for the production of the mare's milk, as well as helping the foal's vital organs to function effectively. Ask your vet for advice on feeding the mare and her future management. This will depend on the time of year and the amount of grass available, as well as on the breed of the mare and her physical condition, and any complications which may have arisen during foaling. Keep an eye on the foal and tell the vet about any worries you have, especially any apparent abnormalities. It may well show signs of scouring (diarrhea), particularly when the mare comes into season at her foal-heat; scouring must not be allowed to get out of control as young foals can sicken very quickly if not looked after properly. Scouring will usually clear after a few days, but if this is excessive and results in dehydration, electrolytes and antibiotics may be needed.

Your mare and foal will require a large stable, which needs to be draftfree and safe in every respect. It is important that there are no sharp protrusions on which the foal could hurt itself, and that the haynet is high up. Many a foal has jumped up and caught its legs in the net causing terminal injury. This is particularly important during the first couple of days when the foal is learning to find its balance and struggles around, lurching from side to side.

The paddock During the daytime, a well-fenced paddock free from hazards and with a good, safe water supply and good grass is essential. The longer the foal can spend out at grass, the better. If there are other mares and foals, better still, as playmates are always popular. There is nothing more entertaining than watching foals play together in the evening as they dash around at often quite amazing speeds. If the mare and foal come in at night, which might be the case except during really warm summer nights, it will be necessary to clean out the stall every day, and a good supply of straw needs to be available.

Feeding Hay and feed are usually given to the mare which the foal will quickly start to nibble, copying its mother. As it gets older and more independent, it is a good idea to give it a small feed away from its mother so that it starts to become used to concentrated feeds after about three to four months. It is very important that the foal eats separately from its mother before being weaned. The mother's milk will protect the foal to a certain extent from various diseases, but when the foal is between three and six months old, it should start a course of vaccinations. A regular worming program should also be conducted and tetanus inoculations given, at three months, before the foal is weaned.

Some mares look after their foals well, while others don't. Some mares get very fat, but fail to nourish the foals sufficiently. Sometimes it may be necessary to supplement the mare's milk with extra food, or even to give extra food to the mare to stimulate her supply of milk. If you suspect your foal is not getting enough milk, discuss the problem with your vet.

Handling the foal The foal should be handled correctly from an early age so that it learns to respect and trust its handlers. It must lead well and not be spoiled, and should be tied up and taught to stand quietly and have its feet picked out right from the start so that this becomes second nature. On the whole, foals are very inquisitive and friendly and are great favorites with children, but they must not be allowed to become over-friendly and boisterous. This can easily happen, especially if there are two or three foals together in a field. The dams may also get jealous, so it is vital that no risks are taken where the young or inexperienced handler is concerned.

Above: This strong, healthy foal has an alert and interested look. Below: While feeding her foal, the mare will need extra food to ensure she has plenty of milk. If milk is not plentiful, the foal will quickly learn to eat and digest hard food.

Weaning

Most foals are weaned at about six months. This means that the foal is taken away from its mother to lead an independent life. The mare's milk supply has to dry up so that she can return to work or, perhaps, prepare for her next offspring. In the wild a mare would wean her foal through a process of gradual rejection. Less frequent sucking means reduced stimulation, so the mare's milk gradually dries up. Colt foals will be rejected totally, but filly foals may remain close companions for many years.

Initially, when mother and foal are separated, it is important they are kept out of earshot of one another so that they do not hear each other calling. For the first few hours, they will have a very strong urge to find each other. The foal is best shut away in a loose box stall with deep bedding; if it is in a paddock, it may try and jump the fence and might injure itself. Even so, no matter how distressing, it is best if the foal is left alone; it will soon settle down. Some settle very quickly, while others may feel upset for a while. It is helpful to have a playmate, if possible, or an old, quiet, sensible mare to provide company.

If the mare is still providing a lot of milk after leaving her foal, she should be taken away to somewhere quiet and kept on a restricted intake of food and water for about 48 hours. For the first few days, it is best not to move her too much to avoid stimulating milk production. If the udder becomes very full and uncomfortable, a little milk may be drawn off, but this should not be done unless absolutely necessary as it only encourages further milk production.

If there are a lot of mares and foals which need to be weaned at the same time, it is a good idea to take one pair of mares away from their foals at a time so that they can stay with a familiar companion. A few days later, another pair of foals may be weaned.

Once the mare and foal have been separated, the mare can be given a chance to settle down to being a single brood mare, especially if she has been covered again and is carrying next year's foal, or she can be put back to work. Remember that in this case the fitness program will take a little longer to put into effect after such a long break.

The foal will very probably lose weight at weaning time. However, if it has two high-protein feeds a day – milk pellets are ideal – and plenty of grass, it will thrive and grow.

The weaned foal will do better if it can join others foals the same age or have an old mare as a companion.

Youngsters

Once weaned, youngsters are best left to grow up and mature, leading as natural an existence as possible with plenty of time out at grass, and extra feeding during the fall and winter. Exercise is most important, and along with careful handling, good food, regular worming, and foot care are the youngster's basic requirements.

During the first three years, the young horse's bones are soft and grow rapidly, so the pasture should not be too steep, and be free from any ruts which would put undue strain on its legs. The youngster should not be put into any strenuous work or be made to carry any weight during this time.

The young foal quickly learns to copy its mother and becomes independent early, but is not generally weaned until it is five or six months old.

Thoroughbred racehorses are known to mature earlier than most other breeds and are put into training as early as 18 months old. Even when they are worked on straight, even ground and carry minimum weight, their soundness record depends on their training and management as much as their physical maturity at this age. Any mismanagement in the early years may have long-lasting effects in the future.

Future training is covered in Chapter 4.

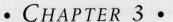

CHAPTER 3

RIDING BREEDS OF THE WORLD

'Round-hoof'd, short-jointed, fetlocks shag
and long,
Broad breast, full eye, small head and
nostril wide,
High crest, short ears, straight legs and
passing strong,
Thin mane, thick tail, broad buttock,
tender hide:
Look, what a horse should have he did not lack
Save a proud rider on so proud a back.'

Shakespeare, *Venus and Adonis*

The histories of the ancient and more established breeds is a most fascinating subject, showing how these animals have thrived over the centuries and how certain dominant features have survived even with crossbreeding through several generations.

The emergence of the competition horse in the latter part of the 20th century is proof of changing needs as horses are used more for leisure and sport than for military and agricultural purposes. Because of this different types of horses and ponies, such as the Hunter, the Hackney, the Cob, and the riding pony have evolved to cater for the highly specialized competitions and activities open to the modern rider. The small (pony) breeds are less than 14.2 hh and the large (horse) breeds are over this height; the various types all have their own governing bodies to control standards.

There are now horses and ponies available of all sizes, shapes, and temperaments to suit every taste, whether you decide to buy or to take up the challenge and responsiblity of breeding one of your own. This chapter describes the most popular riding breeds available in the world today.

THE CONNEMARA PONY
Origin: Connemara, Ireland.
Height: 13 to 14.2 hh.
Color: Originally dun with a dorsal stripe and black points (now very rare), but usually gray. Bay, black, and brown are also seen.
Characteristics: The Connemara is intelligent and kind and makes an excellent child's riding pony. It has a well-carried, alert head, with strong sloping shoulders, deep girth, compact body, sloping hindquarters, and short and hard legs with good bone. This pony has free and comfortable action, is sure-footed and hardy, and makes an excellent jumper. Crossed with a Thoroughbred, it has produced some top-class competition horses.

The Connemara is an ancient breed and has run wild in mountainous country for thousands of years, surviving on the very poorest of fodder. Until recently it has been a multipurpose pony, used to carry peat and turf in harness as well as for all types of riding. It has certainly contributed to the famous Irish hunter and has been instrumental in giving many a famous rider a good grounding at pony level.

THE DALES PONY
Origin: Northeast England.
Height: 14 to 14.2 hh.
Color: Usually jet black, bay, dark brown, and occasionally gray. White markings other than a small star on the face or a white heel or coronet are unacceptable, since a white face, fetlock, or hoof reflects the introduction of Clydesdale blood into the breed.
Characteristics: The Dales is sensible and quiet to handle. These qualities combined with its great physical strength and sureness of foot make it ideal for riding and trekking.

The animal should have a stocky, powerful body with good bone, a muscular back, and quarters which show a free and active movement. The ears should be small, and there should be an abundant mane, a low-set tail, and feathers on the legs. This pony is renowned for its exceptional soundness and strength.

The Dales is a native of the eastern side of the Pennines, and similar in appearance to its close relation, the Fell pony. Originally, the Dales and Fell ponies were identical, their different names being taken from their region of birth, that is, either east or west of the Pennines. Both breeds are of Celtic descent and were used for work for hundreds of years on the fell and dale farms. In the 17th and 18th centuries they worked as pack ponies, carrying lead from the mines to the coast.

Some outcrossing was done to improve the Dales pony for farmwork and transportation. In the 19th century a popular Welsh Cob stallion, Comet, was brought to the Dales to

compete in trotting matches – a favorite local sport at that time – and was put to many Dales mares.

With the advent of the industrial revolution, the Dales pony became redundant. Hundreds were slaughtered, so many that by the 1950s, the breed was nearly extinct. It was saved by the advent of trail riding and is now widely used as a show and riding pony and in harness.

THE FELL PONY

Origin: Cumberland, Northwest England (now part of Cumbria).

Height: 13 to 14 hh.

Color: Usually black, but can be bay, brown, or occasionally gray. White markings are rare and considered undesirable.

Characteristics: A lively, alert pony, usually with good temperament, the Fell is strong and has stamina. It is a good work pony for general riding and driving. It has an alert head, tapering to the nose, which is carried high. There should be a good sloping shoulder and a muscular body with well-sprung ribs and strong loins. Strong sloping hindquarters are also a feature of this breed, together with a thick mane and tail with some fine feathers on the heels. Coarse hair is not desirable. The Fell is smaller and slightly lighter than the Dales pony, though still with at least 8 in. (20 cm) of bone.

This all-purpose pony is used almost exclusively nowadays for showing and riding, though it was once a harness, farm, and pack pony. In the 17th and 18th centuries, Fell ponies were used to take lead from the mines to the coast. The roads were unsuitable for carts, and the Fell regularly carried loads of up to 220 lb. (54 kg) as far as thirty miles and even more, day-by-day. The Fell, which became famous as a trotter during the 19th century, has a smooth, fast trot which it can keep up for many miles. It has great substance and is very hardy. Fell pony breeders are proud of the purity of the breed. In its natural state the Fell pony has to survive high up in the fells, or hills, and, it is said that during a blizzard the snow will pile up on its back, demonstrating the effectiveness of its winter coat.

THE HIGHLAND PONY

Origin: Scotland.

Height: 12.2 to 14.2 hh.

Color: Usually gray or varying shades of dun, some with a dorsal stripe down the length of the back, and often seen with black points or silver hairs in the mane and tail, the Highland can also be chestnut with a flaxen mane and tail, black, or bay.

Characteristics: The breed is intelligent, strong, docile, and sure-footed. It is one of the most versatile of British breeds and makes an excellent general riding or trail pony. The Highland pony has been part of Scotland's history for centuries. There are two types: the smaller, Western Isles type, and the Garran or Mainland variety. The Highland is a powerful, well-made animal with a short, broad head with wide nostrils, bright, intelligent eyes, and short ears. The head is carried well on a strong, cresty neck, the back is short, the ribs well sprung, and the hindquarters full and powerful. The legs are short, hard, and strong with plenty of bone and thick feather at the fetlock joint. The Highland has a long, thick tail and plenty of mane, and its action is straight, free, and well-balanced. It is a sturdy, hardy pony and very sure-footed.

The Highland is traditionally associated with deer stalking. It is strong and well-balanced enough to carry a deer carcass over the steep and slippery slopes of the Scottish glens, and so docile and trusting that a hunter can fire a gun from its back. The Highland is the biggest and strongest of the nine British mountain and moorland pony breeds. The smaller Western Isles type is an excellent riding pony, while the bigger, stronger Garran makes a first-class trail pony.

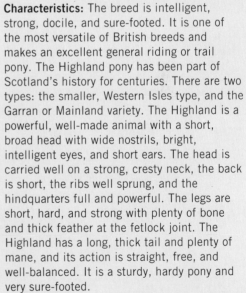

THE SHETLAND PONY

Origin: The Shetland and the Orkney Islands, Scotland.

Height: Average 9.3 hh; it should not exceed 10.2 hh at 4 years or older.

Color: Any color is acceptable, though black is the predominant color.

Characteristics: This breed has a very gentle disposition, and is courageous, sure-footed, and most adaptable. The head is small, with a small muzzle and wide nostrils. There is a very heavy winter "double coat" and a fine, sleek summer coat. The neck is thickset, with a well-developed crest, especially in the stallion. The back is short, strong, and deep through the girth. The legs are hard with short cannon bones and hard, well-shaped feet. The Shetland moves with a straight line action, active but not exaggerated.

The Shetland pony is an ancient breed; the earliest remains found in the Shetland Islands date back to 500 B.C. It is extremely hardy, living on cold, exposed hillsides with very little shelter, its diminutive size being a great advantage in these conditions. In its natural state, it survived on poor grassland and often ate seaweed. It was used by the Shetlanders for all types of work and in the mid-19th century was in much demand as a pit pony in the coal mines of the north of England.

The Shetland has outstanding strength for its size. In 1820, a 9 hh pony was recorded as carrying a 168 lb. (76 kg) man forty miles in one day. However, its size and docile character make it a perfect child's pony.

THE NEW FOREST PONY

Origin: The New Forest, Hampshire, England.

Height: 12 to 14.2 hh.

Color: Any color is acceptable except piebald or skewbald.

Characteristics: This pony is intelligent, brave, willing, friendly, and quick to learn. Because the New Forest itself is an open expanse of common land, crisscrossed by roads and with picnic places between the trees, this free-range pony is exposed to visitors from birth and grows up less nervous of people and traffic than most other native British breeds; for this reason it is considered one of the safest rides for children. It also makes a splendid hunter.

The New Forest pony has rather a large head with an intelligent eye, well set on a shortish neck. There are good shoulders, with a short back and a deep girth. There should be good hard legs with short cannon bones. It is a hardy, thrifty feeder with a solid constitution and plenty of endurance and stamina. Over the years, a certain amount of crossbreeding has been allowed, though the pony is now a definite type.

THE DARTMOOR PONY

Origin: Devon, England.

Height: Up to 12.2 hh.

Color: Bay, black, and brown are preferred. Colors such as skewbald and piebald exist, but are not recognized by the breed society. Excessive white is discouraged.

Characteristics: Kind and sensible, and ideal as a first pony, the Dartmoor has a small, aristocratic head with little pricked ears. There should be strong, sloping shoulders, slim, hard legs, and tough, well-shaped feet. The tail should be set high and plentiful, and there should be an abundant mane along a strong, well-formed neck. The action should be good, low and free as befits a riding pony. The Dartmoor is one of the most popular breeds for children with its good temperament. From time immemorial, ponies of a small, hardy riding type have lived on Dartmoor, but until the end of the last century they were not registered and often varied in type. A Dartmoor section of the British National Pony Society Studbook was started in 1899, and the standard of the pony has remained almost unchanged ever since. After 1902 the Dartmoor Committee would not allow ponies with more than 25 percent alien blood to enter the stud book. The Dartmoor pony was hit hard in World War II because the moor itself was used as a training center for the army; when the war ended, only ponies passed by inspection or placed at chosen shows were allowed into the stud book. It is a credit to the Society that this pony survives in its pure-bred form.

THE EXMOOR PONY

Origin: Devon and Somerset, England.

Height: 11.2 to 13.00 hh.

Color: Bay, brown, mouse, and dun; all with a mealy (cream-colored) muzzle and with no white marking of any kind.

Characteristics: The breed is intelligent, hardy and courageous, with surprising speed and endurance. Once broken the animals are alert and kindly, and make splendid children's ponies, provided they are well-educated and handled early on. They have elegant heads with wide nostrils, broad foreheads, and prominent eyes, known as frog or toad eyes. The ears are short, thick, and pointed. The neck is short and thick, and set on a deep broad chest with the shoulder well back. There is a medium length back with powerful hindquarters and clean, hard legs showing black points and small, tough feet. The breed has a free, straight action; it is very versatile and has the strength to carry a full-grown adult through a day's hunting and also makes an excellent pony in harness as well as a child's pony.

The Exmoor pony comes from the wild, open moorland of Exmoor in the west of England. They may have been the ponies used by the Celts to pull their war chariots, for they are the oldest of the British native breeds and, because of the remoteness of their native habitat, have not been too interbred and so survive in almost their original form. They are hardy enough to survive harsh winters, which can sometimes bring several feet of snow, without shelter or extra food.

WELSH MOUNTAIN PONY – SECTION A

Origin: Wales.

Height: Not over 12 hh (but usually not much smaller).

Color: Any, except piebald and skewbald. Grays are popular.

Characteristics: A high-spirited pony with great intelligence, courage, and endurance, the breed has a small, Arab-type head with open nostrils, sloping shoulders, a muscular back and deep girth with well-sprung ribs. The tail is set high, the legs are fine and hard, and the feet small, round, and tough. The pony is quick and free in its paces.

This small, aristocratic-looking pony is considered by many to be the most beautiful of all the British native breeds. It is popular throughout Britain, Europe, and North America, and is extensively bred outside its native home, though breeders often import fresh blood from Wales to keep their stock true to its native type. The Welsh Mountain pony is the foundation stock for Sections B, C, and D. It is also a prime contributor to many of Britain's hunting and showing ponies.

WELSH PONY – SECTION B

Origin: Wales.

Height: 12 to 13.2 hh.

Color: Any color except piebald and skewbald.

Characteristics: The same as for Section A, but with particular emphasis on its suitability in looks, action, and kindly temperament as a quality riding pony for children.

The Welsh Section B pony is a taller version of the Welsh Mountain pony. It owes a genealogical debt to Merlin, a Thoroughbred stallion and direct descendant of the Darley Arabian, who ran wild on the Denbighshire hills of northern Wales in the 18th century. Section B ponies are still known locally as Merlins.

WELSH PONY OF COB TYPE – SECTION C

Origin: Wales.
Height: Not to exceed 13.2 hh.
Color: Any solid color.
Characteristics: Like those of a scaled-down Welsh Cob, though smaller and lighter in build, the Section C is a hardy pony, active, willing, and a good "doer."

The Section C pony was formerly in demand as a harness pony, and might have declined in numbers through competition with the car, had not trail-riding vacations saved the breed from becoming a museum piece. Its strong build gives it enough substance for adults to ride, and its kind temperament and seeming ability to thrive on heavy work make it a perfect mount for the increasing numbers of vacationers who flock to Wales for a taste of the outdoor life.

WELSH COB – SECTION D

Origin: Wales.
Height: Usually 14 to 15 hh.
Color: Any, except piebald and skewbald. Black, bay, chestnut, and roan are most commonly found.
Characteristics: These are bold and energetic animals, intelligent with a good temperament and a pony character. They are superb jumpers.

The Welsh Cob resembles a heavy, scaled-up Welsh Mountain Pony. The head should be neat and full of quality, with bold, wide-set eyes and small, pricked ears. There should be good shoulders, with the forelegs set square and forward, as well as a well-made neck with a good crest. The body should be strong, deep-girthed, with muscular and lengthy hindquarters, and the tail set high. The feet should be well shaped. In movement the whole foreleg should extend as far forward as possible from the shoulder in order to produce the famous trot action. The hocks should be flexed under the body with straight and powerful leverage. When standing, the Welsh Cob's hind legs are naturally positioned out behind.

The Cob was used both as a pack and a riding pony in the two World Wars. It has been successfully crossed with the Thoroughbred to produce good hunters and high-quality performance horses, and has had a great influence in the development of trotting horses all over the world.

THE THOROUGHBRED

Origin: Britain.
Height: 14.2 to 17.2 hh, but 16.1 is probably the average height.
Color: Most solid colors.
Characteristics: The Thoroughbred is the most influential breed in the world, and the fastest. The world's racing industry is conducted around the Thoroughbred. There are few breeds that have not at some time or other had some infusion of Thoroughbred blood to lighten their type. In the 17th and 18th centuries there were three great Arabian sires – the Byerley Turk, the Darley Arabian, and the Godolphin Arabian – which became the foundation sires of the British Thoroughbred. From these three horses can be traced every Thoroughbred registered today. Bulle Rock, a son of the Darley Arabian, was one of the sires brought to North America by settlers in 1730, and the American Thoroughbred evolved from this one horse.

The Thoroughbred is renowned for its speed, but its supreme quality and presence make it the outstanding horse in looks. It is also much sought after in the show ring, for eventing, dressage, and show jumping. Its temperament tends to be a little fiery, and it is not suited to the inexperienced rider, but with tact and appropriate training it will excel at most competitive sports.

The head is very fine with bright, alert eyes and medium-sized ears. The neck is long, arched, and elegant. The body is strong and deep, with widely sprung ribs and a strong back with high croup and muscular quarters. It has strong and flat-boned limbs with a minimum of eight inches of bone, and although not particularly broad it stands over plenty of ground with good room through the chest. Although it looks refined and is renowned for its great speed, the Thoroughbred is sometimes pushed ahead and raced before it is physically mature, causing problems. As each country tends to have its own special needs, so the Thoroughbred has developed in different ways in different parts of the world. Thus in some countries, Thoroughbreds are developed for greater stamina or jumping ability, for example.

THE ARAB

Origin: The Arabian peninsula.

Height: 14.2 hh plus.

Color: Originally mostly chestnut and bay, but now any strong colors can be seen, including many grays.

Characteristics: The head is small and short with a concave profile, a prominent, broad forehead, and a small muzzle with wide large nostrils. The widely set eyes are large and expressive and the jowl wide and deep, accentuating the lovely curve of the throat. The ears are small and alert, while the tail is carried high and distinctively arched. The body is short, coupled with a good sloping shoulder. All in all, the Arab presents a picture of elegance, beauty, and balance.

The Arab is thought to be the oldest-established breed in the world, and records have been found dating back 5,000 years. Great efforts have always been made to maintain the purity of the breed, and, although there are many famous lines throughout the world, this has been managed successfully. Arab influence can be seen in many other breeds, especially the Thoroughbred.

Today, the Arab is used for almost every type of equestrian event around the world as it excels at racing, long distance riding, in the show ring, and in competition work.

THE CLEVELAND BAY

Origin: Cleveland, Yorkshire, England.
Height: 16 to 16.2 hh.
Color: Bay with black points. No other color is allowed, but a small star is permissible. The feet are blue.
Characteristics: This ancient breed is well-known for its stamina, power, speed, and endurance, and shows lively action. The head is rather large on a long, sleek neck, and the body is well sprung but not too long in the back. There is between 9 and 10 inches of bone on clean short legs, and the tail is held proud of strong, powerful quarters.

The Cleveland Bay is the oldest of Britain's established horse breeds. Two of the original Thoroughbred foundation sires influenced the breed in the 18th century, namely Manica, by the Darley Arabian, in the early 1700s, and Jalap, foaled in 1758 by Regulus, who was by the Godolphin Arabian. The Cleveland Bay Horse Society was formed in 1884.

Originally used for agricultural work or in harness, the Yorkshire Coach horses, as Cleveland Bays were sometimes called, were much in demand during the coaching era, when mares and stallions were regularly exported to the royal studs of Europe and throughout the U.S. As mechanical power took over, the Cleveland Bay, valued for its stamina, action, and style, was bred to produce hunters of great quality, and it continues to be much in demand as a driving horse. Crossed with the Thoroughbred, it is proving to be equally successful in show jumping, eventing, and dressage, having produced several international stars.

THE IRISH DRAFT

Origin: Ireland.
Height: 15.2 to 17 hh.
Color: Bay, brown, chestnut, and gray are the most common colors.
Characteristics: This ancient and multipurpose breed has changed over the years to become one of the lightest and fastest of the coldblood breeds. It has an intelligent straight head with a slightly crested and rather short, stocky neck. The body is strong and fairly long with strong, rather sloping hindquarters, and the limbs are round and large. It is an active and athletic horse producing good jumpers and excellent hunters. The crossing of Thoroughbreds with Irish Drafts has produced an extremely popular and versatile competition animal which has excelled in dressage, show jumping, eventing, and driving, as well as making an excellent hunter and show horse.

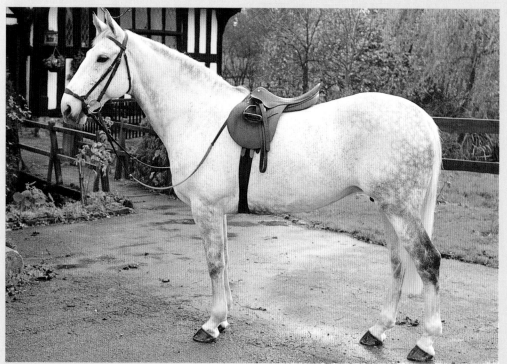

THE SELLE FRANÇAIS

Origin: France.
Height: 15.3 to 16.2 hh.
Color: Predominantly chestnut, but all colors are permitted.
Characteristics: This popular new breed was established as a competition horse in 1958, having amalgamated the successful French riding breeds (saddle horses) to produce a versatile and robust competition horse. Over 50 percent have a Thoroughbred or Arab sire, while the remainder are mostly Selle Français. There are strict guidelines regarding the proportion of the different blood lines allowed for registration in the stud book. There are three divisions, the competition horse being most suited to dressage and show jumping. The second division is more for the racehorse, and there are special races for them; these also excel at eventing. The third division is for the general riding horse. The breed is also divided into middleweight and heavyweight, according to their weight-carrying capacity and height.

Generally the Selle Français is strong and muscular, and with a distinguished eye-catching look. It has flowing supple paces and well-proportioned limbs. It has proved to be a most successful sports horse as well as a driving horse.

WARMBLOODS

Origin: Nationally bred throughout Britain and Europe.

Height: 15.3 to 16.3 hh.

Color: Most solid colors.

Characteristics: Warmbloods have been developed quite recently to cater for today's equestrian sports. The hot blood of the Thoroughbred has been crossed with the local draft breeds (cold bloods) to produce a riding horse with speed and stamina more suited to competitive use. Through careful selective breeding and importing of suitable breeding stock where necessary, national warmblood societies have produced their own lines with special emphasis on temperament, type, movement, and ability, with good bone, strong quarters, and deep girth. Warmblood societies are extremely strict about registration, grading and developing good bloodlines from proven competition stock.

The Danish Warmblood has been most successful, having produced three-day event and dressage champions. It is of the lighter type and much in demand.

The Dutch Warmblood has developed into five distinct types, catering for all tastes. This breed is noted for its calm temperament and good paces. These horses have excelled in all equestrian disciplines including driving, dressage, show jumping, and eventing.

The British Warmblood (above) is relatively new and tends to be of finer type. There is more Thoroughbred in their breeding lines than in their European neighbors. They have excelled in dressage, show jumping, and eventing.

The Swedish Warmblood has developed since 1874 and has produced several champions in all disciplines, including driving. This type has a very fine head and is intelligent yet tractable and very versatile.

The Swiss Warmblood has developed from an injection of Thoroughbred and French blood into native Swiss mares. The Swiss government aims to produce riding and work horses as well as army horses. To date, these horses have done well in dressage.

The Trakehner (right) is the most elegant and lightest in type of the German warmbloods because of a great influx of Thoroughbred blood. It was developed in East Prussia, at the Royal Stud, in the early 18th century, but it suffered badly during World War I. It is now much in demand and has been bred extensively throughout western Germany. With its lovely freedom of action, it excels in dressage, show jumping, and eventing.

The Hanoverian was first developed in the 18th century and is generally slightly heavier in type; nevertheless, it is Germany's most successful competition horse with a very successful record in the dressage and show jumping fields due to the tremendous power in its shoulder and quarters.

All German breeds have to undergo rigorous training and grading before being selected for inclusion in the relevant stud books.

THE QUARTER HORSE
Origin: U.S.A.
Height: 14.3 to 16 hh.
Color: Any solid color, although predominately chestnut. Horses cannot be registered with white markings.
Characteristics: The most popular and numerous breed in the U.S., the Quarter Horse originated from crossing the Thoroughbred with the local wild Mustang. The latter had Spanish and Barb origins and was extremely tough with great powers of acceleration.

In the 18th century, races through town streets and tracks, usually about a quarter of a mile, were common, and for this distance acceleration was of tremendous importance. The Quarter Horse owes its name to its success over this distance. One of the early Thoroughbred imports, Janus, produced several progeny to show great acceleration and speed to win over this distance, and this encouraged more organized breeding. True race tracks developed, and today the world's richest race is the All American Futurity Stakes for three-year-old Quarter Horses.

The Quarter Horse has a short, broad head with small, alert ears, wide-set, generous eyes, and a short muzzle. The neck is of medium length and slightly arched, with well-formed withers, while the shoulders are deep and sloping with a strong, powerful back. The quarters are very broad, deep, and heavy-looking in relation to the rest of the horse.

The Quarter Horse is very muscular through the thigh, and it is this which gives the breed its speed and power. The hocks are also well placed and strong, and are always well underneath, making it easy to turn, stop, and start with speed and balance. With a calm temperament, strength, and agility, the Quarter Horse can excel in numerous spheres from racing to polo, rodeos to trail riding, show jumping to dressage.

THE MORGAN HORSE
Origin: Vermont, U.S.A.
Height: 14.1 to 15.2 hh.
Color: Dark brown, bay, or black with minimal white.
Characteristics: This famous breed can claim to be the only one to evolve from a single sire: Justin Morgan's stallion Figure. This horse's breeding was thought to be Thoroughbred or Arab, but there is quite a lot of evidence to suggest that there was a Welsh Cob influence. Figure gained great fame during his lifetime and passed on his characteristics and conformation to his offspring. He was amazingly strong, reputedly winning every log-pulling contest he entered, and remaining unbeaten – whether ridden or in harness – in races over ¼ mile (440 meters).

The breed is now divided into two groups: the Park and Pleasure divisions. The Park takes some time to train to fully develop the higher action combined with balance and lightness and great animation. The Pleasure Morgan has lower action and is more docile. The Morgan has a slightly tapering head with small ears and a well-crested neck. The withers are prominent with well-sloping shoulders and a broad chest. Its back and quarters are well-rounded and muscular, and its limbs are strong and set square with good rounded and dense feet. Its very high and noble bearing make it a most attractive and eye-catching horse. Like the Welsh Cob, the Morgan stands square with the hindlegs positioned well back. Morgans are extremely popular for all types of riding and driving, and they have been winners in many fields from dressage to long distance riding.

THE AMERICAN SADDLEBRED

Origin: U.S.A.
Height: 15 to 16 hh.
Color: Black, gray, and chestnut are common. Occasionally this horse might be roan, pinto, or even palomino.
Characteristics: Originally bred in Kentucky and known as the Kentucky Saddler, the breed was developed from Thoroughbreds, Morgans, and Trotters to produce a comfortable riding horse able to cover long distances over the vast plantations, strong enough to pull plows, and yet fast enough to win a race and handsome enough to look good pulling buggies. The resulting animal is the horse with speed, style, strength, and intelligence, which became famous for carrying many well-known Civil War generals.

The American Saddlebreeders' Association was founded in 1891, and adherence to a recognized type from carefully selected stock was encouraged from the start. The Saddlebred is now used for many purposes,

ranging from general riding and driving to hunting, jumping, and use as a parade horse, but is perhaps best known as a show horse.

The breed is divided into three divisions, based on the true paces and the artificial gaits, that is, the lope and the rack. The groupings are: the three-gaited, five-gaited, and light harness horse. The American Saddlebred is judged on its conformation, action, manners, soundness, and overall impression. The gaits should be executed in a slow, collected manner with a high head carriage.

The mane is clipped on a three-gaited horse, but left full for the five-gaited and the light harness classes. There are also pleasure, performance, and equitation classes. The horse is bred to have great presence, with a well-shaped head and small, alert ears and, large wide-set eyes. It has a long, arched neck and strong, short back with flat croup and muscular quarters. The legs are straight and strong with sloping, rather long, pasterns and

good feet, which are often left to grow very long to show off the extravagant action. In the U.S., the tail is often "nicked" to create an artificially high tail carriage, but together with docking, this practice is now illegal in the U.K.

THE TENNESSEE WALKING HORSE

Origin: U.S.A.
Height: 15 to 16 hh.
Color: Bay, chestnut, roan, black, and occasionally gray.
Characteristics: A strong and robust horse with a short neck and back and sometimes a plain head. It was originally developed as a breed in the 19th century by Tennessee plantation owners who wanted a horse which was agile and light on its feet so that it could carry them on lengthy tours of inspection of their estates without damaging the plants. The foundation stock used included the Narragansett and Canadian pacers crossed with Thoroughbred, Saddlebred, Standardbred, and Morgan blood. It is traditionally described as the world's greatest show, pleasure, and trail-riding horse.

It is a very versatile horse with a placid temperament with unusual, but very smooth and comfortable gaits which are unique to the breed. These are the flat walk, the running walk, and the rocking chair canter. The flat walk is in four time. The horse glides over the line left by its right front foot with its right hind foot and then does the same on the left, nodding its head in time with its feet. This is known as overstride. The running walk is a faster version of the flat walk with the overstride increasing by up to 12-20 in. (30-50 cm) at an approximate speed of 6-9 miles (9-14 km) per hour. The rocking chair canter is a rolling, highly collected movement.

THE PALOMINO

Origin: Unknown.
Height: Any.
Color: Golden, with a white mane and tail.
Characteristics: Palomino is a color and may appear in numerous breeds and in all shapes and sizes, though in the U.S. there are height restrictions which exclude ponies from being registered with the Palomino Horse Association. The Palomino is particularly popular in the U.S. and is much favored in Western classes.

The true palomino color should be similar to that of a newly minted gold coin, with a white mane and tail (having less than 25 percent dark hairs) and dark eyes. In show classes, it is the color that takes priority, and horses that are too dark or on the pale side will be penalized. The mane is left unplaited. In Western classes these animals look magnificent dressed up in traditional saddlery.

THE PINTO

Origin: Worldwide, though more prevalent in North and South America.
Height: Between 14 to 17 hh.
Color: White, with black, bay, or brown patches of varying size.
Characteristics: The same coloring is found in all types and breeds of horse throughout the world, so it cannot be defined as a breed. In the U.S. there are two named color markings, Overo and Tobiano. In the Overo the white patches start from the belly and extend

upward, the face is usually white and the mane and tail dark. Blue eyes are common with this type.

Tobiano markings are more irregular, with larger white areas, frequently starting on the back; the legs are usually white. The Pinto has been called the Pony of America and the Painted Horse of America.

As they are very attractive yet tough, these horses were popular with Native Americans, and they are still used today for ceremonial occasions. Special studs are being developed to breed the Pinto in the U.S.A.

There are no physical restrictions of characteristics specific to the type, but they do tend to have thick necks set on heavy shoulders, though they still retain a pony quality.

Known as the "odd colored" pony in the U.K., they are sometimes considered "vulgar." British Pintos have lost the refined looks of the American type due to the introduction of heavier, coldblooded breeds.

Odd colored ponies are discouraged on the hunting field as they are thought to stand out too much. In Britain and Europe, they are much favored by gypsy communities where, sadly, indiscriminate breeding is prevalent.

THE APPALOOSA

Origin: U.S.A., although spotted horses can be found worldwide.

Height: 14.2 to 15.2 hh.

Color: White hair dotted with black, brown, or bay spots in one of five basic patterns: leopard, marble, blanket, snowflake, or frosted (see p. 21).

Characteristics: Appaloosas are strong, hardy, and full of stamina, and very intelligent. Although great efforts have been made in this direction in recent years, the spotted horse has not yet been standardized as a breed. Appaloosas have several distinguishing features as well as their coloring. Unlike most horses, the sclera of the eye is circled in white. They also have pink and sometimes mottled skin which is particularly noticeable around the nostrils. Their manes tend to be sparse and wispy. The hooves are striped with vertical black and white marks, and the withers are well defined. The introduction of Arab blood has given the Appaloosa a refined quality with an excellent carriage; it is used nowadays for all types of riding and competition, and its stamina makes it particularly sought for endurance riding.

The Appaloosa can be traced back to the spotted horses of European cave drawings. The Spanish and Neapolitan breeds were noted for their spots, and it is thought some of these came to North America with the Spaniards in the early 1600s. The Indians captured some, and the Nez Percé tribe were riding them by 1730. They were originally bred near their homelands in the Palouse valley and were first called "Palouse" by the French – hence the name Appaloosa.

THE COB

Origin: Britain and Ireland.
Height: 15.1 hh is the maximum for a show Cob.
Color: Any.
Characteristics: The Cob is a type and not a breed and should not be confused with the Welsh Cob, which is a breed. It has been produced by crossing Irish Drafts with lighter, mainly Thoroughbred horses. This has resulted in a tough, strong horse able to carry heavyweight riders. It should be light and easy to ride with a good shoulder, very comfortable, and a good mover capable of galloping. It should have good bone with a minimum of 8½ in. (22 cm) and has short cannons and stands foursquare. In show classes, which are divided into lightweight and heavyweight divisions, the Cob should not exceed 15.1 hh. In ridden classes it is judged like the Hunter and ridden by the judge. The Cob should be the sort of horse you would be happy to put your grandfather on, with a calm but workmanlike disposition.

Cobs are usually shown with hogged manes. The tail should be full and set high, and pulled and trimmed to just below the hocks. Cobs always used to be shown with their tails docked until this practice was made illegal nearly 50 years ago.

POLO PONY

Origin: The Far East.
Height: 14.2 hh up. Height restrictions were lifted after World War I.
Color: Any.
Characteristics: The Polo pony is a type rather than a breed and has been valued for over 2,000 years, since polo was first played in the Far East. The modern-day game of polo derives its name from the Tibetan word *palu*, which means ball. The main criterion for a good Polo pony is its performance, both in speed and agility. It should be able to stop and turn in its own length, perform the half pass at full gallop, and have outstanding natural balance and acceleration, together with a willing, courageous temperament.

Although founded on the Thoroughbred, the modern Polo pony is not always known for its looks, but more for stamina and hardiness. It has a long, free neck and a strong, short back, with plenty of room for the lungs. Although Polo ponies are worked lean, they must show powerful quarters with clean, strong legs, with the hocks well let down. The last 50 years have seen a revival of polo worldwide, especially in Argentina, where thousands are bred, which means that the Polo pony continues to thrive and improve.

THE HUNTER

Origin: Britain and Ireland.
Height: Any.
Color: Any.
Characteristics: The Hunter is a sturdy, strong type of horse with the quality and substance to cover distances at speed. It should be tough and athletic and a good, bold jumper with an in-built sense of self-preservation. It should be able to provide a good, comfortable ride and carry considerable weight through a full day's hunting.

Britain and Ireland are traditionally the home of the Hunter, where the Thoroughbred has been crossed for generations with some of the local draft breeds to produce a tough but quality horse. Many Thoroughbreds of the stronger build fall into this type, producing some outstanding stock. The Hunter should have good bone, a short strong back, sloping shoulder and good feet, and a calm temperament. Many of the top competition horses today are of Hunter type. Popular Hunter stallions are much in demand as competition sires. Good Hunters that have proved themselves in the hunting field are much in demand. They have demonstrated their ability to stay sound as well as perform throughout the season.

In show classes there are numerous sections in both ridden and in-hand classes, particularly in the U.S., Britain, and Ireland. Green Hunters, working Hunter, small, ladies, and weight divisions are common.

A lightweight Hunter must be capable of carrying 182 lb. (82 kg), a middleweight 182-196 lb. (82-89 kg), and a heavyweight over 196 lb. (89 kg).

THE HACK

Origin: Britain.
Height: Not above 15.3 hh.
Color: Any.
Characteristics: The Hack is a type of horse of supreme elegance with great presence and quality, a real "lady's" horse. It should be a beautifully balanced ride, so good conformation is essential, as are an equitable temperament and good manners.

Most Hacks are of the Thoroughbred type, and these horses are particularly sought after in Britain and Australia, where there are numerous show classes for different heights, as well as for youngstock and breeding classes, ridden sidesaddle and astride.

The show Hack must have a refined head with a well-proportioned neck, a short back with slightly pronounced withers, a deep girth, and well-formed quarters. The legs must be clean with an action to give a sound and comfortable ride.

OTHER INFLUENTIAL RIDING BREEDS

- Andalucian
- Holstein
- Lipizzaner
- Gelderland
- Luisitano
- Oldenburg
- Haflinger
- Akhal-Teké
- Fjord
- Icelandic
- Australian
- Stock Horse
- Criolla
- Altér Real
- Knapstrup
- Hackney
- Paso Fino

CHAPTER 4

TRAINING THE HORSE

'I recommend the exercise known as
the Volte because it accustoms the horse
to turn on either jaw. Changing the
direction is also a good thing, that the
jaws on either side may be equally suppled.'

Translated from Xenophon,
The Art of Horsemanship (Circa 380 B.C.)

The first lessons start by leading the foal alongside its mother when bringing them both in from the field.

It is never too early to start training a youngster, even though it may be a year or two before you start to ride the animal.

The mare will teach its offspring how to cope with most situations, and a close study will reveal some fairly startling revelations. Lessons in everything from taking exercise, and coping with the elements, to how to cope with dangerous-looking objects, cleaning wounds, and avoiding persistent flies are clearly demonstrated if you take the time to watch the mare and foal out in the field. The handler must teach the foal similar lessons when it has to cope with what a domesticated animal is expected to do.

Leading

This is definitely lesson one and can be learned quickly if the mare and foal are put out in the mornings if they are stabled at night. When being led and while out in the paddock, the foal should be put into a foal slip. This will make it easier to catch the foal until it has learned to come to you. Most foals are very inquisitive and will come up quickly. Others may be shy and take a little more time. Always be patient. Teach a foal to lead by letting it follow the mare to start with. Then have the foal led beside the mare, then in front, and eventually on its own. An assistant's hand behind the quarters will help propel any stubborn foal. Once the walking forward lesson has been learned, a foal should be little trouble in the future. Do not try to separate the foal from the mare when teaching it to walk with a lead rein. If you do, both will get upset.

The foal must be respectful to humans at all times and must know when it is doing something which is not approved of. Annoying little habits can turn into vices if not corrected early enough. When very young, a sharp "no" will probably be enough; clapping your hands together is also effective.

Handling the foal

The more the foal is handled in the early days, the better. When it is about two to three months old, it should have its first worming treatment and vaccinations, and the farrier should check its feet. When you give your foal its daily check, make sure you spend a little time talking to it to get it accustomed to human company. Run your hand over its neck and back, and pick up the feet if at all possible. Once a bond has been established between foal and human, it will make any future training that much easier and less upsetting for the youngster.

Showing

You may want to show your foal or youngster. This can be an excellent introduction to traveling and seeing the sights – if done in moderation. Practice loading the mare and foal into the trailer a few times and rewarding them both with a feed once they are inside. Take your time doing this. It is often reassuring for the youngster to watch another animal enter the trailer. Mare and foal should have as much room as possible when traveling, with plenty of straw as protection. The mare can be tied up, but the foal must always be left free to move around. Never take a foal or youngster to a show until it can trot up and down calmly on a lead rope in full control and can stand properly.

The yearling

The young horse must be led in hand regularly so that it knows how to behave. Always ensure that whatever you do with youngsters is done firmly and quietly and with the minimum of fuss. Try not to make an issue of anything. If the youngster refuses to do something, it is better to do something quite different and then come back to the first exercise later and try it a different way. Putting a padded surcingle on at this stage is a good introduction to the saddle later on. Make sure it does not slide back. A breast strap across the front of the chest should prevent this. Picking out the feet and a light brushing should be done as often as possible. The weaned youngster should learn to respond to your hand and voice when being caught, stabled, led or tied up. Voice commands such as "whoa," "halt," "trot," "walk on," "steady," and "over" should be used regularly. When asking the youngster to "move over" in the stable, place your hand on its flank or belly with slight pressure as you speak. This will be a good introduction to the leg aids used later when the horse is ridden.

Backing the youngster

The youngster should be backed at a time when it is strong enough to be able to take this treatment without strain, usually in the summer or fall of its third year. Some youngsters are better left until they are four, while others might be lightly backed when they are almost three if they are very mature. If the youngster has been well handled, has a healthy respect for its trainer, and is generally confident, backing is rarely a problem so long as a lot of time is taken at the beginning of this course of training.

Lungeing

This is the first step (see p. 33). The handler should start by teaching the animal to go around in a large circle with loose side reins from a surcingle to the cavesson. Teach the youngster to obey the voice, and give plenty of encouragement and praise when something is well done.

Start with two people, so that one can lead the horse around in the circle from the

Tying up the foal

At six months, weaning will probably have taken place. After this the youngster has to learn about being tied up. This is best done first inside a stable. Once it shows no sign of resistance and does not pull, it can be tied up outside. Start by using a long lead, rope, or lunge rein attached to the foal slip or halter, not a bridle. Thread the rein through the ring; then hold the loose end of the rope. Do not let the foal pull back; but take up more contact on the rope while getting a helper to stand behind the foal and flick it with the lunge rein until it stops pulling and stands quietly. Reward with a pat and soothing words. Do this until the foal learns to stand still for a few minutes without pulling. Slowly increase the time and use other safe, enclosed spaces where it cannot come to any harm if it breaks loose. Always use a safety knot (see p. 25).

outside while the other holds the lunge rein and guides the horse between the rein and the whip, with the horse moving around in as large a circle as possible.

Gradually work on achieving rhythmic and active paces, bearing in mind that the

Lungeing can be used to teach balance and obedience and improve the horse's general way of going, as well as for exercise.

horse is unlikely to be able to canter and should be discouraged from attempting this for some time yet, unless naturally well balanced. Obedience is imperative, and you must make the youngster listen to your words of command. If it has not understood about slowing down, for instance, some short, sharp jerks from the lunge rein may be needed, alternatively run the horse toward a barrier or fence or gradually decrease the circle until you can get the youngster to stop.

Introducing the bit

Start by putting the bit in the mouth in the stable and leaving it on for a short time each day. A soft mild bit is ideal, such as a light, loose ringed snaffle or a rubber bit. It should always be the right size for the horse's mouth and fitted at the right height. Many trainers believe that special mouthing bits with attached keys encourage the horse to play with the bit; others think they give it a good mouth. Young horses should not be

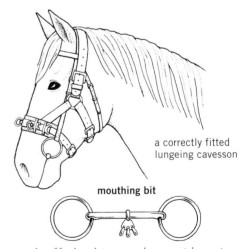

a correctly fitted lungeing cavesson

mouthing bit

lunged off the bit nor have side reins fastened on it until they have can go forward confidently. Next, lunge the horse with a saddle on, so that it can get used to this new feeling. Do not tighten the girths too much until the horse is used to them. Secure or remove the stirrup irons so that they do not flap around, and use a breast strap to hold the saddle forward in place.

Long reining the youngster

This will teach the horse to go forward more confidently and become familiar with the feel of the reins against its sides, which will be a preparation for when it has a rider on its back in the future. Walking around the stable with long reins will also get the youngster used to some of the everyday sights and sounds. With a nervous horse, it may be helpful to have a helper walk by its head for the first couple of outings.

To add the extra rein used for long reining, you will first need to let down both stirrups and shorten them to a height roughly in line with the horse's bit. Secure the stirrups with string under the horse's belly or fasten them to the girth to prevent them from flapping. The stirrups now become

Long reining will teach the horse to go forward into the rein and is excellent preparation for taking a mounted rider.

Backing the young horse

This is the process of mounting a horse for the first time. How successful you are very much depends on early preparation and the trust and confidence the horse has in you and the other human beings. Time and patience are essential. It is also most important that the person doing the backing is an experienced and lightweight rider able to remain relaxed at all times.

Stage one Start by lungeing to make sure the horse is relaxed. If at all possible, have two people to help you during backing for the first couple of days, with one holding the horse and the other helping the rider.

Stage two Put a neckstrap on the horse, and take it to a quiet spot. Have the handler hold it, talking quietly all the time. The rider can then gently move the saddle a little, watching the eye of the horse to make sure it looks relaxed. The assistant then lifts the rider up gently toward, but not into, the saddle a couple of times.

Stage three The next stage is for the rider to lie right across the saddle. If the horse is calm, it can be moved forward a couple of steps and then halted and praised. This may be enough for the first day if the horse looks in any way apprehensive.

Stage four It may take a couple of days for some horses to get this far, while others might seem totally unfazed by what is going on – in which case the rider can be lifted right into the saddle with legs astride, taking care not to hit the horse's back as the leg is thrown over.

Taking time over the early stages is the secret of successful backing. Quietness and kindness are generally rewarded.

The rider should not sit upright too quickly, but must keep talking to the horse. Sit up gradually, gently settling into the saddle and holding either the pommel of the saddle or the neckstrap, taking care not to brush the horse's sides with the legs. Talk to the horse. If it seems confident, move it forward a couple of strides and then halt and reward it with a pat. The trainer may say that that is enough for the day, or ask the rider to dismount quietly and then mount again. Reassurance given to the horse, and patience at all times, are essential.

The horse must feel confident about

The rider must remain quite relaxed when mounted and be very gentle with the legs until the horse is used to them.

having a rider on its back. Take your time, and allow the horse to get used to this and for it to see you on its back. Watch its eye all the time. The rider will know if the horse is relaxed or tense by the tightening of its back. At no time should the rider use his legs. The horse should respond to the trainer's voice and can be led forward and around the area until confident. It can then be lunged in walk and trot until it goes forward and is well balanced, and can cope with the rider's extra weight. Some may try to buck a little and must be kept moving forward firmly.

"runners" through which the lunge reins are threaded. To start with, allow the horse to feel the rein around the back of his leg just above the hocks, moving it around so that he gets used to the feeling. Start to lunge him at the walk (with the reins through the stirrup irons), with the outside rein taken over the saddle to start with, and then flick the lunge rein down over his quarters so that it falls to just above the hock. The horse may be a bit nervous at first, but so long as you remain quiet and use a calm voice, it will soon settle and learn to accept this new experience. If you have a helper, he or she can ease the rein down and walk beside the horse for a few strides before moving away.

Quite soon it will be possible to take the horse out for walks along quiet tracks and to make it twist and turn as it responds to the rider's hands and the feel of the reins on its flanks. It is most important that your hands remain very light and responsive so that the horse is never pulled into a position but goes confidently forward by itself. After a week or so of this training, the horse should be ready to be backed.

Independence
Once the horse seems confident, the rider must take control, steering and bringing the horse to a halt before it is let loose from the lunge rein. This is best done at the end of a session and preferably in an enclosed space. To start with the trainer can release the lunge rein but stay close by, walking alongside, and then gradually moving away.

The backing process may take anything from two to three days to two to three weeks, depending on the horse. Once this period is over, the horse should spend a few days learning to go forward at walk and trot, and stopping, starting, and being steered, with the rider using the legs as well as the voice. The trainer should remain nearby during these sessions in case of difficulties until the horse is obedient and confident with the rider mounted.

The rider must exaggerate instructions, taking the hand out sideways to indicate direction, and using the voice rather than too much leg for encouragement forward. A good kick or squeeze may well mean the rider will be thrown to the ground.

As soon as the horse goes forward, stops, starts, and steers reasonably well, it can start to go out to see the world around it, preferably with another, more experienced horse

The young horse must be taught to go up and down hills and through shallow water with confidence.

and rider as companions. The rides should be quiet and encouraging. Try not to take a route where there are a lot of spooks. Out on the road, the young horse should be protected from traffic by being on the inside of the schoolmaster. The horse that has not previously had the chance to experience traffic should first stand in a safe gateway to get used to vehicles before venturing out on the road. If you happen to have a field alongside a road or driveway, the horse will probably be used to the noise and movement. Traffic noise should always be borne in mind when youngsters are placed in fields.

Variation during exercise
Take the horse on as many different rides as possible. The more it can see or do, the better. Take it through woods, fields, along tracks and bridleways, up and down hills, and, if possible, through shallow, safe water, letting it gradually take the initiative and going forward inquisitively. After a week or so, make the youngster go in front and let it canter on forward if it wants to. Never ask for any collection or outline at this stage. Allow the horse complete freedom of head

and neck to balance itself. Care should be taken with the use of the hands and bit, especially as the horse may now have been teething for some months.

Shoeing
If it is not already shod, the horse will soon need shoes, particularly going on roads, but do not hurry to have it shod unless it is absolutely necessary. It may be a good idea to put on front shoes first, to allow the horse to get used to these at grass before putting shoes on the hind feet. Some animals find the extra weight quite strange to start with and lose their movement for a time.

After backing, the horse may need a break; very often after four to six weeks of being ridden, the young horse is turned loose again to grow more mature. If backed as a three-year-old, the horse will not really have mature tendons and muscles, even if it does appear big and strong.

When you bring the horse back into work after a break, start with a few days lungeing before mounting again. During the first few lessons, make sure it has not forgotten its lungeing and backing lessons.

More advanced work

The horse now has to continue its flat work and start building up an outline and improving all its paces. A low, rounded outline, pushing the horse from behind into a light contact, is what is required. The training should be done a little at a time and often, in between hacking out. Do not overtire the horse, and give it frequent rests on a long rein, allowing it to stretch its neck and topline fully.

To start with, get the horse to go straight and in large circles. The most important points to consider are: the ease with which the horse goes forward, how straight it goes, and the rhythm and balance. Each of these is dependent upon the others.

Forward movement How the horse goes forward depends on its confidence. If it has not been too restricted, you should not have any problems.

Straightness will not be achieved unless the horse is going forward well and in balance. Straightness may be difficult to achieve, especially when going along the side or a wall of an arena because the horse's shoulders are narrower than its hips. Very often it hugs the wall with its shoulders and so the quarters swing inward. This is less likely to happen if the horse is pushed forward strongly up into its bridle. Aim for straightness from the top of the nose to the tail. "Sit straight, ride straight, and the horse will go straight" is a saying worth remembering.

Rhythm Work the horse in a good rhythm in large circles and allow it to seek the contact. Change the rein as often as possible and let it "swing" in the trot, keeping a constantly light feel, making sure the balance is not lost and that the horse does not get onto its forehand.

Balance To achieve balance, the horse will need to come off its forehand and to learn to carry itself by using its quarters, hocks, and hindlegs. This will help to shift the weight toward the back and allow more freedom in front. Half halts (below) and riding up and down hills (see p. 36) are two of the most useful methods to help the horse to make the best use of its hindquarters.

When the horse is carrying itself in a balanced way, it should be able to carry out movements with ease and without any change of rhythm.

Exercises to help the young horse

The following exercises are designed to help the horse use itself correctly and also to build up muscle and become fit and supple so that it can perform on the flat and jump with ease. Start by working for 20 minutes, then for half an hour. It will be some time before the young horse will be able to hold its concentration for longer periods, and it will find even simple exercises very hard work at first. Make sure the horse shows no signs of stiffness the next day that indicate overwork.

Circles These are particularly useful exercises for making the horse supple, and may be done anywhere in the stable area (see p. 34). They are usually done in 21 yd. (20 m), 16 yd. (15 m) or 11 yd (10 m) circles. Eleven yard (10 m) circles are too small for a young horse, as they put too much strain on the back, ribs, and inside hindleg, but it will eventually manage these once it learns proper balance and builds up strength and muscle.

Serpentines These are excellent suppling exercises because they require a change of bend at each side of the field, and across the center line (see p. 34). As the horse gets more advanced, the serpentines can increase in number. Three in a 21 x 43 yd. (20 x 40 m) arena is sufficient for the young horse, but this can increase to four or five serpentines later.

Spiraling This means decreasing the size of the circle from 21 yd. (20 m) in diameter to about 11 or 13 yd. (10 or 12 m). It is done by increasing the pressure from the outside leg. When the circle is small enough, start to increase it again by pushing the horse into the outside rein with the inside leg. This is a form of "leg yielding."

Canter to trot transitions Starting on a large 21 yd. (20 m) circle in canter, the horse is brought back to trot and then pushed on again into canter. This is repeated four or five times on each rein and is excellent for helping the horse to balance itself and to learn how to strike off on the correct leg (see p. 32). Later the same exercise can be done on 16 and 11 yd. (15 and 10 m) circles.

Lengthening the strides This is usually done in trot with the horse being pushed into a longer stride and outline for a few strides and then brought back again. It helps to create suppleness and balance.

The half halt This is one of the most important exercises used in training at all levels. The half halt is used in preparation for a change of movement or to check and adjust the horse's balance. To perform a half halt, you use your back and seat to push the horse into a restraining hand, and it responds by engaging the hocks. The act of engagement will generally lighten the forehand. A half halt will teach the horse to be more attentive to its rider.

The half halt can be started with the young horse in walk. Once it has learned to respond to the rider's aids, it can be performed in trot and canter.

Medium trot is the pace between working and extended trot. The horse has to lengthen and stretch forward a little while maintaining a rounded but purposeful outline. Start by lengthening the stride on the straight after balancing the horse with a half halt. The rider has to create and maintain the right amount of impulsion from behind to stop the horse from falling onto its forehand.

Extended trot This is the most exaggerated form of trot and requires maximum lengthening of the frame as well as stretch from the limbs. When the horse is carrying itself in a balanced way and has the strength and suppleness to cope, it should be able to carry out the movement with ease and without any loss of rhythm, so long as it is not on its forehand with all the energy and impulsion going out "through its nose."

The halt The halt is a continuation of the half halt. All horses must learn to halt and remain still until asked to move. The weight should be evenly distributed on all legs with the front and hind pairs together standing square. The horse should be on the bit (see p. 116), but it must be relaxed and must not step back or sideways. It will take time and patience for a good halt to be achieved.

The rein back This exercise follows a halt which should be well executed before the aids to rein back are given. Keep a light contact and never force the horse. The steps should be even and picked up for each stride, not dragged back. The rein back is in two time using diagonal pairs of legs; left hind and right foreleg together, then right hind and left foreleg together. The horse must be allowed to go forward quietly after a few steps backwards.

Neither the halt nor the rein back can be achieved satisfactorily until the horse is old enough to be sufficiently balanced and collected.

Further schooling

As the horse builds up confidence, so its way of going must become more sophisticated. A rounder, more collected outline will become necessary, with the horse able to use its hocks more effectively and to shorten and lengthen its stride so that it can easily cope with what it is asked to do. Lateral schooling exercises such as renvers and travers help to increase suppleness and bend. These along with leg yielding and shoulder-in are excellent preparatory work for the half-pass.

Leg yielding

This movement, which is an obedience and supling exercise, is generally carried out in trot. The horse's body remains straight while having a slight bend at the poll, away from the direction in which it is moving. The inside legs pass and cross in front of the outside legs.

Leg yielding is the most basic of all the lateral movements, and many riders use this exercise as a start to this type of work.

The inside leg is placed on the girth, and the horse is then encouraged to step across to the outside while maintaining straightness of the body. The rider asks for a slight bend at the poll, enabling him just to see the eye. The outside rein regulates the degree of bend and controls the shoulders.

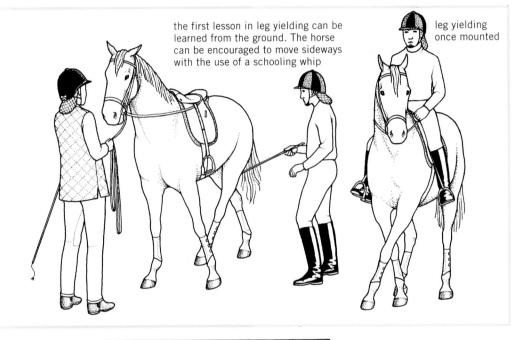

the first lesson in leg yielding can be learned from the ground. The horse can be encouraged to move sideways with the use of a schooling whip

leg yielding once mounted

Introduction to lateral work

Turns on the forehand and haunches These are excellent supling aids and useful for teaching the horse to answer and go away from the leg. For the 180° turn on the forehand, first bring the horse to a halt and slightly bend it in the direction it is to go. The horse must then move its hindquarters away from the rider's leg in a semicircle, and make a very small half-circle with the forelegs so that it turns 180° slowly, step by step, to face the other way. This movement is usually performed along the side of the arena. The horse's hindlegs must cross, with the inside hindleg crossing over in front of the outside leg.

For the 180° turn on the haunches, the horse reverses the above procedure, and the forehand is brought slowly around the haunches, which make a very small semi-circle while the forehand is brought around in a larger circle and the horse is slightly bent around the inside leg. This is done from a shortened walk to maintain impulsion. It is the start to the pirouette and is often referred to as a half-pirouette in walk.

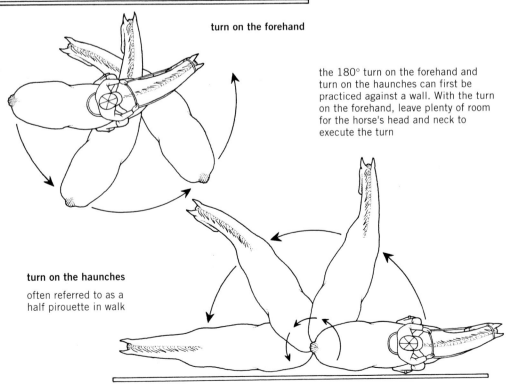

turn on the forehand

the 180° turn on the forehand and turn on the haunches can first be practiced against a wall. With the turn on the forehand, leave plenty of room for the horse's head and neck to execute the turn

turn on the haunches

often referred to as a half pirouette in walk

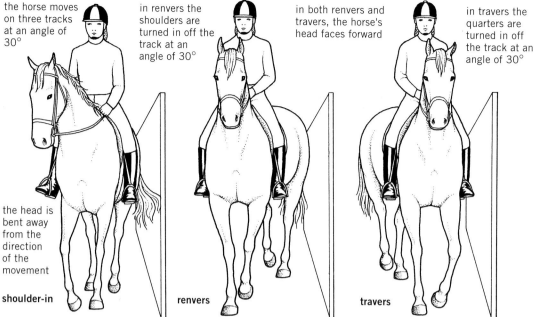

the horse moves on three tracks at an angle of 30°

the head is bent away from the direction of the movement

shoulder-in

in renvers the shoulders are turned in off the track at an angle of 30°

in both renvers and travers, the horse's head faces forward

renvers

in travers the quarters are turned in off the track at an angle of 30°

travers

The shoulder-in (above) is the next exercise to learn. In this the horse moves at an angle of approximately 30° in the direction of the movement, usually along the side of an arena or in a circle. The horse should be bent slightly from head to tail around the rider's inside leg, which should be forward on the girth. The horse is looking away from the direction of the movement and is on three tracks; the inside foreleg is to the inside, the outside foreleg and inside hindleg are on the inner track and the outside hindleg is on the outer one.

The outside rein controls the degree of bend, and the inside one indicates the direction. The horse should be ridden forward purposefully after the shoulder-in so that it does not tend to drop behind the bit. Do not make the mistake of asking for too much bend at the cost of going forward.

Renvers and travers are two exercises whereby the horse is bent around the rider's leg, which is positioned at an angle of 30° to the wall. In travers the horse's hindquarters are turned in off the track. In renvers the shoulders are turned in off the track. Control the degree of bend with the outside rein and leg. Forwardness is important if the exercise is to be of value. Both exercises are useful when preparing for the half-pass.

The half-pass is the most advanced of the lateral movements and requires the horse to move forward and sideways at the same time, while looking in the direction in which it is traveling. As the horse improves in suppleness, a greater degree of bend can be asked for, but never at the expense of a loss of regularity or forwardness. The half-pass can be done in trot or canter.

All these movements need to be attained gradually and progressively so as not to build up tension or stiffness. It is essential for the

Canter work becomes increasingly important to establish a consistent balanced pace, with the horse going well forward in a good rhythm up to the bit. The horse must remain consistent and totally obedient, listening and waiting for your instructions.

Flying change The horse should be taught to do a flying change so that there is no rhythm lost in the canter when a change onto the opposite leg is required. Start by cantering on a figure-eight or a three-loop serpentine with a simple change (that is, three strides of trot) before cantering off on the new, correct leg. This must be perfected before first attempting the flying change, which is when the horse changes its leading leg and bend during the moment of suspension after the third beat of canter. This movement is natural to the horse.

When cantering, a definite shift of the weight and leg aids will be all that is required for many horses. Start by preparing the horse with a half halt and then ask for a change to

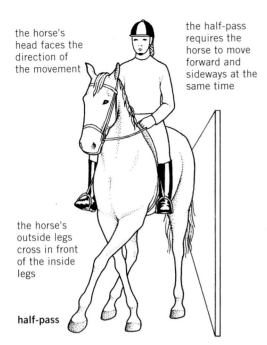

the horse's head faces the direction of the movement

the half-pass requires the horse to move forward and sideways at the same time

the horse's outside legs cross in front of the inside legs

half-pass

rider to be relaxed if the horse is to maintain large, open free strides with good shoulder and hock movements. To perform the half-pass correctly, the horse should first be in collected trot or canter with its hocks well engaged. All movements have to be prepared with a half halt or, if necessary, a series of half halts, to ensure that the horse is well off its forehand. Ask for the bend and then, with the outside leg, push the horse's quarters over, maintaining the series and giving and taking with the inside hand to keep it soft and forward going in the direction away from the outside leg.

Retraining the spoiled horse and coping with problems

A good horse is often spoiled for various reasons. It might have been rushed in the early stages of training, or have been restricted by the rider, with the result that there is loss of natural movement. Or the horse may have been made too tense in all its work.

Ignorance on the part of the trainer is a major problem. It is amazing how often usually sensible people make very bad mistakes through ignorance about what an animal is physically capable of or because of a total lack of understanding of what the animal can be expected to do. Too much is often asked of a horse, either for its age or state of fitness. It becomes worried and reacts by evasions of some sort.

Signs of worry and evasion are: head tossing, mouthiness, lack of rhythm and suppleness, or one-sidedness, rearing and bolting.

The way ahead

Often the best way to settle a horse is to not to ride it, but instead to put it on the lunge for a week. Without the rider's weight, there is nothing to make the horse tense up or fight against except itself, and it can learn to relax and settle into a rhythm and concentrate on what it is being asked to do rather than worry about what might happen to it. Long reining may be equally useful. Start with fairly loose reins and gradually tighten them until the horse is going in a correct outline and is accepting the bit calmly and

confidently. After a week, try riding again, either on the lunge or independently, and see if the situation has improved. Try to improve the horse with suppling exercises and unstressful changes of pace and speed until it accepts quite calmly what is being asked. Never force it, but calmly work the horse through any tension by quiet and repetitive work on both reins.

Specific problems

Whatever the cause, the problem will manifest itself in some form of evasion. The horse will try to avoid the bit and the rider's aids.

Being behind the bit This means that the horse does not go forward onto the bit and avoids consistent contact. To solve this problem, the horse should have as mild a bit as possible, such as a thick, loose-ringed bit or a rubber snaffle. Some horses dislike the nutcracker action of the jointed bit and are happier in a straight bit. Very light and sympathetic hands are required, and the horse must be pushed on forward and encouraged to "take a hold" with a relaxed jaw and neck.

Too much work in a restricted area tends to encourage a horse into being behind the bit, so if possible get out into the countryside and allow the horse to open up.

Overbent horses tend to bring their noses back behind the vertical and carry their heads and necks too low, with too much bend from the withers and poll. They are inclined to bring their heads in toward the chest and either drop behind the bit or lean on it with a dead mouth. This usually means either too

the other leg in the same way as you would ask for a canter. Alternatively, place a pole on the ground and canter over it in a figure-eight, exaggerating the change of bend and swinging your body a little toward the leg you want to change to as you go over the pole. Once the horse has mastered this exercise, it should be quite easy to ask for the change.

Pole work Once the horse is going forward with confidence on the flat, it should be introduced to poles on the ground. It is well worth teaching the horse to go over poles in early days so that it is thoroughly used to them. Even if you do not intend to jump your horse when it matures, pole work is necessary as part of the horse's training for balance and cadence. Poles at ground level are useful throughout the training program of all horses,.

Ground poles are also invaluable when teaching a horse to lengthen or shorten its stride.

severe a bit is being used or that the horse is being ridden with an overstrong hand. Alternatively it might mean that the horse is not being ridden forwards enough.

To help cure this fault, treat as for being behind the bit and have a slightly higher hand if the horse continues to get its head too low. Raise the hand and push the horse forward on a softer contact.

Pulling A horse which pulls through setting its neck muscles and lower jaw is unresponsive and disobedient. It does not obey the rider's aids, either because it is in pain or through ignorance. It may tuck its head in its chest and get overbent; it may throw its head up in the air so that the bit action is totally ineffective, or it may bear down on the bit or toss it around with an open mouth in obvious discomfort.

First check the horse's mouth carefully to make sure there are no loose or sharp teeth, painful wolf teeth, or sore lips. Check that the bit is the right size for the horse and that it rests comfortably in the mouth. Retrain the horse to balance itself and reward it with a giving of the hand, working up through walk to trot to canter until the horse can be ridden into a soft and giving contact.

Tongue over the bit This is a problem which may be difficult to eradicate. The bit may be too low in the mouth; pressure on the tongue may be too severe; the horse may have too narrow a mouth for the bit. If all seems well in the mouth, start by taking the bridle up a hole or two on either side. A gentle, straight snaffle bit may be effective or a double-jointed snaffle that remains flatter in the mouth with a more gentle action on the tongue. With the double-jointed snaffle, make sure it is of a type where the extra central plate or ring link lies flat on the horse's tongue and not the type which sits at an angle with severe tongue pressure (see p.118). Sometimes if the horse opens its mouth a lot a drop noseband will solve the problem. Encourage the horse forward so that a good contact is being made. Be very soft and light with the hands. If all this fails, there are a number of tongue ports or tongue grids which correct this.

A rubber tongue port (guard) can be attached over a straight bit. The port faces towards the throat, lying flat on the tongue, which discourages the horse from putting its tongue over the bit.

The tongue grid is a thin metal bar with a large port. This is fastened in place by a sliphead on the bridle. It is impossible for the horse to get its tongue over the grid. Tongue grids are a temporary measure and should only be worn for a short period.

Dry mouth This makes it difficult for the horse to remain light in the hand. The salivary glands fail to work leaving a hard, dry and unresponsive mouth which is liable to injury. Offer succulents such as apples or carrots at intervals once the bit is in place.

Copper bits, because of their taste, often encourage the horse to salivate more, as will coating the bit in syrup.

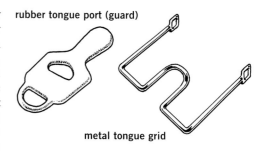

rubber tongue port (guard)

metal tongue grid

A poor outline First study the horse's way of going and see what is wrong. Always see that the horse is wearing the right tack and that it is fitted correctly. Opt for a milder bit, and remove any restraining pieces of tack (that is, nosebands and martingales) to see if this improves the situation before trying others. Check that the saddle sits correctly and does not have a broken tree causing discomfort. Then study the horse's conformation and see what bearing, if any, this might have on the situation.

A low-set on neck is always going to be a disadvantage. Ewe necks will never look good, but with correct training they can be minimized. The poll should be the highest point, with the nose just in front of the vertical. The top of the neck should be curved upwards with a soft bottom line. The back must be supple and the tail loose, straight and swinging. All joints must move equally and freely. The horse must look balanced and easy in its work. Always take note of any difference in the outline when

The horse and the bit

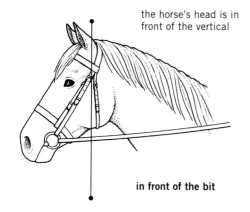

the horse's head is in front of the vertical

in front of the bit

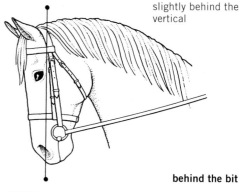

the horse's head is in the correct position, slightly in front of the vertical

on the bit

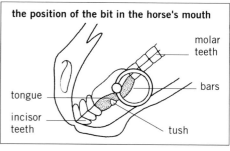

the horse's head is slightly behind the vertical

behind the bit

the position of the bit in the horse's mouth

molar teeth

bars

tongue

incisor teeth

tush

The action of the bit will depend on how well the horse is schooled and whether it 'accepts' the bit. This will only come about if the horse feels comfortable with the bit being the right shape and size for its mouth and in the correct place.

Depending on the degree of schooling, the young horse is likely to be in front of the bit. As training progresses it will come more on the bit through greater use of legs, seat and balance. The rider's hands must be supple and quiet if the horse is not to try and avoid pressure by coming behind the bit. If the horse is behind the bit it will be very hard to get a good ride out of it as it will tend to evade all the other aids and carry its head too low or too high in order to avoid the bit, and will not have positive rhythm or cadence.

the horse is with and without a rider on its back. First and foremost, the rider must think what he is doing wrong when the horse is going badly. Most horses are less supple on one side than the other and this must be taken into account. Bad riding can cause greater stiffness on either side which in turn may cause any one of the evasive tactics mentioned above.

Rearing There may be several reasons why a horse will rear so the particular cause must first be determined. Generally if a horse cannot go forward because the rider is preventing it, it will either go backwards or rear upwards. When horses get excited, nervous riders may clutch at their mouths which causes them to rear. Always keep a nervous or excitable horse moving and never restrict it. Walking round in a circle is often a good idea. Nappy horses will sometimes stop and rear because they do not want to go forward, strong riding and a few sharp smacks with the whip encouraging the horse forward will usually solve this. Riding out with a well-behaved horse for a couple of weeks may help the horse to forget its hang-

ups, and one may well be perfectly all right after a short period

Horses which rear should always be ridden out with a standing martingale which, if correctly adjusted, prevents them raising their heads out of control. If a horse rears up grab the mane and stay well forward, if possible pulling its head down and round so that you can encourage it to bring its forehand down, then urge it forwards with your legs. If the horse has reared because it did not want to do something it is often best to ride it round energetically, taking its mind off what you were attempting, before trying again. Always best to avoid a confrontation if you can achieve the desired result by employing different tactics.

Bolting When a horse bolts or gallops off uncontrollably it can be extremely frightening and dangerous. Horses may well do this through pain, fear or fright but it is most important that the rider can and does regain control as soon as possible. Try and keep calm and think rationally, either circling or pulling the horse up as best you can. If the horse is known to be a bolter ride in a tight-

When problems arise, the first thing to do is to establish the cause. Is it pain, fright, fear or naughtiness? Rearing and bolting are dangerous and require the rider to stay forward and remain calm and think rationally

ish standing martingale and use a bit with which you are sure you can pull up the horse. If the animal is nervous, patience will be required and you must reassure the horse that such behaviour is unnecessary. If the horse is genuinely frightened the same approach is required initially; you must react quickly and not let him run away from anything but turn and face up to the problem.

Confirmed bolters must be cured of this habit before they get out of control. Experiment with different bits; if the mouth is always open, start by shutting it with a drop or flash noseband. Anticipate situations when the horse may try to bolt and be ready to stop it firmly at the first indication of wanting to go. Be patient but very firm and never trust such animals with a child or an inexperienced rider.

Bits and schooling aids

There are a number of bits which can considerably influence your horse's way of going. Today, there are snaffle bits on the market with loose rings, full or half shanks, eggbutt rings, together with a variety of metal, rubber, and plastic mouthpieces. In general, the softer the bit, the lighter the horse, but this is only the case if the rider's legs are sufficiently effective to be able to contain the horse in a good outline.

In the majority of schooling situations and novice competitions, the snaffle bridle is worn. For more advanced riding, other more severe snaffle bits, Pelham bits, or double bridles are worn. For maximum control over cross-country or in the hunting field, the gag can be worn, and it is commonly seen on the polo field.

Each bit works in different ways, in most cases on different parts of the mouth or nose, and also on the poll and chin grooves if worn with a curb chain.

Snaffle bits

These are the simplest form of bit and are found in varying degrees of severity. The snaffle may have an unjointed mouthpiece, known as a mullen, which acts on the bars of the mouth, or a jointed mouthpiece which produces a nutcracker action. The action of the snaffle can be accentuated by the use of drop, flash, or grakle (crossover) nosebands which prevent the horse from opening its mouth.

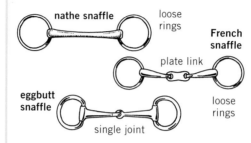

nathe snaffle — loose rings

French snaffle

plate link

eggbutt snaffle — loose rings

single joint

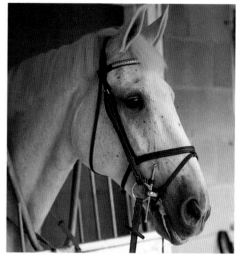

Above: The Fulmer snaffle has full shanks and is usually fitted with keepers attached to the bridle shankpieces.

The gag is a part of the snaffle group, but adapted so that the action becomes quite severe. The shank rings have holes set into them top and bottom, and the shankpieces of the bridle are threaded through with the reins attached to the end. This allows for a pulley action when the reins are taut. Pressure is put on the poll, and the bit slides up in the mouth, which accentuates the effect. It can be very useful for horses which pull hard, especially when working at speed. The rider must realize, however, that to be effective, a give and take action is required so that the bit drops down when released and is only effective again with the next restriction. The gag is best used with another rein fitted to the bit shanks in the usual way. This allows the rider to use the gag rein only when needed.

The Pelham is based on the Liverpool driving bit. It works quite effectively on some horses and can be used with two reins, or when fitted with "roundings" (as above) with one rein. It comes in a variety of mouthpieces and is fitted with a curb chain. Pelhams may be useful for children who require a little more control than that of the snaffle.

The Kimblewick (or Tom Thumb) is a popular version of the Pelham.

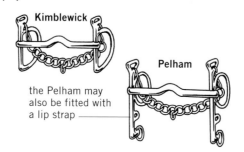

Kimblewick

Pelham

the Pelham may also be fitted with a lip strap

The bitless bridle works by putting pressure on the nose. Most bitless bridles are padded with sheepskin (as seen above) to reduce the severity. They are usually combined with some pressure to the chin groove and poll. Most bitless bridles have fairly long shanks which make them very severe as they provide considerable leverage.

Because they work by putting pressure on the nose, it is important to realize that the horse will not be as responsive to the rein aids as when a conventional bit is used, and the leg aids must be secure. This bridle can be useful on the horse with a "dead" mouth. It can also be suitable for the horse which has trouble with its teeth or has a difficult or oversensitive mouth.

The double bridle

This is often seen on the hunting field and in the show ring, and is a must for medium and advanced dressage. It consists of two bits (a bridoon and a curb) and two reins which are held separately.

This very sophisticated bridle enables the rider to use each rein and each bit independently. The snaffle action of the bridoon raises the head, while the action of the curb bit puts pressure on the curb groove and on the poll, lowering the head.

The bridoon is a smaller, lighter, jointed snaffle. It has smaller shank rings and a narrower mouthpiece than the ordinary snaffle, which makes its action more direct and more severe.

The curb bit, usually a Weymouth, is fitted with a curb chain. The length of the curb will considerably influence the degree of control, the longer shanks giving the most leverage and therefore being the most severe.

There are many different mouthpieces available with different sized ports, both fixed and sliding. They all have a slightly different action which must be assessed to find the one most suitable for your horse.

Curb chains The action of the curb bit is mostly determined by the tightness of the curb chain. This should be fastened so that the slant of the curb bit is at an angle of approximately 45°. Too tight and it will be too severe; too loose and it will not give sufficient control.

The curb chain should be fitted between the bridoon and the curb bit. The chain must be turned so that it lies flat in the chin groove; it is tightened to the required length by linking it evenly over the hooks on each side of the curb bit. The central link (fly link) should be placed with the lip strap threaded through to hold it in place.

There are several different types of curb chain. The strongest is the double-link variety. Leather or rubber chain guards can be fitted over these to give a milder effect. There are also elasticized "chains" or leather types which are much softer. Make sure all curb chains are of a suitable length.

Holding the reins The bridoon (snaffle) rein is usually held through the palm and between the thumb and index finger. The curb, which normally has a thinner rein, is then taken up and held between the third and fourth finger of each hand.

Used correctly, the double bridle enables the rider to exert maximum control, but in the wrong hands it can be lethal and so should never be put in the hands of the inexperienced. It takes great dexterity and coordination to use the double bridle correctly. Only a cavesson noseband is ever used with a double bridle.

parts of the double bridle

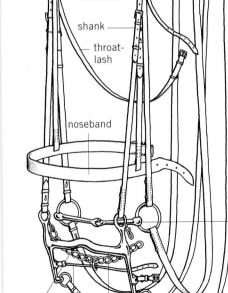

noseband sliphead · headpiece · bridoon rein · curb rein · bridoon sliphead · browband · shank · throat-lash · noseband · single-link curb chain · lip strap · Weymouth curb bit · loose-ring jointed bridoon bit

Above: A correctly fitted curb chain. It should ideally be worn with a lip strap as below.

single-link curb chain

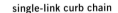

central link (fly link)

double-link curb chain

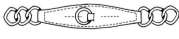

leather curb chain

holding the reins

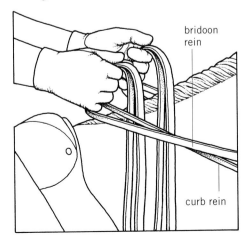

bridoon rein

curb rein

Nosebands

Nosebands can make quite a difference to a horse's way of going and will accentuate the action of the bit.

Always choose a good quality noseband. A well-made one will hang at right angles to its own shankpieces, which should be hidden by the bridle shankpieces.

Although there are a great many different sorts of noseband in existence, there are five types which are generally in use.

The cavesson is the simplest, and fitted loosely it plays no part in the control of the horse. It is generally worn to enhance the look of the head. However, it is used when a standing martingale is worn (see below), which prevents the horse from carrying or throwing its head too high when ridden. The cavesson noseband should be fitted so that you can place two fingers between the nosepiece and the horse's jaw bone.

The sheepskin-covered cavesson noseband is often seen on the racecourse. It is a cavesson noseband fitted with a thick roll of sheepskin over the nosepiece. It is designed to help horses lower their heads and to prevent shying. The sheepskin is fitted high enough to prevent this.

The drop noseband is fitted firmly below the bit to prevent the horse from opening its mouth and getting its tongue over the bit, and for extra control. The nosepiece must not be too low on the nostrils, or it will interfere with the breathing. A standing martingale should never be fitted to a drop noseband.

This flash noseband is made of a good quality leather, the lower strap does not bend or twist the nosepiece.

The flash noseband is a combination of the cavesson and drop noseband. It consists of a cavesson with a thin extra strap which goes through a loop on the front of the nosepiece.

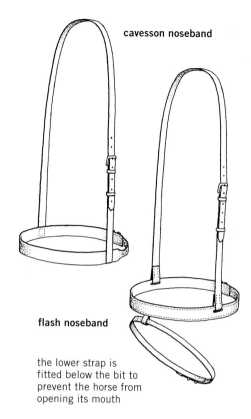

cavesson noseband

flash noseband

the lower strap is fitted below the bit to prevent the horse from opening its mouth

Like the drop noseband, it is fitted below the bit to prevent the horse from opening its mouth. It is particularly useful as it has the action of the drop noseband, and yet a standing martingale can be attached to the cavesson nosepiece.

The grakle (crossover noseband) has two diagonal straps which cross over the front of

The martingale

These can be very helpful with horses that throw their heads around or hold their heads too high. A martingale keeps the head in the correct position without the intervention of the rider's hands. There are two types of martingale most commonly used for riding: the standing and the running martingale.

To adjust martingales correctly, fit the neck strap and then attach it to the girth. It should then be adjusted so that the rein rings or noseband strap touch the top of the withers when held up.

The standing martingale is fixed to the cavesson noseband and acts by pulling on the nose, thus preventing the horse from tossing its head or carrying it so high that it evades the bit and gets out of control. Fitted correctly, it will not interfere with the horse's normal way of going, only coming into use when the head comes up too high. The standing martingale should never be fitted to a drop noseband or used when jumping, as a free head and neck is then required.

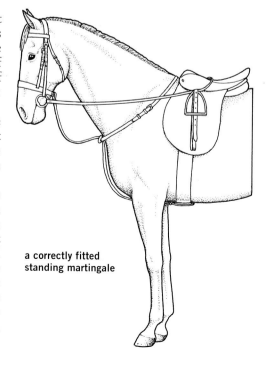

a correctly fitted standing martingale

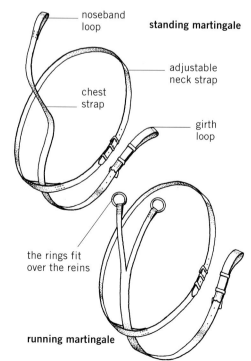

noseband loop

standing martingale

adjustable neck strap

chest strap

girth loop

the rings fit over the reins

running martingale

grakle noseband

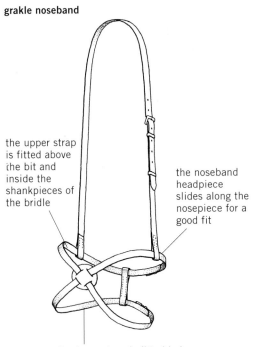

the upper strap is fitted above the bit and inside the shankpieces of the bridle

the noseband headpiece slides along the nosepiece for a good fit

the lower strap is fitted below the bit to prevent the horse from opening its mouth

drop noseband

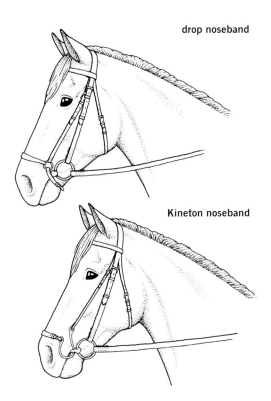

Kineton noseband

the nose and fasten below and above the bit inside the shankpieces. It is useful for pullers as it exerts pressure on the nose and also for those horses which cross their jaws, so giving greater control. A standing martingale cannot be fitted with a grakle.

The Kineton is usually fitted over the top of a snaffle bridle with a cavesson noseband. It

The grakle noseband has all the advantages of the drop noseband without the danger of affecting the breathing if fitted too low.

consists of a nosepiece which goes over the top of the muzzle and so does not close the mouth. This is attached to semicircular metal loops which hook behind the bit and are

fastened to a sliphead. When the bit is pulled, pressure is exerted on the muzzle, causing a little difficulty in breathing. It can be very effective with some headstrong horses, particularly with runaways, and is often seen on racehorses. This is a very severe way of controlling the horse and should only be adopted as a last resort.

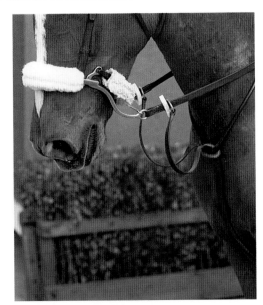

The running martingale must always be fitted with rubber stops on the reins and often with another stop at the breast joint to prevent it from slipping back through the loop.

The running martingale is more flexible and is attached to the reins which are fed through rings which move freely when not in use. It acts more on the bars of the mouth than the standing martingale, which has the effect of lowering the head, and the direct pressure applied helps to accentuate the steering aids. When the horse's head is in the correct position, there should be a straight line from the bit through the rings to the hand. Leather or rubber stops on the reins must always be used to ensure the rings do not get caught on the rein buckles.

The bib martingale is useful for young horses and is often seen on Thoroughbreds and other breeds which show great head and neck flexion. The bib martingale is a combination of the Irish and the running martingale, with the area between the two straps which slip over the reins filled in with a piece of leather. This is done for added safety, as it prevents the two rein straps from catching on the bridle or the horse's teeth during excessive headshaking.

The Irish martingale (or Irish rings) is not a true martingale as it does not act on the horse's head position. It is a leather strap about 6 in. (15 cm) long with two rings on each end which slip over the reins in between the head and neck. It stops the reins from being thrown over the head during headshaking or a fall. It also helps maintain a consistent contact, as the reins cannot flap about very easily. It is therefore invaluable on the young and excitable horse, where any other martingale might prove dangerous.

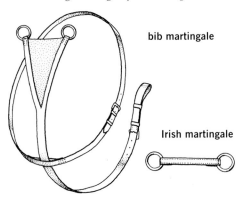

bib martingale

Irish martingale

Other useful training aids

There are various training aids which can be helpful in experienced hands, but some can be very damaging to the horse if abused or overused by the uninitiated. They must only ever be used with a snaffle bridle.

The Market Harborough is a combination of running reins and a martingale. The reins feed through the bit rings and are attached to a martingale D-ring near the horses's breastbone. Fitted correctly, this martingale only comes into effect when the horse takes up too much contact or raises its head too high.

It is important that the Market Harborough is fitted correctly; otherwise, its action will be that of running reins (draw reins), pulling the horse's head down from what may already have been a correct head carriage.

The running rein is a continuous rein which is fitted through both bit rings. At its most severe, it is attached between the horse's legs to the girth and used as a second rein (A). It can also be attached to the girth straps (B) on each side; in this way, it will not pull the top of the poll and neck muscles too much when in use.

Used properly the running rein places the horse's head in the correct position. So long as the horse is encouraged forward and the rider's hands remain soft and "allowing," it is very effective. If, however, there is a permanent pull, the horse will soon become fixed and stiff, or drop behind it to try to avoid the pressure.

As the running rein works directly off the bit to control head movements, it must never be used while jumping, when freedom for the horse's neck and head is crucial.

Chambon and de Gogue are two devices of European origin which put pressure on the poll to encourage the horse to lower its head. They are useful for schooling and encourage the correct way of going by coming into effect and applying pressure if the horse raises its head to evade contact. The Chambon consists of an attachment to the bit which goes through pull rings at browhand level on both sides and then down to a joint which fastens to the girth between the legs and prevents the horse from raising its head above the angle of control. The de Gogue is more complex and puts pressure on the poll, the mouth, and the base of the neck, but only if the horse raises its head too high. It can be used in two positions, one specifically for jumping. By encouraging the horse to keep its head low and stretch forward, the animal is able to use itself better.

Market Harborough

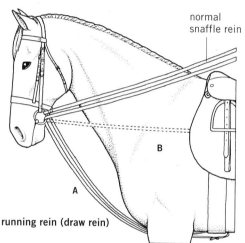

running rein (draw rein)

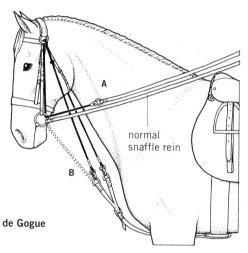

de Gogue

Spurs enable the rider to achieve an immediate effect, either in terms of movement or by accentuating the effect of the leg aids. They should only be used by experienced riders who have an independent seat and good control of their hands and legs. They are the correct dress with long (hunting) boots.

Spurs with rowels should never be used. A spur has a shank on the back of it which, if curved, should point inward and downward when worn. The buckle on the spur straps should be fitted on the outside of the rider's boots with the point of the strap pointing downward. Pointed shanks or any type likely to cause injury should never be used.

Schooling whips For general schooling, the long dressage whip is excellent, as its length enables the rider to touch the quarters gently with a slight movement of the wrist.

For difficult horses, and especially for the horse that does not go freely forward, it may be an advantage to carry two schooling

Bit guards are rubber circles of 2½ to 3 in. (5.5 to 7.5 cm) in diameter with a hole in the middle. They are stretched over the bit shank rings in pairs and sit between the bit shanks and the horse's lips on each side. They prevent the horse's lips from being rubbed and stop the bit from being pulled through the mouth.

All training aids can be effective if their use is properly understood and if they are used with discretion. Ask a knowledgeable person to explain clearly what needs to be achieved and how, and what pitfalls to avoid. Always remember that the use of force is never successful, either in the short or long term.

At the end of the day, correct schooling, time, and patience are the most important elements needed to produce a well-schooled horse.

whips, one on each side of the horse. A whip is often carried on the side of the horse with the greatest stiffness to encourage a little more activity. The way to move the schooling whip to the opposite hand is as follows:
• Put both reins into the hand with the whip.
• With the free hand, cross over the back of the other hand, taking hold of the whip so that it faces in the correct direction.
• Gently swing the length of the whip over to the other side and take up the reins again.

This should be practiced first at the halt. Your horse will soon get used to the movement and will show no signs of being spooked by it.

As with other whips, the schooling whip should be held flat against the thigh in a neat manner. Take extra care with the longer schooling whip not to tickle the horse's quarters unintentionally.

The whip is only ever used for correction or guidance; it must never be used in temper.

Jump training

When the horse is fit, obedient, and sufficiently mature, you may wish to start jump training. Like all other training this should be done slowly: time and patience are the important criteria.

To start with, it is best to teach the horse to jump single fences, either in a riding school or over logs, ditches, or hedges when out hacking. The more small jumps it can cope with initially, the better. If it is lacking in confidence, a lead from another horse will very often make it understand what to do.

Never attempt anything too big to start with and always ride positively so that the horse is never confused about your intentions or learns to stop before a jump.

Grids

These must now be introduced to teach the horse to become more agile and quick thinking and to cope with combinations of fences. The grids should be built up progressively, adding one fence at a time. Poles on the ground in between the fences help the horse to find the correct striding to meet the fences (see p. 40).

The purpose of the grid is to teach the horse to cope with different types of fences.
Cross poles will teach the horse to jump in the center of the fences, in this case where the jump is at its lowest.
Horizontal poles will encourage the horse to jump higher and more neatly in front.
A parallel or spread will encourage the horse to stretch and round its back over the fence.

Grids can be varied to suit the horse and to teach it to figure out what is required by allowing it freedom on an even but soft contact, going with the movement, and staying in balance throughout.

The distances between the poles and fences must be set so that the horse gains maximum benefit and confidence from the exercises. Roughly 9 to 10 ft. (2.7-3 m) distance between each will be about right for the average horse's stride. Shorter distances will encourage the horse to bascule over the fence, and longer distances will encourage it to flatten. Remember to allow a little more room in between as the fences get bigger.

Jumping courses

Build your course to vary the degree of difficulty so that your horse has to think really hard and use itself well. It must get used to jumping combinations of every kind. A horse often comes to its first competition, sees a line of fences with a confusing number of poles, and feels it cannot cope. Practice with doubles of every kind and then progress to trebles. Jump all variations, starting low and increasing in height as the horse gains confidence.

The horse now needs experience in jumping different types of fence and must learn to become confident about "fillers," which can look rather spooky.

The sooner you can let the young horse pop over small natural fences to build up its confidence, the better.

Introduction to cross-country fences

Riding across country is exhilarating and fun; however, it is vital that the horse is taught to cope with every situation that might arise and that the rider knows what to expect.

In the horse's early training, it should have met with small cross-country fences such as logs and ditches and have been through water. Try to jump cross-country type of fences while out hunting as this is an ideal and versatile grounding for the horse. Often there are "jumps" in forests and woods to be found, but always check that the takeoff and landings are safe.

Nowadays there are numerous cross-country training courses provided for practice. If the horse has done some show jumping, it should be confident enough to tackle most types of cross-country fences found on the flat, but it is as well to make it familiar with the different types of fence at elementary level before jumping anything too big across country.

Teach the horse to "pop" over ditches quietly. These may be a bit frightening, so stick to small ones to begin with. When schooling, it is often helpful to teach the horse to jump the individual parts of a complex fence separately to learn the technique. This is particularly useful when practicing fences such as coffins which may cause problems for some horses. Jump over the ditch, then the ditch and rail out together, and then finally move to jumping over the whole thing.

Some horses may refuse to jump off a step and will need time to learn how this should be done without jarring themselves. Be firm but patient until they have mastered how to "pop off" such an obstacle.

"Into space" fences are those where the

landing is not visible from the approach. Confidence is required to jump into space. First jump small fences cleverly sited to look inviting to the horse and cause it no worries when it gets close before takeoff.

Riding at speed

Cross-country fences are designed to be ridden at boldly and at controlled speed. Once the horse is jumping small fences well, it must learn to jump something bigger in preparation for those likely to be met at cross-country competitions. You have to find a pace and rhythm which is comfortable for the horse. Later, with increased fitness, this may need to be changed to meet the speeds required for your standard of competition. Keep a good contact to give it the necessary support, and ride it on strongly without driving it onto its forehand. Keep the horse's head up and your weight farther back to give extra security when jumping at speed.

If the horse is a little hesitant, push him on strongly so that he learns to jump everything asked for without question.

Rider's position for cross-country riding

To ride at speed, the rider will need a good base for support to be able to control a galloping horse. The stirrups will therefore need to be a little shorter than normal. The rider will still require a deep heel pushing down on the balls of the feet and will have to be prepared to grip with the knee and the lower leg for extra security, especially on landing. The weight of the rider should not be too far forward, but ready to react to whatever the situation demands. The rider must keep the horse going forward and up into the bridle at all times. It will be necessary to ride on a slightly longer rein than usual when riding and jumping at speed

Jumping a drop When jumping fences with a drop landing, always sit up well and keep the horse steady so that he does not jar himself on landing.

so as not to interfere with the horse over fixed jumps, unlike show jumping where accuracy and turn of speed are too vital to allow much freedom in enclosed spaces.

Coping with the ground

Inevitably the ground conditions will make a considerable difference to the course, especially if it is wet and muddy. Bad conditions can make an ordinarily straightforward course a nightmare for an inexperienced horse unless it is ridden with care and learns to approach fences correctly. The use of cleats can make a lot of difference in slippery conditions, and large cleats should most certainly be used. When turning, balance and control are essential. The rider will have to compensate for the ground by making gradual, gentle turns and avoiding sudden changes in pace. The rider must keep upright and take care on the approach to the fence.

In deep going, the fences are going to be bigger and will require more effort to jump. The horse will have to be ridden forward positively to compensate for the difficult terrain. On hard ground the surface may be very slippery, and small, sharp cleats will help to give the horse good grip. The horse may not want to gallop or stretch on hard ground, so it will need pushing up together, especially near the end of a course. Ideally, horses should be run on hard ground as little as possible if they are to stay sound and continue to enjoy jumping.

Jumping fences on hills

Unless a horse has been schooled on hills or has lived in a field with slopes, it may find it difficult to cope with going up and down hills at speed and in particular to jump on a slope. It has to learn to balance itself without the rider having to interfere. Keep your mount under control, and go up and down hills of different size and steepness whenever you can. Stay upright when coming down, and contain the horse so that it comes downhill in balance. When going uphill, stay

Fixed fences Solid single fences require steady but bold riding so that the horse meets the fence off a good stride.

forward and off its back, and push it on. Ride strongly at fences when going uphill, and keep steady on the approach downhill. If a horse overjumps going downhill, it will get frightened. The secret is just to pop over the fence so that there is no jarring. That way, too, the horse will not injure itself.

Different types of cross-country fence

There are numerous different types of cross-country fence requiring different approaches and techniques from horse and rider. The following give some guidelines on what might be required, but bear in mind each fence is unique on account of its siting, height, and ground conditions.

Uprights (verticals) How these are jumped very much depends on their siting. In general they should cause few problems, so long as horse and rider are balanced in their approach.

In most cases, uprights should be jumped straight. If coming downhill at one, keep the horse balanced and steady so that you get an accurate jump. If jumping an upright uphill, or at the top of a hill, make sure you have sufficient impulsion and that the horse is well pushed together to jump well.

Spreads Spread fences need to be ridden at with plenty of impulsion to jump the width with ease. Approaching too slowly will mean the horse will need to make a great effort to jump the fence, and consistent slow jumping over spreads will eventually undermine the horse's confidence. Do not allow the horse to stand too far off, as this will make the jump very wide.

Sloping spreads are the most inviting and ride well, but "square parallels" are more difficult and should be ridden at straight, with the horse pushed up into the bridle off the forehand.

Combinations These require a balanced and controlled approach with the horse "listening" to the rider and concentrating hard on the fence ahead. The rider should have previously planned a good route to the fence. Make sure that the fence is approached at the right speed and at the right

position for an easy and safe ride over. Some fences, especially those with angled rails, can be very difficult to negotiate if not ridden at sensibly to allow the horse sufficient room to jump and put in the necessary stride or strides in between the various elements.

Some combinations require a "bounce," whereby the horse has to jump two or more elements without a stride in between. It is essential for the horse to be properly balanced on its approach. If it is on the forehand, the horse will have a lot of difficulty shortening itself up to jump off its hocks.

Coffins usually combine an upright with a downhill approach to a ditch, followed by an uphill stride to a rail out. They include a ditch which is usually invisible until the last moment. The horse needs to be confident about what it is doing, and the rider must approach in balance and then be sure to ride each stride all the way through to avoid trouble anywhere within the coffin.

A coffin is a classic event fence and a favorite with most course builders.

Ditches are often rather frightening, especially for a young and inexperienced horse. It is most important for the rider to be positive in the approach and to be in no doubt of the intention to go over. Never look down into a ditch, but ride the horse up into the hand. Keep the head up a little and keep going forward. With careful schooling in the early days, any worries about ditches should have long passed by the time you actually ride a course. The saying "sit up and ride on" is very apt when jumping any fence with a ditch, whether an open ditch, one with a rail over the top, incorporated into a combination, or just a big gaping hole in the ground. All ditches need lots of patience and determination at first, especially with horses which are a bit suspicious.

Banks need a lot of impulsion as the horse has to make a big effort to get to the top and then balance itself before jumping off again. Controlled speed on the approach and a good jump up, with the hocks well under-

neath to propel the horse upward, are the main essentials. Keep straight and ride forward once you are on top. The horse needs to jump out well when it lands – too steep a landing could result in a "peck" landing, so the rider must sit up and keep the momentum forward.

Normandy banks with their rail usually have a bounce stride on top with the horse taking off immediately. These require a balanced but strong approach, with the horse ridden on forward throughout.

Steps require a controlled speed so that the

Jumping down steps The rider has approached these steps at a steady but forward trot, is well balanced throughout her take-off and landing, and has maintained a firm lower leg.

balanced throughout. As with riding up and down hills, keep upright on the way down and ride the horse forward. Keep forward with a strong leg on the way up.

Water Jumping into water needs practice so that you can judge not only how your horse reacts to going in the water, but how it copes with it. Some horses tend to jump in too heavily, making a big splash, and then find it difficult to balance themselves to come out well.

It is normally best to approach water at a controlled canter or strong trot, keeping the body fairly upright as you jump with the legs braced forward for the drop landing. How fast you go will depend on the type of fence, the depth of the water, whether it is fast flowing or not, and how your horse reacts to water. Fences actually in water should be approached in trot so that the water isn't too churned up, and the horse can focus on the jump. If you go fast, this can cause so much spray that the horse does not see the fence. A controlled approach and allowing the water to settle on landing are the two important points to remember here.

Corners require an accurate assessment of the situation to be negotiated as well as the ability to ride straight. It is important when walking the course beforehand to make up your mind about the best place to jump each fence. You should look in front and behind, then assess the situation and decide from which point you are going to approach the fence and the safest line to jump it. Do not start to check as you approach the fence; this is too late, and will make the horse lose its concentration or force it to alter its line of approach.

The best line is usually a safe distance in from the apex over an imaginary line drawn down the middle of your fence. Jumping across this at a right angle should be about right for most corners, but you must choose your own safe line as every fence will be different.

Jumping through water It is usually best to approach water at a controlled canter or strong trot, keeping your body fairly upright and your lower leg secure.

Corners These require accurate but bold riding straight through your chosen line. Never start to check in front of a corner in case the horse wavers off its line.

horse approaches them with the hocks well underneath and is able to jump up one, two, three, or four steps with ease. The more steps, the more important it is to keep riding forward with plenty of leg. Coming down requires control and straightness so that the horse does not jar itself and remains

• CHAPTER 5 •

RIDING FOR SPORT AND PLEASURE

'No hour of life is lost that is spent in the saddle.'

Sir Winston Churchill

If necessary horses may need their manes and tails washed or even require washing all over to look their best

Once you have learnt to ride and jump, you may decide to specialize in one or more equestrian activity.

Those who are ambitious may be lured into show jumping and eventing, with the possibility of international competition. The dedicated rider will perhaps find the training and elegance of the dressage horse an absorbing prospect. Long-distance riding is becoming extremely popular worldwide, and the months of fitness training, good stable management and veterinary knowledge required makes this equestrian activity a most absorbing and rewarding undertaking. The show world is again a very different activity. Whether native pony breeds, hunters or Palominos, Arabs, Morgans, green hunters, hacks, cobs or children's ponies, there are usually several classes for every type of horse and pony which cater for breeds, types, colours and those ridden or in hand.

Riding side-saddle has again become in vogue, both with the show horse and equitation classes. Vaulting is attracting much interest as a sport and also as a therapy. Polo, the fastest of all equestrian games, is more popular now than ever before, and hunting continues to thrive. Entertainments such as gymkhanas will always appeal to the young and old alike, as will western riding and rodeos with their varied and highly skilled performances.

Preparation and turnout

While most activities require both horse and rider to look their best — clean, tidy and well turned out — and be good examples of their chosen sport, some competitions require a specific style of turnout for both horse and rider, which has to be presented to perfection if they are to be in line for any award.

The following sets out in general detail how to prepare for competitions.

Grooming A well-groomed and thoroughly clean horse is essential for the proper turnout for any class. For best results, the horse should be washed all over and its coat made to look really sparkling. Special attention should be paid to manes, tails and legs. White chalk can be rubbed into the socks for extra brightness. Hooves should be polished, oiled or painted. Whiskers should be trimmed as required for the particular class, and manes and tails plaited, braided or pulled. Horses are usually best shown with their full coats; occasionally, though, it is necessary to clip them. For this the full clip is used.

Trimming The jaw, ears, legs and heels are most likely to require attention, especially with ponies and other coldblooded types. All these can be tidied with clippers (the dog trimming type are best) or scissors and a comb. All trimming must be neat and discreet to improve the look of the animal. Start by trimming a little at a time rather than taking too much off at one go. If using scissors, be careful not to finish up with a stepped look. Have a sharp pair of scissors with rounded ends. Take your time and work steadily back from the head, including the ears. Trim the heels and pastern but do not trim up the backs of the tendons unless these have a lot of unwanted feather. Be discreet. Try not to make it too obvious that you have cut the coat. Pluck out any 'cat' hairs with sharp, downward pulls. Cut a small section of the mane behind the ears, just large enough to fit the bridle headpiece in, if required. Do not take away more mane than is absolutely necessary. With some classes of horse, however, trimming the mane is obligatory.

If you want to show your animal, find out if it is appropriate to undertake extensive trimming. Certain classes, such as the British Mountain and Moorland, require ponies to be left in their natural state.

Mane pulling First comb your horse's mane right the way through so that there are no knots and tangles. If possible, pull after exercise when the horse is warm and the pores of the skin are open; it is easier to work then. Look at the mane and carefully feel

Quarter marks

These are patterns that can be marked on the horse's quarters when it is to appear at shows or events. It is important that these marks accentuate the horse's looks and conformation rather than detract from them. They should be neat, tidy and fairly discreet. Always check that they are in order for your show class as sometimes they are frowned on in certain sections.

Stencils Plastic sheets with various diamond or square stencil patterns are placed on the rump of a well groomed horse. A body brush or comb is then drawn smartly downwards and the stencil taken off leaving an imprint on the coat.

Squares can be produced with a downward stroke of the body brush or comb, squared off by brushing top and bottom lines along the lay of the coat.

Shark's teeth are usually put on the lower part of the quarters. Start by brushing the coat normally, then use an upward stroke, followed by a downward one, leaving 'teeth' marks evenly displayed on either side.

where it is at its thickest. Pull a few hairs at a time, moving evenly up and down the neck, taking the longest hair each time. You are aiming for an even length and thickness of the mane all the way down. If it is very long and untidy, pull a few hairs each day so that the horse does not get sore.

Tail pulling The purpose of pulling the tail is to improve its appearance and shape. To pull the tail, first comb lightly through the top. Then pull out a few hairs at a time from each side, moving up and down the dock. (The dock is the solid part of the horse's tail.) Take only a very few hairs from the front and do not take too much from any one place or you might end up with a bald patch. Never pull out the long hairs in the tail – only those at the sides and front of the dock. If you intend to plait the tail, do not pull at all.

Sometimes a horse's tail is clipped up the sides. This leaves a most unnatural look and ruins its appearance. The practice is most definitely to be discouraged.

Once pulled, manes and tails take only a few moments a week to keep neat and tidy.

Plaiting and braiding

Plaits are generally used on show and competition horses and when out hunting. The number depends on the shape of the horse's neck and how it will look its best. Seven to nine are usual on a hunter.

To plait the mane successfully, it is most

A braided mane is much favoured in the USA

continental-style plaits

English-style plaits

important that it has been evenly pulled to a suitable length. Divide the mane up evenly and damp each section well as you go. Plait firmly, and when you have finished, wind a double thickness of thread round the end a few times before folding it up and securing it with a couple of stitches. The forelock should be made into a single, neat plait.

At this stage you may wish to fasten white adhesive tape round each plait in the continental fashion. This must be done evenly after folding so that it does not affect the overall look or shape of the neck. Elastic bands do not look professional.

The English plait is rolled up into a neat, round ball. Secure this well by passing a needle and thread through a couple of times. The plaits should be even in size and evenly spaced down the neck. Leave the plaits over the withers free until the very last minute as they are liable to be rubbed by a rug, if used, and get untidy.

Always unplait the mane as soon as possible after your event as plaits left in too long can damage the mane. Cut the thread with a sharp knife or scissors and then unravel and brush out with a damp brush to straighten the mane.

Plaiting the tail

The tail hairs need to be as long as possible for successful plaiting. Start by dampening the hair and take a small strand from each side at the top of the dock. Pick up a third strand from the middle and start a central French plait, taking in hair from the sides as you go. Keep the side pieces even and the central plait straight. Once you have gone some way down, nearly to the end of the

dock, stop taking in the side pieces and continue the plait to the end. Loop it back under the dock plait and stitch neatly into position.

Tail plaiting is an excellent way of tidying grass-kept animals or those with a full tail. It will require a bit of practice for a really good finish. The plaited tail should be cut square at the bottom to complete the picture. In the UK 10 cm (4 in) below the dock is considered correct, while in the USA tails are usually left rather longer or not cut at all.

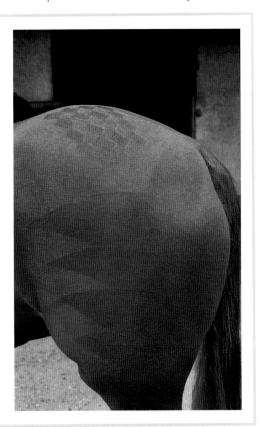

A neatly-plaited tail requires practice

SHOWING

In the United Kingdom there are classes for many breeds and types of horse at nearly all the big agricultural and horse shows around the country. Several breeds have their own specific in-hand shows. The Mountain and Moorland and riding pony youngstock classes are always very well supported. The Horse of the Year Show at Wembley probably has the most prestigious in-hand championship, catering for all riding pony and horse types as well as the ridden classes for each type. In the United States there are even more classes. Conformation classes referred to as model or strip classes include Quarter Horses, Walking Horses and Paso Finos. However it is the riding sections that really create the greatest interest.

Showing in-hand

This can be very rewarding, especially if you have youngsters you have bred or brought on. In the UK one handler per horse is the norm. In the USA two handlers are permissible in most sections. For all in-hand classes, exhibits are usually shown in front of the judge at walk and trot and stand up or 'park' in the appropriate stance for the class and type.

Presentation should be neat and tidy with the horses and ponies looking their very best and led round the ring showing themselves off to their best advantage. This can be difficult with youngsters which may get excitable. Arriving at the showground early and lungeing or performing another exercise to quieten the horses down before the class will help to make sure they behave well.

Some breeds have their own shows but all breeds and types have their own rules and regulations and it is usually necessary to be a member of the appropriate society and have your horse registered with it before being able to compete except at a small show.

Most rule books are fairly comprehensive and it will not take long to get to know what is required. It is well worthwhile to visit a show before you enter your own horse to see how everything is conducted.

Colts or stallions likely to misbehave should be shown in show bridle and side reins to keep them straight. In this way they are much more manageable. It is the handlers' responsibility to keep their charges safely under control. If they cannot do so and a good square up does not sort the animal out they should not appear in public until the horse is better behaved.

The show cane or stick is usually made of cane, sometimes covered with leather. It is not generally more than 0.74 m (2½ ft) long, although longer ones are used for riding side-saddle

Ridden show classes in the UK

The United Kingdom is the home of the thoroughbred which has produced the country's world-renowned hunters and competition horses. These and the numerous other breeds and types help to make the showing scene one of the most active in the world. There are shows catering for most types of horse or pony almost every week of the year somewhere around the country. The United Kingdom also boasts an impressive collection of native ponies which are highly sought after, and the qualifying classes for the Mountain and Moorland Championships at Olympia are highly competitive. The most popular classes include:

Hunters The hunter classes are divided into three weight classes, a small class for those of 15.2 hh and under; novice, four-year-olds, and ladies side-saddle; and working hunters which may be further divided into a lightweight and a heavyweight section. Hunters are ridden by the judge. Working hunters are expected to jump a course of rustic fences at a strong hunting pace.

Hacks The hack is an extremely elegant riding horse with exemplary manners and way of going. It should be well schooled and a pleasure to ride. There are two height classes: one for those over 14.2 hh but not exceeding 15.00 hh, and one for those over 15.00 hh but not exceeding 15.3 hh. There are also classes for novices, ladies (side-saddle) and sometimes for pairs. Hacks are expected to give an individual show and are then ridden by the judge. Special attention is given to manners and way of going.

Riding horse This is a relatively new class, catering for those horses that have too much substance to be a hack but not quite enough to be a hunter. Manners and way of going are most important. There are two height classes: one for those between 14.2 hh and 15.2 hh and one for those over 15.2 hh. There are also novice and ladies side-saddle classes. The riding horse is judged like the hack but is expected to gallop.

Cobs The cob is a weight-carrying horse. It should be well mannered and be a good straightforward, comfortable ride. Cobs should not exceed 15.1 hh but are divided into two weight divisions. Those capable of carrying up to 82 kg (13 stone) are termed lightweights, and over that, heavyweights. Cobs should be able to gallop well and will be ridden by the judge.

Show ponies In the UK these are divided into three types: the show pony, the working hunter pony and the show hunter pony. These may be ridden by children of different

The Hunter is probably the most renowned of all the British show horses and many have gone on to excel in other fields

ages according to the height of the pony.

The show pony is the finer type with the most quality, yet one which maintains true pony characteristics. It must be beautifully mannered and suitable for a child. The working hunter pony is an altogether chunkier type. It is a scaled down hunter and is expected to jump a course of rustic fences. It also has to be well mannered.

The show hunter pony is not expected to jump. It must be beautifully mannered and suitable for a child. There are also leading rein classes (led) first ridden, side-saddle, pairs and classes for novices.

Arabs have their own breed shows and are a regular feature at most big county shows.

There are classes for purebreds, part-breds and Anglo-Arabs. The ridden Arab is treated as a riding horse and ridden by the judge. There are also novice and side-saddle classes. The purebred Arab classes are among the most spectacular; the horses are shown in their natural state with their distinctive manes and tails flowing free.

Mountain and Moorland The nine native breeds of Connemara, Dale, Dartmoor, Exmoor, Fell, Highland, New Forest, Shetland and the four Welsh types all have their own classes and shows which cater solely for each type, ridden, in-hand and driven. There are often mixed Mountain and Moorland classes at the bigger shows. These cater for all the breeds but are usually divided into two sections for the bigger and smaller breeds. In the ridden classes the ponies are generally ridden by the judge. The larger breeds section caters for Dale, Fell, Connemara, New Forest, Highland and the Welsh Pony Sections C and D (Cob type and Welsh Cob). The smaller breeds section caters for the Dartmoor, Exmoor, Shetland, Welsh Mountain Section A and Welsh Pony Section B.

Some shows also cater for foreign native breeds such as Haflingers, Norwegian Fjord, Icelandic, Caspian and Falabella.

Hackneys are very popular and provide a fine spectacle in the showring. Almost exclusively driven, there are classes for amateur, open, single, pair, team and ordinary driving. There are also in-hand classes for youngstock, mares and stallions.

The unique hackney action of the free shoulder and knee, with foreleg thrown well forward with a slight pause, takes time and training to get right but once mastered the rewards are great.

Warmbloods are becoming increasingly popular. Bred for competitive work they have good bone and exceptional movement. They have been derived from crossing the Thoroughbred with the heavier European

The Ridden Mountain and Moorland classes are extremely popular. The exhibits are ridden by the judge and expected to be good rides

breeds. There are now many shows catering for these in youngstock, stallion and brood mare classes and they have their own grading and breed shows.

Palominos with their distinctive colouring, are not a breed but a colour. Classes generally cater for youngstock, stallions and mares in-hand, as well as mixed ridden classes. The Palomino is shown in its natural state for these classes, and horses and ponies come in all sizes and types.

Other popular classes There are, of course, numerous other classes, notably for Cleveland Bays shown in-hand only. Irish Draughts are also only shown in-hand. American horses such as the Appaloosas, Quarter Horse, Morgan and Saddlebred, are shown in hand, ridden and sometimes driven and have special rules adapted for their use in Britain. Polo ponies are catered for, notably at the Royal Windsor Horse Show where they are presented ready for play. There are also classes for Andalusians, Lusitanos and Lipizzaners.

Heavy horses with their massive size are part of British tradition. Not only are there classes for them in-hand and driven but they often appear as features in main ring attractions with their trade vehicles. Their stunning turnouts and distinctive braided manes and tails make them a very splendid sight on any occasion. A very great deal of work goes into looking after the harness and the overall turnout must rank amongst the most specialized.

The show saddle and cane

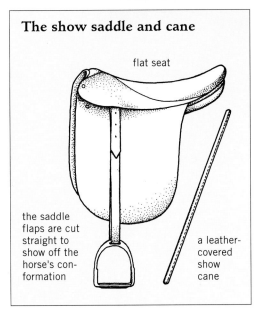

flat seat

the saddle flaps are cut straight to show off the horse's conformation

a leather-covered show cane

Showing in the U.S.A. by E.C.Ward

Showing is a much more diverse activity in the U.S. than in the U.K., and the rules differ significantly. For instance, the horses are not usually ridden by the judges.

Showing can nevertheless be divided into five main classes.

Equitation classes are where the ability of the rider is judged rather than that of the horse.

Hunter classes are a very large division where most horses are judged ridden and over fences.

Western classes are for horses shown in western tack in a variety of roles for both working and pleasure.

Individual breed, type, and color classes are where each group has its own breed society and specialized shows.

Driving and gaited horses are for horses shown in harness, in-hand, or under saddle.

Equitation classes

Equitation classes are primarily designed for junior riders (under 18 years of age). There are, however, classes for adults. Many of America's most famous riders started their career in equitation classes.

Equitation falls into three categories: hunter seat, western, and saddle seat. The prime object of these classes is to judge the seat, hands, application of the aids, and balance of the rider. In the hunter classes the rider is judged riding on the flat and over fences. Though the style differs from classical dressage classes, the same principles apply, and at the higher levels specific movements are required to be performed. The aim of the hunter seat competitions is to qualify for the championships at the end of the season, known as the American Horse Shows Association Medal Class and the Maclay. Riders are asked to perform extensive tests both on their own horses and on those of other competitors.

In the saddle seat and western equitation classes, the riders are judged on their abilities and control, but no jumping is required. For saddle seat classes the type of horse ridden is a "gaited horse," such as the Tennessee Walking Horse or the American Saddlebred. Western classes are ridden in traditional clothes and tack.

Hunter classes

Hunter classes originated by simulating situations and conditions found in the hunting field. In the United States, the Hunter division has become a highly stylized discipline. Judges are looking for an even hunting pace, manners, jumping style, movement, and soundness on the part of the horse. The rider's form is also taken into account.

Under saddle classes require the horse to walk, trot, canter, and hand gallop. The jumping course consists of eight fences of a natural character. This competition has

Each country has specific ways of showing off their horses. It is important to understand precisely what is required if you want to succeed.

become so highly stylized that even the number of strides between fences and flying changes of stride are critical.

Horses are exhibited and judged in a large number of categories, the principal ones being size, weight, breeding, and age. There are further divisions for green hunters, ponies, sidesaddle, and horses qualified in the hunting field. There are also classes for youngstock, brood mares, and stallions. These are judged on conformation, quality, substance, soundness, and, in the case of youngstock, their suitability to become hunters.

Western classes

Western classes are held for any breed or type of horse of 14.1 hh or over. The principal divisions are for trail, stock, pleasure, and western horses. Trail horse classes require the competitors to work their

In the U.S., there are numerous different classes catering both for the rider's ability as well as the conformation and way of going of the horse. The tack used on these occasions is generally on the "showy" side. In certain classes, such as those for western riding and the gaited horse, the tack is very highly specialized, as is the riding of these particular animals.

Individual breed, type, and color classes

These are run and judged on similar lines to those in the U.K. The more popular American breeds are Morgans, Tennessee Walkers, Appaloosas, Palominos, Quarter Horses, Arabians, and the American Saddlebred. The United States has no indigenous heavy horse breeds, but classes for Clydesdales, Percherons, and Belgian Draft Horses are extremely popular; and Welsh, Shetland, and Connemara breeds are also well represented. The U.S. has also developed its own exclusive breed, namely the Pony of the Americas, and classes are held in all disciplines.

Driving and gaited horses

The Hackney horse and pony have a very strong following in both riding and driving classes. In certain parts of the U.S., the three- and five-gaited horses are popular. While principally bred as riding horses, these breeds are also shown extensively in harness, as is the American Shetland Pony. Harness classes cover all types of events, ranging from the four-in-hand coaching marathons to fine-harness classes in which single horses or ponies are driven to lightweight sulkies and viceroys.

horses over and through a series of obstacles. Only one hand is permitted on the reins, and this must not change throughout the competition. Judges take into account conformation, the appointments of horse and rider, and the way the horse goes. Stock horses are required to perform movements simulating those found on a working ranch and are asked to work with cattle. Pleasure horses are judged on their paces. Judges look for easy riding horses that carry themselves in a balanced fashion with a good attitude. Conformation is also a consideration. Western horses are similar to trail horses as they have to go through and over varied obstacles. Here judges are looking for manners and the disposition to make a good working ranch horse. Their quality of gait, including flying changes, are of primary consideration, but conformation is also considered important.

RIDING SIDESADDLE

The elegance of sidesaddle riding has once again increased in popularity. On both sides of the Atlantic, every sort of sidesaddle class has emerged with equitation classes encouraging riders back to this ancient riding style.

Sidesaddle riding is not difficult, but does require some practice to maintain a correct position. The horse should be well schooled on the flat and obedient to the leg aids. To carry a sidesaddle well, the horse has to have a good shoulder and reasonably pronounced withers with strong back muscles. The rider will need a sidesaddle habit, usually of blue or black cloth or mellow tweed, but while learning, jodhpurs and long boots will be perfectly in order. The one essential is a long whip to compensate for the missing leg on the offside.

The sidesaddle

The sidesaddle is designed so that both legs rest on the same side. It has a flat seat with two pommels; the upper one, called the fixed head, supports the right leg, while the lower one, known as the leaping-head, rotates and helps to keep the left leg in position in the stirrup. When extra support is required, the heel comes up and pushes into this pommel for security.

The stirrup usually has a quick release attachment which lifts off when the rider is off the saddle, but is held down by the stirrup bar flap when the rider is mounted.

The side-saddle

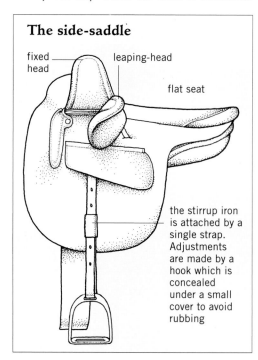

fixed head
leaping-head
flat seat

the stirrup iron is attached by a single strap. Adjustments are made by a hook which is concealed under a small cover to avoid rubbing

Mounting

This is quite difficult. Ideally you should have a strong person to help put you up. This should be done directly onto the saddle. The helper should make a "step" with the hands. The rider should place her left leg in the hands, facing forward, and be lifted high enough to sit on the saddle, bringing her right leg up at the same time to put it over the fixed head. The left leg rests in the stirrup under the leaping-head.

Alternatively, the rider can mount in the usual way and then quietly bring the right leg over into the correct position.

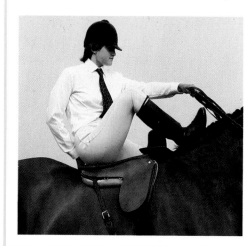

Adjustments to the stirrup length are different to the normal arrangement in that there is a hook through a point on a single strap. This is unhooked and raised or lowered as required. Once the necessary adjustments have been made, a cover is pulled down over the hook to prevent it from rubbing the rider's leg.

The sidesaddle needs a balance strap to prevent the back of the saddle from moving up and down on the horse's spine. This is either a separate strap which goes from under the saddle flap to fasten diagonally to the back of the saddle, or a special attachment on the girth. There is often an outside strap holding the saddle flap down to keep it secure.

Always check the girths are tight before mounting.

The rider's position

Start by getting yourself correctly balanced in the center of the saddle. Your shoulders and hips must be straight and square to the horse's shoulders, only allowing for the left leg to be in its downward position. The right hip must stay back and not be allowed to go forward, as this would mean the body would become twisted. The heel should be well

The rider's position

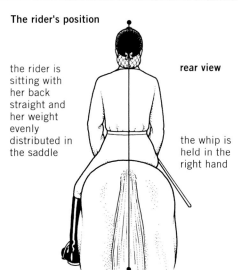

the rider is sitting with her back straight and her weight evenly distributed in the saddle

rear view

the whip is held in the right hand

down in the usual position in the stirrups, which should be long enough to allow a gap of at least 1 in. (2.5 cm) between the top of the knee and the leaping-head. Extra security is gained when needed by pushing the knee upward into the leaping-head, but ordinarily the leg should be loose and relaxed.

The hands can be carried either just above the right knee or a little lower on either side, depending on what feels most comfortable.

A longer rein than usual is necessary, as the rider is sitting a little farther back than usual. The rider's head must always be up and looking ahead.

Moving

Allow the horse to walk, trot and, when you feel secure, to canter on both reins to get used to the feel of a different riding position. Aim to keep your weight central, especially when on the left rein.

Do not ride too much on your first few outings, as the strange position can make you quite stiff until you get used to it. The best way to improve your position in all paces is under instruction on the lunge without the stirrups.

In trot it is essential to relax your back into the movement of the horse and "bump" in the saddle.

In canter, do not get left behind on the first canter steps.

In gallop, keep straight, making sure you have enough leverage on the reins to pull the horse up. Keep the horse balanced on turns by using a firm outside "supporting" rein.

The whip, held in the right hand, can be used to gain extra movement, or if the horse tends to "fall in" to the right, but if it is correctly balanced, this should not happen.

Jumping sidesaddle should not make too much difference for the horse, as long as it is given enough freedom when actually jumping. For the rider it will mean a little more effort is needed to go forward over the fence; the hips need to be extra supple.

Start over small fences in trot. Jumping is, however, much easier in canter. The technique is exactly the same as when riding astride: weight forward, hands forward, look ahead, and keep straight.

It helps to have a horse which keeps up a consistent rhythm and to approach your fence in a good forward manner. It will be a little more difficult to get and stay forward long enough to make sure you do not come back on the saddle too soon. This is because on a sidesaddle you are a little behind the horse's central point of gravity.

Sidesaddle classes

Sidesaddle equitation classes are extremely popular on both side of the Atlantic. These specifically judge the rider. A short test is undertaken to evaluate the straightness, ability, and overall look of the rider. Qualifying rounds and classes for these are hotly contested. There are also ladies' classes (which usually means sidesaddle) for Hunters, Hacks, Cobs, working (jumping) riding horses, Arabs, and children's ponies, which are also extremely popular. With these it is the horse rather than the rider which is being judged.

Nothing looks more elegant than a class of well-turned out riders in their habits riding side-saddle. These are wearing top hats and veils which is usual at "Royal" and other big shows during the afternoon. Bowler hats with veils and ties are worn in the mornings at British classes.

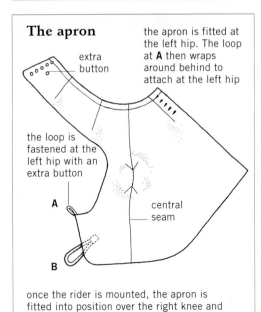

The apron

the apron is fitted at the left hip. The loop at **A** then wraps around behind to attach at the left hip

extra button

the loop is fastened at the left hip with an extra button

A

central seam

B

once the rider is mounted, the apron is fitted into position over the right knee and pulled around the back of the right leg, and the elastic loop (**B**) is placed over the right foot

Western Riding

Western riding is very popular in various other parts of the world as well as in the United States. The sport is about developing a special harmony between horse and rider, and the riding is undertaken in western style and western dress.

When fully trained, the horse should be calm, responsive, and comfortable without tension. Use of the rider's weight, minimum use of the bit, and a relaxed approach are the keynotes to success. The best breed of horse for western riding is the Quarter Horse.

Equipment

The western saddle is the most important item. It is considerably heavier than the English saddle and spreads the weight over a much larger area of the horse's back. With the skirting and padding, it provides a comfortable base for the rider. Often highly decorated, many saddles, especially those used in the show ring, are real works of art.

Stirrups vary greatly, ranging from the metal type used on English saddles to those covered in thick, rolled leather. They are attached to the broad "fender." This has to be the correct length for the rider's leg. Although the leg position is longer than English style, it should still be slightly bent, with a straight line through the shoulders, hip, and heel. The western stirrup is designed so that mounting can be done with ease, facing more to the front. The western rider steps off the saddle from the stirrup. The fender should hang comfortably at the right angle for the rider to mount and dismount with ease. The leather may require soaking to be bent to the required position and then allowed to dry.

Bridle The western horse starts its training with a simple type of noseband called a bosal. This is made of rawhide and finishes under the chin. Attached to this are plaited horsehair reins known as mecate. Simple leather bridles are used thereafter, with single curb bits, usually with low to medium ports to minimize their severity. Curb chains are rarely seen, but the bit has a leather strap around the chin groove to prevent excessive poll pressure. Western bits come in a variety of designs and for show purposes are often highly decorated.

There are three basic bridle designs: slip-eared, with a sliding browband, slit-eared, where the headpiece has slits to allow the ears through, and one-eared with a more sophisticated shape cut for one ear only.

Reins are normally either Texas-style split

This well-presented horse and rider are clean and neat and ready to enter the show ring for western riding.

reins, approximately 7 ft. (2.1 m) long or the California-style romal, which are closed reins with an extra attachment known as a quirt, which can be used as a whip.

Chaps are often worn as they provide ideal protection from rubs and sores on the legs which can arise from the friction between rider and saddle. Supported on a belt, the individual "leggings" wrap around the legs and normally nowadays are secured by strong zippers or ties positioned up the outside. They may be decorated with fringe or decorative stitching and are extremely comfortable to wear.

Training the horse

Early training of the horse centers on gaining the animal's confidence and respect. The Quarter Horse is a fast-maturing animal, and

there are classes for ridden two-year-olds. At this early age, however, training should be kept to a minimum; few other breeds would be mature enough to be trained without putting their future development in jeopardy. Early lessons include teaching the horse to follow its trainers, and follow on from leading in hand. The horse has to learn to stop and relax every time it is brought to a halt. It is made to stand square on every occasion. This is vital for success in future training. An important western movement is the rein back. All early training is done with the bosal, which should be used with a gentle tug and release movement. Once backed, the horse keeps the bosal until it responds confidently to the rider's aids, which usually center on weight distribution and seat, with leg and rein aids kept to the minimum.

A bridle is not introduced until the horse is sufficiently obedient and balanced in all gaits and can halt, turn, and rein back.

Neck reining The horse must learn to go effectively with two even reins and to

Western tack

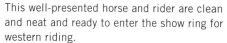

bosal

the bosal may be worn with or without a throatlatch (fiador)

fiador

slit-eared bridle

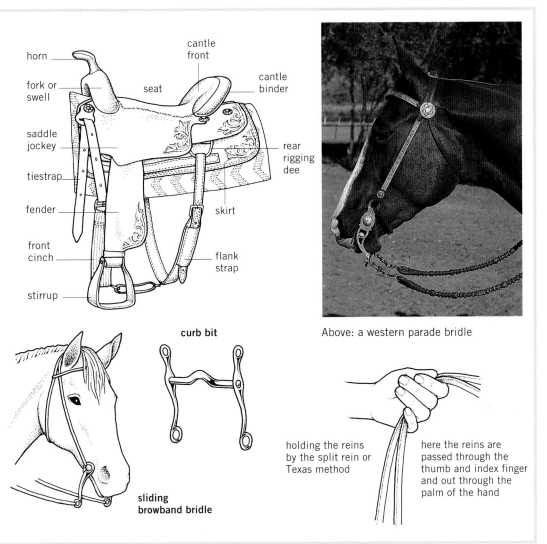

horn

fork or swell

seat

cantle front

cantle binder

saddle jockey

tiestrap

fender

front cinch

stirrup

rear rigging dee

skirt

flank strap

curb bit

sliding browband bridle

holding the reins by the split rein or Texas method

here the reins are passed through the thumb and index finger and out through the palm of the hand

Above: a western parade bridle

Neck reining

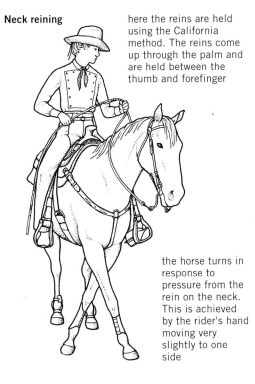

here the reins are held using the California method. The reins come up through the palm and are held between the thumb and forefinger

the horse turns in response to pressure from the rein on the neck. This is achieved by the rider's hand moving very slightly to one side

respond to pressure on the neck from a one-handed neck rein. It is taught to move away from the rein aid without changing its bend. This is achieved by the rider's hand moving very slightly away from the center, causing the outside rein to put pressure on the horse's neck.

The jog and lope, which are slow versions of the trot and canter, are two of the most basic paces for the western horse. These paces have to be properly established before the horse can do them with extreme lightness of the forehand. The rider almost always sits to the jog.

Backing up (rein back), **rollback** (turning on the haunches), **spins** (a series of pirouettes), and **lead changes** (flying changes) are similar movements to those in the classical style; however, they are done faster, with more elasticity in the steps, but with little rein contact. The weight is generally much farther back.

The sliding stop is one of the most spectacular movements, but was developed more for the show ring than for practical necessity. The horse slides to a stop with its hind legs well under its body and its back and poll rounded and the forehand free. It may well slide anything up to 30 ft. (9 m). Special sliding shoes need to be fitted, and the correct depth and consistency of surface are vital for this movement to be successfully carried out.

Show classes

There are six main events for the western horse, all of which demonstrate particular attributes for each class. The various classes have been adapted to suit the different styles in Europe and Australia, and top American judges come over for championships, and trainers help to develop the art of western riding.

Western pleasure This is one of the most popular classes. It is designed to show what a pleasure it is to ride the western horse. The horse should be calm, smooth, and responsive to the rider. It is required to jog and lope on both reins, and rein back, with the rider having the reins in one hand.

Trail A good trail horse must be calm and capable of coping with any possible hazards encountered on a trail ride. A gate has to be opened and shut, logs must be ridden over, and the horse must to reined back through or around an obstacle. Other hazards may also be required to demonstrate the horse's suitability as a good trail ride.

Western ride This event is designed to test the ranch horse in all paces, lead changes, and rein back. A set pattern (course) is followed through to include typical obstacles found in daily work.

Reining demonstrates the most advanced western movements shown at speed in a completely relaxed and smooth manner. Everything has to be precise and fluent, with the pattern performed correctly and in balance. Reining is the equivalent of high school dressage.

Cutting is the highest test of a western horse's skill and involves the horse taking a selected cow away from a herd and preventing it from returning. The rider has two and a half minutes and should, once the cow has been indicated to the horse, leave it to do all the work. Cutting horses when fully trained can be so quick that it is extremely difficult to stay with them. They almost seem to possess a special "cow sense," like a good sheep dog with its sheep.

Working cow horse This is a class for the general-purpose ranch horse and cow horse. It is divided into two parts: reining and cattle working. The scores for both sections are added together to determine the winner.

Rodeo

Throughout the year thousands of rodeos are held all over the country, and cowboys travel long distances to compete in these often dangerous but highly entertaining events. All over the world, children have been brought up to read of the exploits of the American cowboy: tough, brave, handsome, and wearing the famous chaps over blue jeans, with high-heeled boots, a wide brimmed hat, and silver-buckled belt. A romanticized picture of this man and his best friend, his horse, has been immortalized on films and television. The exploits of, for example, Roy Rogers and Trigger, and the Lone Ranger and Silver mean that the lifestyle of the cowboy is well documented and appreciated by millions.

History

The word rodeo is Spanish for "round up." When the Spaniards spread through the southwest in the early 1500s, they brought horses and cattle with them. The breeding of these animals flourished, and it eventually became necessary to drive herds of cattle to the stockyards to sell them in markets which were often great distances away. With the advent of the railroads, the distances became even greater as herds were driven to collection points at rail stations, and long waits were often encountered. Contests developed to relieve the boredom of waiting. Riders used their riding skills, and the rodeo began, featuring everyday skills such as roping calves, maneuvering cattle, and riding unbroken horses.

It was not until 1883, however, that William Cody, a former Pony Express rider and buffalo hunter, organized a traveling extravaganza of trick roping, trick shooting, and mock battles between cowboys and Indians, which he called Buffalo Bill's Wild West Show. It toured the U.S.A. and Europe at about the same time as Barnum's traveling circus, which was billed "The Greatest Show on Earth."

Cowboy shows increased, featuring their various skills, and contests were formed, with the first major rodeo taking place on July 4, 1886, in Prescott, Arizona. In the early 1900s, rodeo events took place at horse shows, in stadiums, and at state fairs. Cowboys often earned more on a bucking bronco in a few seconds than they did from a week's ranching. This was the start of what is now a highly professional sport.

In 1936 the Cowboys' Turtle Association was formed to draw up rules and guidelines

to defend their sport as it had become very disorganized and criminal activity was prevalent. In 1945 the name was changed to the Rodeo Cowboys' Association. A world champion saddle bronc rider, Bill Linderman, introduced tighter regulations and rules on safety, and thenceforward the sport became properly managed and grew in popularity and attendance.

Charismatic performances on the part of several champions continued to enhance the sport in the 1950s and 1960s, and "World Champions" in several contests became household names. Nowadays there are at least 8,000 professional cowboys, not to mention the unregistered amateurs. Successful cowboys earn huge sums of money.

Rodeo championships are now held in Las Vegas where the 15 champions of the individual rodeo events compete for the supreme title.

Rodeo events

There are six main rodeo events: saddle bronc, bareback, steer wrestling, bull riding, calf roping, and team roping. Rodeo events are divided into two types: riding and timed events. Other events such as barrel racing, pole bending, and chuck-wagon racing may also take place.

Bareback riding

This is similar to saddle bronc riding in that the rider has to remain on the horse's back for eight seconds, and the spurring technique in constant motion is vital. The "rigging," a leather surcingle with a stiff handle to grasp, is the only aid, and the rider wedges one hand through it, leaving the other hand free. Strength and balance are essential to perform skillfully during rides. A tremendous strain is put on the arm holding onto the rigging during this competition.

Steer wrestling

For this event, two horses and riders and a steer are required. Only one rider competes; the other, known as a "hazer," is there to keep the steer in line for the contestant to be able to jump off his horse and grab its horns and throw it on its side. This takes a matter of seconds! It is a timed event, so the winner is the one who does the job the fastest. Balance, timing, and speed are essential for success. The hazer often produces the horses for these events and receives a percentage of the winner's earnings.

Saddle bronc riding

This sport derived from old methods of breaking wild horses for ranch work. The horses are saddled in a chute and have just a halter and rope for the competitor to hold.

Rodeos are enormously popular throughout the U.S.A.; literally thousands are held every year. Nowadays the main rodeo events are saddle bronc riding, bareback riding, steer wrestling, bull riding, calf roping, and team roping. Barrel racing, left, is the one sport where cowgirls compete with cowboys on equal terms. In team roping, right, two cowboys work together to bring down a steer. The Quarter Horse, below, is the animal most favored for rodeos.

The cowboy lowers himself onto the saddle in the chute, the bucking strap is fastened tightly, and the horse released. The aim is for the cowboy to stay on the horse for eight seconds and at the same time give a good performance. As he starts, his feet have to be forward over the points of the shoulders and then move back so that the spurs are felt on the flanks and then go forward again. Ideally the rider should use his legs in rhythm to the movements of the horse. Riders hope their mounts will perform consistently rather than wildly. Only one hand is allowed on the rein throughout.

Bull riding

This sport is undoubtedly the most exciting, but also the most dangerous of all rodeo contests. As with bareback riding the rider has to try to ride a 2,000 lb. (900 kg) bull for eight seconds, hanging on with the reining hand to a braided rope strapped behind its withers and leaving the other hand in the air. Extra points are awarded for spurring and an upright position. Both, however, are extremely difficult to achieve on these unpredictable animals. The bulls that turn around in the air, known as spinners, are probably the most difficult to handle. The really dangerous time for the rider is when he has been thrown to the ground as the bull, aiming to kill, will often charge him. Mounted pick-up riders and professional bull fighters are employed to divert the bull's attention away from the hapless rider.

Calf roping

This was and is still one of the most effective methods of catching the untamed calf, and competitions demonstrate to perfection the skill with the rope. The calf is given a head start out of the chute, and the horse and rider follow, adjusting their speed to successfully rope the calf. The horse backs up to keep the rope taut as the rider sprints off to the calf and ropes any three legs with this "pigging string." When secured, he signals to the judge and remounts his horse. The calf has to remain secure for six seconds; otherwise, the contestant is disqualified. The fastest time wins. This is a partnership event, and the bond between horse and rider is close.

Team roping

Two cowboys are needed to work as a team to bring down a steer. The "header" sets off and tosses a rope around the horns of the steer and throws it on its side. The "heeler" immediately ropes the animal's hind feet. The clock is stopped at the moment both horses are facing each other, with the steer in the middle and both ropes taut.

Barrel racing

This is the one rodeo sport where cowgirls mix with cowboys on equal terms. Although there are rodeos for cowgirls only, it is usually only at barrel racing that both sexes are allowed to compete together. The sport is a test of speed and agility over a "cloverleaf" course of three barrels in a triangle pattern. It is a timed event, starting from when the horse sets off over the start line, then goes around each barrel in turn and crosses the finish line. There are other, simpler forms of barrel racing, but this is the only professional event.

The horse plays a big part, and Quarter Horses excel at this sport as they are bred for quick turns, great acceleration, and speed over short distances.

LONG-DISTANCE RIDING

Endurance riding is nothing new, as tremendous distances used to be covered all over the world before the days of motor vehicles. Long-distance rides were often undertaken as bets or undergone by the cavalry to test both men and horses. It was in the United States, however, where competitions in long-distance riding were first set up, and by the early 1960s, these had spread to the U.K. and from there to Europe. In 1985 the FEI officially recognized endurance riding as a sport, and it has grown in popularity ever since.

The horses cover distances ranging from 25, 50, 75, to 100 miles (40, 80, 120, to 160 km) in a day, or sometimes this is spread out over two or three days. The condition of the horse is checked by a vet at regular intervals along the route and at the finish. These checks include pulse rate and respiration, soundness, soreness, and overall general condition. Speed is not the main criterion, as the winner has to be sound and fit as well as fast. There are special awards for the horse in best condition, as well as completion awards along with the overall winning places.

Types of horse

Although there are numerous different types of horse that do well, the Arab undoubtedly has the greatest stamina for this tough sport. Part breds, pony crosses, and Morgans, Quarter Horses, and Appaloosas are also popular. A horse with correct conformation and tough limbs which is a straight mover will be less likely to acquire knocks or sores. Good feet are essential if the horse is to cope with the differing terrain to be found in rough ground, forests, prairies, and rocky mountain trails, as well as hard, soft, or even icy conditions.

Equipment

The saddlery used must fit well and be comfortable. Avoid using new tack which may rub in places. Well-proven tack that you have used in training is ideal. Check it carefully to make sure it is in good condition and that the leather straps and stitching are strong. Do not forget that bits can cause sores if they acquire rough edges, and unoiled leather on bridles, saddles, or girths can also cause great discomfort.

Your clothes should be comfortable, soft and suitable for the conditions. Tight or stiff clothes or those that are very heavy are unsuitable. Make sure you have weather-proof garments and a dry set of clothes

available to change into along the way. Make sure your underwear is made of natural fibers such as cotton and that you wear the lightest type of riding hat.

Helpers

Your helpers are vital to the success of your ride. They must be well briefed on the various requirements at the different checkpoints along the route. If they know enough to be able to take charge of the horse during the breaks, you should try to get as much rest and refreshment as possible while they are looking after your mount. Relaxing during the breaks means you will help your horse by riding well. Nothing tires a horse more than a tired and floppy rider in the saddle. Your helpers should be ready with drinks and electrolytes and any other necessities, and should be willing to wash

The endurance horse must be very fit and well prepared for the long rides expected of it. How it is ridden, its general condition, and the equipment used all contribute to success.

down as and when required and allowed.

Fitness

The gradual conditioning of the horse to make it fit enough for endurance riding requires a considerable amount of planning and time. It may take anything from three to six months to train and prepare for your ride, depending on the distance to be covered. Management will include all the usual care, with particular emphasis on feeding and watering. The endurance horse needs extra electrolytes during hard training to replace lost body salts and must also learn to drink as it is ridden along the route. It has to be supple and athletic. Remember to change diagonals at the trot and legs at the canter so that the horse is using itself evenly on both sides. Failure to do this can lead to lameness and stress on one side of its body.

Work on building up a good rhythm on your rides and establishing a pace that is easy and comfortable for your horse. Vary your routes to familiarize your horse with different ground and conditions. Gradually increase the distance in rides. Train on hills

and work on developing the heart and lungs. Monitor the horse's pulse and respiration rates to check for fitness, and plan a long-term program to build your horse up to the standard of riding required.

Rider's fitness

The rider has to work on his or her own fitness as well as that of the horse. Extra exercise is essential if you are not to become a burden to your horse. Walking, jogging, aerobics, skipping, swimming, cycling are all good for making you fit.

A high-energy, balanced, and nutritious diet is essential. Glucose candy on rides will help as well as drinks containing electrolytes.

Work on hardening your skin and have adequate protection to prevent chapping or soreness. You should get on and off the horse when this becomes necessary, especially if you need a change of position.

Never forget that all fitness work, whether yours or the horse's, has to be built up gradually.

Competitions

There are many types of competition. In the U.K. the Golden Horseshoe ride is the ultimate. Sponsored rides of varying distances have become very popular as charity fund

raisers, and these have awakened a lot of interest in long-distance riding.

A lot of respect and admiration for endurance riding was gained in 1990 by the excellent performances shown at the World Equestrian Games in Stockholm. Other nations were able to see the great amount of work and preparation which goes into long-distance riding. In the U.S. the Western States Trail Ride follows an old Pony Express route from Nevada to California, with temperatures ranging from the heat of the El Dorado Canyon to the freezing, snowy conditions in the Sierra Nevada Mountains. This ride, for the Tevis Cup, was started by one of the sport's great founders, Wendell Robie. Other notable events are The Old Dominion Ride in Virginia, and the North America Open Championship. In Australia, the Great Two-Day Endurance Race in Queensland covers a distance of 250 miles (400 km) over the two days.

Competitive trail riding

This is also extremely popular. Less distance is covered, but it has to be done within minimum and maximum times. Points are awarded for soundness (40 percent), condition (40 percent), manners (15 percent), and way of going (5 percent). These are given by judges along the route and determine the winners.

A sport which has recently appeared in the United States is the ride and tie race. A team consists of two people and one horse. The first rider and horse set off to a pre-determined spot, and the horse is tied up until the second team member runs from the start to meet it. The first team member sets off to the next tie-up point on foot. He or

The rider's fitness is as important as that of the horse and requires just as much thought and planning. Knowing your route and skill at map reading are also vital. At stopping points it is necessary to have effective and well-briefed helpers to give maximum assistance with minimum fuss. Watering is essential whenever possible to maintain condition throughout.

she is then overtaken by the team mate riding the horse and aiming for the next tie spot. This continues until the horse and both riders reach the finish.

There will probably be other endurance sports devised in the future. In endurance riding, the amateur can compete and at the same time learn a great deal about the horse and its care and management. It is a particularly friendly sport, as well as being extremely challenging, and it is certainly one where horse and rider develop a unique partnership founded on respect and understanding.

Vaulting

Vaulting (*voltige*) has long been an established art in Europe, where children learn to ride and do the equivalent of gymnastics on horseback. It can be enjoyed by several children together, providing the chance to achieve the feel and rhythm of riding from an early age.

Although learning to ride in this way is not really a substitute for conventional riding, it will certainly help the child to be relaxed and to develop a good seat on the horse. The rider will become supple and athletic, and develop the rudiments of team work, whether for leisure or for competitive work.

To be successful, vaulting requires a steady, well-schooled horse that can keep up a consistent rhythm throughout the practice periods. The vaulter may go singly, in a pair, or in a team. In competitions each vaulter is required to have an individual number.

Equipment for horse and rider

The vaulting horse requires a vaulting pad and surcingle with two grip handles. It may also have two foot loops which act as stirrups. Some have an extra loop to hang onto between the two handles.

Two side reins are required, along with the lunge rein fitted to a snaffle bridle. A lunge whip is needed for the handler to maintain a consistent rhythm. Bandages or boots should be worn if a shod horse is used. The rider should be dressed either in sports clothes, such as a track suit, or a leotard and tights. Only sports shoes should be worn, and they must have flexible soles.

Vaulting as a leisure sport

Vaulting is becoming increasing popular as a leisure sport. Girls seem particularly keen.

The sport is also extremely therapeutic as it combines balance, coordination, move-ment, and exercise in one activity. Vaulting has only been utilized as a therapy very recently. It has been found that a lot of physical problems have been cured or very much improved through regular vaulting exercise sessions.

The horse

The vaulting horse may be of any breed, but is preferably medium-sized to large with strong limbs and a good, powerful back. The horse must be placid and kind so as not to react wildly to inexperienced vaulters learning the exercises. The canter has to be flowing and regular. The vaulting horse often

has to canter for long periods on the left rein, and a degree of fitness for this is required. The horse must do regular ordinary work to make sure it remains supple on both reins.

The vaulting trainer

The vaulting trainer is most important as he or she can make or break a class through his methods of teaching and instilling confidence. The best teachers are usually those who have had vaulting experience themselves. He or she must be experienced with horses and be capable of expert lungeing. A trainer also has to be good with children and able to keep their attention as well as know the various exercises to be performed.

Competitive vaulting

This may be divided into group (team) vaulting competitions, individual competitions, and pairs vaulting. Each competition has both compulsory and freestyle exercises.

Some of the most popular compulsory exercises are briefly outlined below.

Vaulting on and sitting Each exercise starts with the vault on. The vaulter runs up parallel to the horse's shoulder, grabs the ribs of the surcingle and "canters" beside the horse's leading left leg. After a very few strides, the vaulter has to spring up toward and onto the horse, with the weight of the body supported on the arms, pulling the body toward the surcingle, and then sit with the head held high. The sitting position is the starting position for all compulsory exercises.

Dismounting involves taking the right leg up high and over the horse's neck in a half circle to the other side. The upper body remains as upright as possible. Both legs are then brought together and pointed toward the horse's front legs. Finally the vaulter pushes off and away from the horse with legs and knees close together. The landing must be done with softly bending knees and ankles and run out in the direction of the movement.

Vaulting (flanking) off From an upright sitting position, both legs are swung forward and then high into the air at the rear in a flowing, elastic movement. While the vaulter is up in the air, the hands push upward; the vaulter swings off the horse on the inside away from the animal, absorbing the landing through the knees and ankles and running out in the direction of the movement.

Scoring In competitive vaulting the marks are given on a scale from one to ten, with ten for an excellent result and nothing if no movement is performed.

Each compulsory exercise is marked

This Pony Club vaulting display in England requires equal if different coordination to that needed in a competitive *voltige* performance.

separately, one for each of the six. Freestyle marks are given, as long as at least seven scoring exercises are performed. If the minimum is not reached, there will be no score.

Freestyle is judged for difficulty, composition, and execution in the ratio of 2:1:3, and the work undertaken must differ from compulsory exercises.

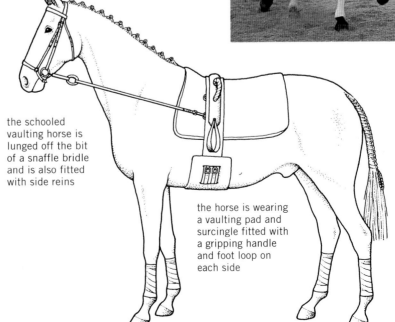

the schooled vaulting horse is lunged off the bit of a snaffle bridle and is also fitted with side reins

the horse is wearing a vaulting pad and surcingle fitted with a gripping handle and foot loop on each side

bandages on all four legs

PONY CLUB

The Pony Club is an organization which caters for young riders the world over.

Quite apart from being an ideal training ground in all disciplines, with annual championships held for each event, it also provides the necessary background to help the rider to choose what particular equestrian activity he or she wishes to specialize in.

There are competitions for dressage, show jumping, horse trials, polo, tetrathlon (a combination sport including running, shooting and riding cross-country), as well as gymkhana events. These consist of mounted games and races on ponies.

The Pony Club aims to encourage young people to enjoy riding and to teach them to care for their animals properly. It also encourages sportsmanship and self-discipline, and with its many organized exchange visits provides a chance for children to meet and exchange ideas with other children living in different countries. There are approximately 1,900 Pony Club branches worldwide in around thirty countries.

The Pony Club was started in Britain in the early 1920s as a junior section of the Institute of the Horse, and in 1928 the first organized gymkhana was held.

Gymkhana and mounted games

The origins of games on horses goes back into the mists of time. It is known that ball games existed before 600 B.C. and that a game resembling mounted tennis was being played in the thirteenth century.

The British Army in India adopted many of India's sports, which included games involving camels, mules, donkeys, and even elephants. Playing games was found to be an ideal way to keep soldiers and horses occupied, fit, and relaxed, and in addition they provided light relief from regimental duties.

The Pony Club was quick to realize the potential for children's ponies in these games, and it was not long before organized mounted events were arranged. Today there are numerous games and races held throughout the world which teach young riders the essentials of good sportsmanship, horse mastership, and companionship with their team mates and their ponies.

Prince Philip Cup

The Mounted Games Association, which was started in 1985, runs a World Mounted Games Competition held each year in a

different country. In 1957 a big boost to the sport came with the inauguration of the Prince Philip Cup, so that children and ponies could compete in games and races and enjoy themselves. This was so successful that today well over 250 branches enter teams for qualifying rounds before a final six go to Britain's prestigious Horse of the Year Show at Wembley and compete each day, culminating in the final on the last night for the coveted Prince Philip Cup.

Other competitions take place to cater for those who do not get to the finals. Rules are strict for all games worldwide to make sure that riders look after their ponies' welfare in a competitive atmosphere. The age limit is

The gymkhana rider develops many skills in practicing mounted games. They include balance, coordination, competitiveness, and speed.

usually 18. Ponies must be at least four years old and not exceed 14.2 hh. Tack has to fit well; inspection of tack and turnout generally precede the competition.

Games Each game starts with the drop of a flag and finishes when the pony gets its head across the line. For games where the rider is dismounted, it is the first pony over the line that is the winner. There are numerous variations of team games – for example, flag races, where one person carries a flag to a holder, gallops back over the line, and other competitors do the same until the last has galloped over the line. New games are being devised all the time and are all highly competitive, requiring great skill on the part of the rider and obedience from, and suppleness in, the pony.

Successful combinations and teams work long and hard to improve their skills and times in all games, and practice sessions are organized regularly. There is very strong competition to have the chance to represent a pony club in competitions.

Games are organized for beginners of all ages, and the competitive nature of the events ensures improvement and the will to progress.

Tetrathlon This is another highly popular sport which tests all-round skills in which riding plays an important part. It consists of four sports, riding, running, swimming, and shooting, and is divided into three age groups. Minimus is for those up to and including eleven-year-olds, Juniors for those aged 12 to 14 inclusive, and Seniors aged up to 21.

The riding section includes jumping a novice-size course (the size of which depends on the age group) of cross-country fences, with penalty points deducted from the maximum score for this section of 1,400. The running section includes the fastest over 1,093 yd. (1,000 m) for the Minimus age group, 1,639 yd. (1,500 m) for the Juniors and Senior girls, and 3,280 yd. (3,000 m) for Senior boys. The swimming part of the tetrathlon includes swimming as far as possible in two minutes (Miminus), three minutes (Juniors), and four minutes (Seniors). The shooting event consists of ten shots from 7½ yd. (7 m) for Minimus and Juniors,

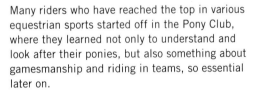

Many riders who have reached the top in various equestrian sports started off in the Pony Club, where they learned not only to understand and look after their ponies, but also something about gamesmanship and riding in teams, so essential later on.

and ten shots from 11 yd. (10 m) for Seniors. There are various regional competitions around the country for teams and individuals, with championships being held annually. No one can take part in the same competition both as an individual and as a member of a team.

Exchange visits for members from other countries are sometimes arranged with borrowed horses.

Other sports Other sports performed in pony clubs, such as dressage, show jumping, horse trials, and polo are discussed in detail elsewhere. For Pony Club members there are area competitions to bring the numbers qualifying for the Championship down to a manageable level. Many champions have emerged from these excellent Pony Club events, which provide so much experience and team practice.

POLO

by Lord Patrick Beresford

For those who rejoice in a ball struck cleanly, and in the courage of a horse in combat, there is nothing to equal polo. It is the fastest game ever invented and also possesses an alluring element of danger. Its origins are lost in antiquity, though it is known that the game was played in Persia as long ago as 600 B.C. In Isfahan, there are the 2,000-year-old ruins of a field 300 yd. (274 m) long, with stone goal posts 8 yd. (7.3 m) apart, and these are the measurements in yards which are still used in polo today. Akbar the Great, the sixteenth-century Mogul Emperor, pronounced polo to be "a game to test a man and to strengthen the ties of friendship," and despite many far from friendly exchanges between irate players, the truth of his description has become even more apparent now that the sport is practiced in over sixty countries around the globe.

First introduced to the western world in 1869 by British cavalry officers returning home from India's Northwest Frontier, the game found a governing body four years later in The Hurlingham Polo Association, based in London. The rules drawn up at that time have changed very little over the years,

apart from the abolition of a height limit for ponies and an off-side clause, both of which had tended to slow the game down.

From England, the sport quickly spread to the rest of Europe and subsequently to the United States and Central and South America. In Argentina especially the terrain, environment, and climate blended perfectly to provide an ideal habitat. In India polo became an integral part of life for British officers and maharajahs alike, and from there it took root in Australia and New Zealand.

The years between World Wars I and II proved in many ways to be the game's most glorious age. During this time the North Americans, who first wrested polo supremacy from the British in 1909, were overpowered by the Argentines, though for sheer artistry it was still the Indians who reigned supreme.

Polo ponies

These are really small horses, ideally about 15 hh–15 h 2½ in. Some are Thoroughbreds, but mostly they are three-quarter or seven-eighths-breds imported from Argentina, their bottom line tracing back to Criollo mares.

They require speed, stamina, and courage, as well as the ability to stop, turn, and accelerate quickly, often while carrying men of considerable weight. At any match you will see that at least three-quarters of all polo ponies are mares, not because mares are believed to be better than geldings, but simply because for some reason they take more readily to the game.

Equipment

The polo ball is made of willow or bamboo, or occasionally of plastic, and must not exceed 3½ in. (8.8 cm) in diameter or 4¾ oz. (134 g) in weight. Sticks (mallets) have flexible bamboo or rattan shafts and hardwood heads. The ball is struck with the side of the head, not on the ends. The stick varies in length from 48 to 52 in. (122 cm to 132 cm), depending on the size of the pony being ridden. Helmets and chin straps are compulsory for players, who must also wear brown polo boots.

Ponies must wear boots or bandages for protection. Bell boots may also be worn on the front legs to protect the heel and coronet. A single ½ in. (1.3 cm) cube cleat may be

Tack and equipment for polo

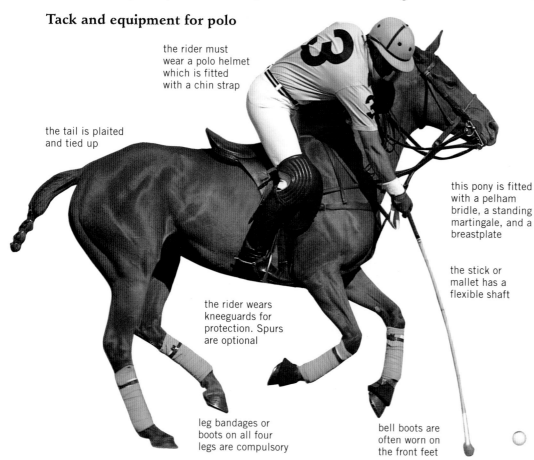

the rider must wear a polo helmet which is fitted with a chin strap

the tail is plaited and tied up

the rider wears kneeguards for protection. Spurs are optional

this pony is fitted with a pelham bridle, a standing martingale, and a breastplate

the stick or mallet has a flexible shaft

leg bandages or boots on all four legs are compulsory

bell boots are often worn on the front feet

Left: Prince Charles (second from right) tussles for the ball with Mrs. Claire Tomlinson, formerly the world's leading lady player, at Cirencester Park.
Right: An American girl groom gets her charges ready to play at the Kentucky Horse Park.
Below: Polo on the frozen lake at the winter sports resort of St. Moritz, in Switzerland, has become a popular rendezvous for players, spectators, and sponsors. It is played with an inflated rubber ball.

placed on the outside of the hind shoes to give good grip. The plaiting and tying up of the tail prevents it from becoming entangled with the stick. The hogging of the mane means that it cannot impede the rider's grip of the reins. There are no strict rules on what tack is worn, but usually an English-style saddle is used with a saddle cloth in the colors of the team, plus a surcingle and breastplate to keep the saddle in the correct position.

The pelham used to be the preferred bit for polo, though now the gag snaffle has become more popular. They are both fitted with a cavesson noseband, a standing martingale, and two reins. Both sets of reins are carried in the left hand. Hackamores are not allowed.

The game
The game is divided into periods of seven minutes each, which are known as chukkers. There are four, five, or six chukkers per game, depending on the level of the tournament. Ends are changed only when a goal is scored, not at the start of each chukker. A pony may be required to play two chukkers, but is always rested for at least one chukker in between. At halftime the spectators may be asked to tread in the divots on the field before play is resumed. There are two mounted umpires and, in the stands, a "third man" or referee, to whom appeal may be made in the event of disagreement.

There are four players in each team, numbered 1 and 2 (the forwards), 3 (the pivot), and 4 (the back). For reasons of safety, left-handed players are not permitted. Each player has a rating, reflecting individual ability, from minus 2 for the beginner to an optimum of plus 10. The handicap of a team is the aggregate of the individual ratings. In most matches, the side with the lower handicap receives a starting advantage in goals of the difference in handicap. Since the difference applies to a six-chukker match, in matches of four chukkers, the advantage is therefore 4/6ths of that difference. The team that ends the match with most goals on the scoreboard is the winner.

The field is 300 yd. (274 m) long by 200 yd. (182 m) wide, often with boards placed down each side to keep the ball in play. The goal posts, positioned 8 yd. (7.3 m) apart, are padded and designed to give easily on impact. The penalty lines are marked 30, 40, and 60 yd. (27, 36.5, and 55 m) from each goal or back line, and a center line is also indicated.

The rules
In polo, safety depends mainly on strict observation of the "right of way." This is determined by the line of the ball or, if it has stopped, by the line on which it last moved. A player has the right of way when riding on, or closest to, this line, provided the shot

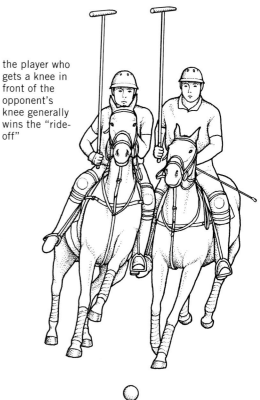

the player who gets a knee in front of the opponent's knee generally wins the "ride-off"

The polo field

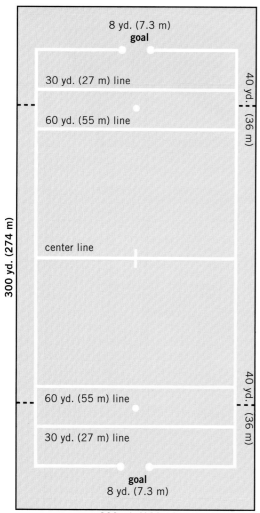

8 yd. (7.3 m)
goal

30 yd. (27 m) line

40 yd. (36 m)

60 yd. (55 m) line

center line

300 yd. (274 m)

40 yd. (36 m)

60 yd. (55 m) line

30 yd. (27 m) line

goal
8 yd. (7.3 m)

200 yd. (182 m)

The speed and courage of top-class polo ponies is evident in this action shot of an attempted "ride off" during one of the Coronation Cup Cup matches in 1990, held at the Guards Polo Club at Windsor, England.

is taken on his off-side. Another player crossing this line in such a way that he may possibly cause a collision is committing a foul. A player may "ride off" another player, by placing himself and his horse against his opponent, provided the horse is ridden at a safe angle, that is, not more than about 40 degrees. A player may also "hook" an opponent's mallet, provided the player is on the same side of his opponent as the ball. Penalties vary according to the degree and place of the foul committed, and consist mainly of free hits, either from the spot, or from the center of the field, or from marks 60, 40, or 30 yd. (55, 36.5, and 27 m) in front of the fouling side's goal.

The match is started, or resumed after a goal is scored, by an umpire throwing the ball in at the center of the field. If the ball goes out of play over the sideline, it is thrown in by the umpire as soon as the teams have "lined up," or, if it has gone over the back line, it is hit in, except when it has gone off a defender's stick, in which case the attacking team will then be awarded a 60 yd. (55 m) "free" shot from opposite where the ball crossed the line.

Books have been written about the tactics of polo, but quite simply the side that wins is

generally the one that remembers best that, first, it is a team game for four players, and second, whatever ability each player may have, he must be given the opportunity to use it to the full.

Polo today

Polo today is very popular, both for participants and spectators. Tournaments and teams which were previously supported only by wealthy patrons are now just as likely to be the recipients of commercial sponsorship. There are a high number of professionals among the players, and those at the top can nowadays earn hundreds of thousands of dollars. In England scholarships are available to young men and women who have shown special ability in their Pony Club teams, and this means they may spend a winter under instruction on a polo ranch in Argentina or elsewhere.

Of the small handful of players in the world who hold the maximum 10-goal handicap, the majority are usually Argentines, and undoubtedly the best polo is played in Buenos Aires, where the finals of the Open are contested in the giant Palermo Stadium in front of an audience of approximately 40,000. In England the Coronation Cup at the Guards Polo Club frequently attracts over 25,000 spectators, and a similar number watch the World Cup games at Palm Beach in Florida.

For many the game has become an addiction which, as has been remarked, "can only be cured by poverty or death."

Hunting

Hunting is probably the most ancient sport in the world. Today there are hundreds of packs of hounds around the world. In the U.K. alone there are around four hundred packs.

Hunting was well established in England by the eleventh century, and it is known that Edward I (1272–1307) had a royal huntsman, one William de Foxhunter. Most packs of hounds used to be privately owned by big landowners, but many small ones were owned and managed by local farmers. It is these that have now become the typical packs run by a hunt club. Today there are huntsmen and staff who are employed to run the hounds and kennels, and the Master is elected by the hunt committee. The Master of Foxhounds Association governs the sport.

In Europe, hunting used to be almost completely privately organized and owned, but is today gradually having to adopt the hunt club system as private land disappears and big landowners use their land for more commercial purposes.

In the U.S., hunting flourished as early as the late 1600s, for several colonists brought packs of hounds with them when they left England. There are now quite a few packs, but in the main hunting is confined to Virginia, Pennsylvania, New York State, New Jersey, Maryland, and the Carolinas. Originally run by the National Steeplechase and Hunt Association, in 1934 hunting came under the auspices of the Master of Foxhounds Association as it does in Britain.

Types of hunting

There are numerous different types of hunting. The three most popular are fox hunting, stag hunting, and wild boar hunting. The latter takes place almost exclusively in continental Europe.

Fox hunting is the most popular, with between 25 to 250 mounted followers, called "the field," with each pack per day. (In addition, there are always many car and foot followers.) Most packs hunt from between two to five days a week.

Stag hounds are bigger, and the packs hunt more in open woodland and hill country, usually once or twice a week.

The hunt members and staff

The Master is the person elected by the hunt committee to organize and run the hunt and organize the day's hunting. In some cases, the Master may own the hounds.

The Huntsman is in charge of the hounds and usually hunts them. He carries the horn to communicate with and control the hounds.

The whippers-in are assistants to the Huntsman. They help manage the hounds and assist generally, staying close to the Huntsman.

The Hunt Secretary is usually a paid official of the hunt and the person to whom you should apply should you wish to become a member of the hunt. The Hunt Secretary also deals with financial matters and subscriptions as well as general organization.

The field is the word used to describe the mounted followers, who are members and subscribers to the hunt.

The Field Master is in charge of the field, and his orders must be obeyed. It is unacceptable to ride in front of the Field Master out hunting, except when the hounds are running. Members pay an annual subscription to the hunt, and there are various rules and regulations which have to be observed; for example, how many horses you can bring out, whether you hunt during weekends, etc.

Hunting is extremely popular, particularly in the U.K., Eire, and many parts of the U.S., as well as in Europe. Most packs hunt between two to five days a week.

The correct dress for hunting

velvet hunting cap

silk top hat

hunting crop

bowler hat

spurs

Tying a hunting tie

1   2   3   pin   4

Equipment

To go hunting you have to wear the right outfit and be turned out correctly. This should include breeches, boots, and spurs. Only the Hunt Master, his staff, and hunt members are entitled to wear the traditional scarlet coat (often incorrectly called pink); otherwise, both men and women should wear tweed coats before the opening meet, and blue or black coats afterward. A colored stock (or tie) (worn only with tweed), a white or cream stock (worn only with blue or black), a tie pin, together with a shirt and hunting cap are all worn.

The skull cap is now becoming increasingly acceptable, and for safety reasons this is sensible. Bowler hats are worn by men wearing tweed coats (ratcatcher), or top hats when wearing a black coat. Riding caps or bowlers can be worn by ladies wearing blue or black. Ladies riding sidesaddle should wear a veil over their bowler or top hat, and a white or cream stock if their habit is blue or black, and a colored stock or a collar and tie if tweed. A top hat is not worn with a tweed habit. Farmers are traditionally entitled to wear hunting caps, as are the Master and hunt servants, and only these are entitled to wear the ribbons at the back of the hunting cap outside their coats. Hunt members should cut the ends off or tuck them away inside.

A hunting whip, which is a special crop with a thong or lash used to keep the hounds away from the horses and for opening gates, should be carried. This has a solid part with a horn or bone hook. The whip is carried with the hook to the back and the thong hanging through the hand and downward. Gloves, usually of string or the non-slip variety, should also be worn.

Above all, you should look neat and tidy, with clean boots and spurs and with hair tucked away.

The horse

The hunter is a special type of horse, tough, strong, placid, a good jumper, and fast when necessary, with plenty of stamina. It comes in all shapes and sizes, but has to be up to weight and capable of carrying its rider on a long day through all types of going and countryside.

The horse must be under control at all times, and as it may be rather more excitable than usual when out hunting, a stronger bit may be needed, and good, strong leather tack should be worn. A comfortable, well-fitting saddle is essential for both horse and rider, and a breastplate to keep the saddle in place is a wise precaution in what can often be undulating countryside. Horses are usually best left without leg protection when hunting in wet ground, as mud and dirt can build up under boots or bandages, causing friction rubs. It is therefore important that the horse is a good mover so that it avoids knocking itself too often.

Riding to hounds

There can be nothing more exhilarating than a good run behind hounds over good country. The countryside, the power of the horses, hounds in full cry, and the excitement of lots of people riding together all make for a good day. Very often, however, a good hunt may mean using public roads and going across land which may have been planted with crops. Always be aware that not everyone enjoys the sport as much as you do. A motorist coming upon a large group of followers riding to hounds across the road can find this extremely frustrating.

The hounds will start by going to a suitable covert which they will draw to find their quarry. The field must stay with the field master until the hounds have really settled and are running.

If you stand still and watch the hounds working, you can learn much about what is going on and how hounds work. The most experienced foxhunters rarely seem in a hurry, but watch and listen intently.

It is regarded a cardinal fault if a horse kicks a hound, so be sure to face your horse toward hounds whenever you find yourself in a vulnerable situation. If this does happen, and the horse is not under control, you may be sent home to avoid further mishaps.

When you go home, it is polite to thank the Master for the day, but this is not always possible. Take your horse away from the line if hounds are still running. Loosen the girths and arrive back at the horse box "cooled off." Cover the horse and if necessary, apply leg bandages. Once home, give small amounts of tepid water until the horse is satisfied, and a bran mash or a small feed.

The opening meet In the U.K., the official hunting season traditionally starts on November 1. It continues until the end of March or April, depending on the state of the crops. Cubbing (or early hunting) may start as soon as harvesting has been completed. During this time young hounds are trained, and they tend to remain in the coverts with the field placed around them to prevent the foxes and cubs from getting away.

The field should stay with the Field Master, who will decide when and where they should be, depending on the movement of the hounds.

Drag hunting

A popular alternative to fox hunting is drag hunting with hounds. This means following a pre-arranged line or lines over suitable countryside with a pack of hounds following a scent (usually aniseed or something similar) which has been "dragged" that morning. There are usually several specially prepared fences, and the field follow as they would in ordinary hunting. This type of hunting is popular where it is impossible to stage a traditional hunt because of built-up areas or a lack of foxes.

Points to remember

• Always keep to the edges of fields of crops.
• Never jump fences except when the hounds are running.
• Do not set off on your own, but keep with the rest of the field in case you head (turn) the fox.
• Obey the Field Master's instructions at all times.
• Never park your truck or van too close to the meet in case you block the road, and always park sensibly.
• Ride to the meet, allowing plenty of time to settle your horse down. Never be late for a meet.
• Find the Hunt Secretary to give him your "cap" (that is, money for the day's hunting) as soon as possible.
• Always give way to the Master or any of the hunt staff.
• Always make sure that gates are shut and secured, and any breakages to gates and fences are reported so that these can be repaired.
• Always thank any followers who open and shut gates for you or those who own land you may be crossing.
• Do not forget your horse or what it is capable of doing.
• Do not over-jump or overtire your horse, especially in heavy going.
• Avoid galloping or cantering on hard surfaces such as roads and tracks more than is necessary.
• If your horse is excitable, keep it in good check at the middle or back of the field.
• A young horse or one with no previous experience of hunting is said to be "green." It must wear a green ribbon in its tail and should be kept away from others until settled.
• A horse that kicks out must wear a red ribbon in its tail as a warning to all other riders to keep their distance.

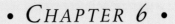

• CHAPTER 6 •

ADVANCED COMPETITIVE RIDING

'There is no secret so close as that between
a rider and his horse.'

R.S.Surtees, *Mr. Sponge's Sporting Tour*
(1853)

Few riders reach the top competitively in comparison to the vast numbers who ride worldwide. For those who do reach the top, however, after years of training and hard work, the rewards are great. The top names become almost legendary for their outstanding displays of horsemanship. Sponsorship for the top names is now commonplace, and prize money for winning the big competitions can be big. Riding at the top is expensive, however, and only a few people really make a living out of the sport unless they supplement their success by teaching, producing, or breeding horses for the sport.

There are three equestrian events which qualify for Olympic status, namely dressage,

show jumping, and the three-day event, or Combined Training. These require high standards of excellence, and to reach the top in these sports may mean years of training for both horse and rider in order to be selected or invited to compete.

These three events usually have annual championships, interspersed between the Olympic four-year cycle, which are competed for worldwide. The World Dressage Championships, the World Show Jumping Championships, and the World Three-Day Event Championships take place every four years, two years after the Olympics. Regional games, such as the European and Pan-American Games, slot in every two years in between. The first World

Equestrian Games, held in Stockholm in 1990, incorporated the three Olympic disciplines, as well as driving, vaulting, and endurance riding.

International events for different standards of horse riding are fitted into a very full calendar and are controlled by the Fédération Equestre Internationale (FEI), which is based in Switzerland and which organizes the rules and regulations for all events and championships. In every discipline there are competitions for pony riders, juniors, young riders, and riders at senior level. There are championships for all, and these usually tend to be held in either the nation which previously won the events or in countries which offer to host them.

The three Olympic sports of show jumping, dressage, and three-day eventing are hotly contested by riders from all over the world. To be an Olympic champion is every rider's dream. Riders and horses have to qualify by a set date before their national federations can nominate them to represent their country in a team or as an individual.

DRESSAGE

Riders who intend to compete at advanced level in dressage will be required to perform all the movements asked for in a test of this standard. These will include: counter canter, half-pass at trot and canter, counter changes of hand both in trot and canter, flying changes and sequence changes, pirouettes, passage, and piaffe. Dressage with music has really caught on, and it is the interpretation and choice of the music in relation to the move-ments shown, as well as the correct execution of the required movements, which gain good marks. Timing is all important for harmony of the music with both horse and rider.

Following on from the basic movements already discussed in Chapter 4, the horse needs to become even more balanced so that it takes more weight through its quarters and hindlegs and is really light in the forehand to perform more advanced movements. In the field of dressage this is referred to as self-carriage.

The movements

Lateral schooling exercises such as renvers and travers (see p. 114) help to increase suppleness and bend. These, along with leg yielding (see p. 113) and shoulder-in (see p. 114), are excellent preparatory work for the other, more advanced movements discussed in this chapter.

Counter changes

Once the horse has mastered the half-pass (see p. 115), counter changes of hand (zigzags) down the center line in trot can be asked for. Usually the horse turns down the center line and does a half-pass in one direction for three or four strides. It then straightens and changes the bend and does double the amount of steps over the center to the opposite side, then straightens again and changes bend to go the other way. It should finish by going straight for a couple of strides before turning away from the center line. These steps can also be done in canter, requiring a flying change to go the other way.

The counter change in canter looks extremely elegant and impressive. It must never be rushed. The important point to remember always is to keep the sideways movements consistent with a straightening before the change is asked for. You must aim for the sequence: sideways, straight, change, sideways, straight, change as you go through the movement.

Goodwood House in England forms a superb backdrop for this rider, warming up in the practice arena before performing his test.

Flying changes

This is one of the more spectacular movements in dressage and involves the horse springing from one diagonal lead in canter to the other during the moment of suspension. The horse has to be very well balanced and off its forehand, so that it can do this as the rider changes the leg aids to influence the horse to move onto the other leg.

Straightness is essential, and the rider must not swing the weight to cause any loss of balance. The horse needs to be in tune with the movements asked for.

Sequence changes

Once flying changes are well-established, changes in sequence can be introduced, with the horse being asked to do several changes. Start gradually, making two or three single changes at random until the horse is confident and calm. Work up to doing this every four, three, and then every two strides before the change of leg. Do not try to do this in a hurry, and ask for only a few changes to start with in each sequence.

Once changes in sequence are established, the one-time changes (that is, every stride) can be started. Perfect harmony between horse and rider are essential for the horse to be able to do this. There should be no swinging from side to side. Straightness is the secret, and the horse should be

Flying changes The flying change, performed here by Robert Dover on Walzertakt, is one of the most impressive dressage movements.

Pirouette in walk Britain's Jennie Loriston-Clarke and Dutch Gold demonstrate this movement, which requires regular steps and suppleness.

absolutely obedient to the aids. Keep the seat very light in the saddle and the horse relaxed.

The pirouette

This is a very collected movement in which the horse's forehand moves around the hindlegs creating a 360° circle for the full pirouette and 180° degrees for the half pirouette. It can be done in walk or canter, the latter being used for advanced work. The hind feet are lifted up and put down again almost on the spot and should not swivel. The horse must remain on the bit and with a light contact and slight bend toward the direction in which it is going. It must take regular steps and be balanced. For a full pirouette in canter, six to eight steps should be taken; if undertaking a half pirouette, only three to four are required. To prepare for this, the horse must first be in a balanced collected canter full of flowing movement, and through a series of half halts must shorten the strides so much that the legs are almost cantering on the spot and then should be asked to go forward again.

Progress on from this, and do a half circle as you shorten the canter and then go on again. Eventually work through three quarters until you achieve the full circle. If the horse gets excited, come back to a walk; if it loses impulsion, create more by going forward with stronger leg aids. The horse must always be going forward and must not be allowed to drop behind the bit. Straightness into and out of the movement are vital for good marks.

The dressage saddle

short, deep seat

Lonsdale girth

buckle guard to prevent chapping

two girth straps to take a Lonsdale girth

The pirouette in walk should be taught early in the horse's training (see turns on the forehand and haunches, p. 113). In canter it should not be attempted until the horse can shorten and lengthen with ease and maintain a collected canter consistently.

The passage

The passage is an extremely collected trot, with the horse being able to produce such power that there is a definite moment of suspension from one diagonal to the other. The legs should be more elevated than usual, and rhythm is vital. Suppleness and lack of tension are the secrets of success, but most important of all is the transition into and out of the movement. Practice this by doing a series of half halts in collected trot while generating extra power through the leg aids. The distinctive spring from one leg to the other will come when the balance is found between movement and control.

It is a good idea to have a helper on the ground with a dressage whip, tapping each leg in turn to help the horse get the right rhythm. Be satisfied with only a few correct strides to start with, always reward the horse, and always move forward.

This work is particularly strenuous and must not be overdone, especially in the early days when the horse has to build up balance and technique without tension. Do not make the mistake of rushing the transitions and maintain the rhythm as you change into and out of the movement.

The piaffe

This is the most collected movement of all and consists of an elevated trot on the spot. The power required for this is enormous, and it takes at least three years' training for the horse to build up the necessary muscle to maintain this elegant movement for any length of time.

It may be taught as a continuation from passage by restricting the forward movement and asking for more collection and elevation in front. Another way to teach the piaffe is to have the horse in side reins with the trainer on the ground controlling the horse along the side of a wall and tapping the horse's legs as more elevation is required. Always reward when a correct step is taken, and use the voice for encouragement. Some horses will not understand what is required and need a rider to tell them what to do. Work along similar lines with the rider up, but keeping the weight light in the saddle to enable the horse to use itself to the maximum. The rider can influence the collection and impulsion, while the trainer can ask for more if necessary by tapping the legs with the whip.

Extended trot This movement requires maximum extension and impulsion, while at the same time maintaining the horse in a rounded and balanced outline. Regularity of the steps is most important, and it is essential that the transitions before and after the movement should be smooth and well-defined.

Passage The collection and elevation required to perform the exaggerated trot known as passage take time to perfect. The height and regularity of the steps, as the horse springs from one diagonal to the other, are essential elements for good marks. The horse must remain relaxed and calm, showing no signs of tenseness.

Piaffe This is the most strenuous and elevated of all the dressage movements, and consists of the trot on the spot. The transitions before and after this are vital, as are the regularity of the steps, if good marks are to be achieved in competitions. The piaffe is very similar to passage on the spot.

It is vital to get an even stride before asking for extra elevation, so work first on establishing a rhythm and then on getting more lift. Do a little at a time, and do not tire the horse. Reward frequently.

Riding to music

The popularity of riding to music has increased dramatically over the last few years. Audiences are generally very responsive and appreciative of good performances. Some horses love working to music, and many have proved to be far more musical than their riders! At the lower levels, classes for

Canter pirouette For pirouette at the canter, even and forward moving strides are essential while maintaining the the correct bend and balance.

Half-pass This movement, with the horse bent toward the direction in which it is traveling, can be done in trot and canter.

dressage to music are offered widely, with riders bringing their own tapes. Tests are usually about four to five minutes long and include certain movements which are compulsory. The overall impression given should be exciting and flowing, with the movements correctly executed. Artistic interpretation of the music to the movements plays an important part. The tests are judged and timed from the halts at the beginning and end of the test.

In international classes, horses are in most instances required to qualify for the Kür or freestyle to music. Usually it is the top dozen or so who have performed in a Grand Prix who come forward. Sometimes, however, there is a choice between the musical or "special," which is a shorter advanced test.

Judges and scoring There are five judges in top-level dressage, who are sited in boxes at the end and sides of the arena. The scoreboard clearly shows the scores and total good marks, which indicate the winning combination.

The dressage scene
Each country stages its own national championships and runs numerous classes for all levels of dressage and dressage to music. It is a progressive sport, and horses move up in grade as they accumulate points or become capable of performing at the higher levels. There are classes for novice horses through to Advanced or Open, though each country has its own particular rules governing the sport. As with most equestrian disciplines, international classes are run under FEI rules, with many competitions qualifying for various championships or points on leader boards.

Scoring
Scoring for dressage classes is based on what the judges decide are good marks for each movement performed, up to a maximum of ten points. Scoring is the same for every test, namely ten excellent, nine very good, eight good, seven fairly good, six satisfactory, five sufficient, four insufficient, three fairly bad, two bad, one very bad, zero not performed.

Judges are encouraged to use the full range of marks available. Some of the more difficult movements or transitions sometimes earn double marks as do the collective marks at the end of the test. Collective marks cover the paces, the impulsion of the horse, such as its desire to move forward, elasticity of steps, and engagement of the hindquarters; submission, which covers attention and obedience, lightness, and ease of the movements, acceptance of the bit; and position and seat of the rider and the correct use of the aids. Judges' remarks on these points can be helpful in influencing future training.

The number of movements in each test varies according to the degree of difficulty. There may be around twelve movements in a novice test and up to thirty or so in the advanced tests.

Judges

To become a judge, you have to be put on a list of judges, which means qualifying for a set standard of test devised according to a particular country's qualification system. At the lower level, there is often only one judge. At international level, however, judges have to be on the FEI list of judges, and there is usually a minimum of three judges placed along the end of the arena opposite the entrance at H, C, and M markers. At the top level, there are five judges, with the two extra ones placed at E and B markers. This number helps to give a very accurate assessment of the horse and rider as they are seen from all angles.

Dress

Dress and presentation should complement the overall picture. The horse should be clean and neat and looking its very best, beautifully plaited with clean tack and bits and sparkling stirrups and spurs. At the lower levels, tweed or blue coats are the correct wear for riders. At the medium or international levels, blue coats are usually required, but at advanced level, a black top hat and a tail coat are necessary.

Gloves and spurs are compulsory at this level. Always check in your rulebook to make sure that your turnout is correct. The most stylish combinations of horse and rider are usually those which appear neat and tidy without too much brass or white adornments. Colors other than black, brown, or white are totally inappropriate on any part of the horse or rider and are deemed highly unprofessional. For novice or lower levels, a snaffle bridle is generally used, but in advanced classes and all FEI tests, a double bridle may be compulsory.

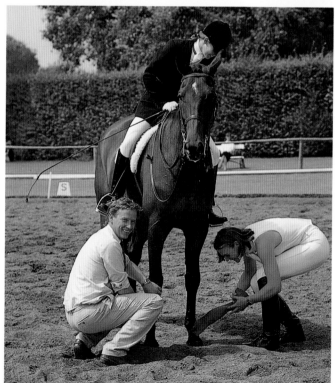

Dress and presentation should complement the overall performance. For novice and preliminary competitions (above left), tweed jackets and hunting caps are acceptable. However, as the standard of the competition gets higher, so does the standard of dress required, with top hat and tails being compulsory in FEI and other advanced tests (above right). Leg protection, generally used for schooling and warming up beforehand, must be removed before the competitor enters the arena (left). Most lower-level tests stipulate the use of snaffle bridles, with the double bridle becoming compulsory for advanced tests. Always check that your bits and clothes are within the rules laid down for the particular competition which you are entering.

An alternative method of tying a hunting tie (stock)

For advanced dressage, the tie or stock is tied in the same way as for the hunting tie (see p. 152). The final knot (**2**) is pulled a little tighter to allow the top layer to twist and lie neatly on top of the underside layer.

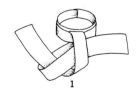

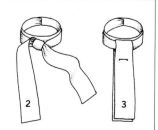

1   2   3

DRESSAGE TEST

Fédération
Equestre
Internationale

Grand Prix

Arena 20 m × 60 m

Left: Olympic, World, and European Champion Nicole Uphoff, on the spectacular Rembrandt, parades with her winner's blanket and sash of honor.
Below: Headgear is not yet compulsory for dressage schooling, but it is recommended for all riding for safety's sake. Here Anne Grethe-Tornblad on Supermax Ravel performs a pirouette to the right, a movement requiring a high degree of collection and balance.
Right: This young horse is looking relaxed and happy in his work, the basic ingredient for successful dressage.

			Max Marks
1.	A	Enter in collected canter	
	I	Halt - Immobility - Salute	
		Proceed in collected trot	10
2.	C	Track to the right	
	MXK	Change rein in extended trot	
	KA	Collected trot	10
3.	A	Collected canter	
	FXH	Change rein in medium canter with flying change of leg at X	
	H	Collected canter	10
4.	C	Collected walk	
		Transition to collected walk	10
5.	M	Turn right	
	Between G and H	Half pirouette to the right	10
6.	Between G and M	Half pirouette to the left	10
7.		The collected walk CMG (H) (M) G	10
8.	GHS	Collected trot	
	SP	Half pass to the left	
	PFAKV	Collected trot	10
9.	VR	Half pass to the right	
	RMCH	Collected trot	10
10.	HXF	Change rein in extended trot	10
11.	FAK	Passage	10
12.	KVXRM	Change rein in extended walk	10×2
13.	MCH	Collected walk	10
14.	H	Proceed in passage	
		Transition from collected walk to passage	10
15.	HSI	Passage	10
16.	I	Piaffe 12-15 steps	10
17.	I	Proceed in passage, transitions from passage to piaffe and from piaffe to passage	10
18.	IRBX	Passage	10
19.	X	Piaffe 12-15 steps	10
20.	X	Proceed in passage transitions from passage to piaffe and from piaffe to passage	10
21.	XEV	Passage	10
22.	V	Proceed in collected canter	
	VKA	Collected canter	10
23.	AG	Down centre line, 5 counter changes of hand in half pass to either side of the centre line with flying changes of leg at each change of direction. The first half pass to the left and the last to the right of 3 strides and 4 others of 6 strides	
	G	Collected canter	10
24.	C	Track to the right	
	MXK	Change rein in extended canter	
	K	Collected canter and flying change of leg	10
25.	A	Down centre line	
	L	Pirouette to the left	
	X	Flying change of leg	10×2
26.	I	Pirouette to the right	
	G	Flying change of leg	
	C	Track to the left	10×2
27.	HXF	On the diagonal 9 flying changes of leg every 2nd stride (finishing on the right leg)	10
28.	KXM	On the diagonal 15 changes of leg every stride (finishing on the left leg)	10
29.	HXF	Change rein in extended canter	
	F	Collected canter and flying change of leg	10
30.	A	On centre line	
	L	Halt - rein back 6 steps - proceed in passage	10
31.		Transitions from collected canter to halt and from rein back to passage	10
32.	LX	Passage	10
33.	X	Piaffe (12 to 15 steps)	10
34.		Transitions from passage to piaffe and from piaffe to passage	10
35.	XG	Passage	10
36.	G	Halt - immobility - salute	10
		Leave arena and walk at A	
		TOTAL	**390**

Collective Marks

1.		Paces (freedom and regularity)	10×2
2.		Impulsion (desire to move forward, elesticity of the steps, suppleness of the back and engagement of the hindquarters)	10×2
3.		Submission (attention and confidence; harmony, lightness and ease of movements; acceptance of the bridle and lightness of the forehand)	10×2
4.		Position, seat of the rider, correct use of the aids	10×2
		TOTAL	**470**

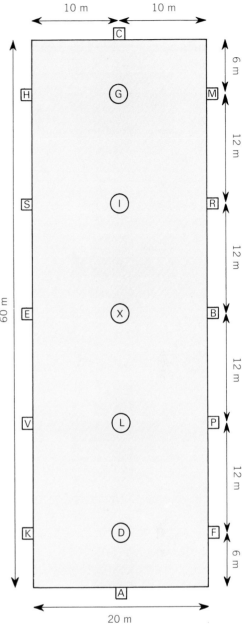

Warming up

Novice tests are necessarily quite short, and the judges must see the horses performing at their best if they are to award good marks. Therefore warming up before the test is most important. It may take time to assess how much work each horse requires before entering the arena. Some require a lot, while others may go rather flat with too much warming up; this is particularly the case with a young horse. At top competition levels, the horse will need to run through every movement and pace before entering the arena. Using the corners of the arena becomes vital at advanced levels, especially as so many movements and transitions happen at the quarter marks (that is K, H, F, and M). From the earliest days, practice straightness down the center line and at the halt. Your entry and exit are the first and last movements the judge sees. Make sure these are good, as they may influence the marks.

Riding tests

Show your horse off to its best by presenting yourself well in the arena. Hold your head and body up, and ride every inch of the way. Apologetic performances just sitting and praying that things will go all right do not get top marks. Ride into and through your corners; prepare every transition from one pace or movement to the next; keep up a steady rhythm and flow. If one movement gets spoiled, do not let it upset the rest of the test. It is seldom worth correcting the horse in the arena at the lower levels. This is the time to build up confidence and cooperation, so being relaxed about absolutely everything, including faults, is important. An older, more experienced horse may need correcting if it makes a bad mistake and continues to do so. Whips may be carried in some tests, but never in FEI classes. Make sure you really know what to do in your test so that you can concentrate on riding, and be calm and positive about doing your best. It is most important that you concentrate totally on the job in hand and are not thinking of other things when in the arena.

Above all, make it look easy; obvious leg and seat aids with excessive hand movements will undermine the overall impression, so keep as still as possible in the saddle. The best performances are where the aids are almost invisible and where the horse looks as if it is performing all by itself – that is how it should be!

SHOW JUMPING

The competitiveness of the show jumping scene at every level makes this sport very exciting and justifiably popular. Anyone who has jumped fences can understand the ever-present urge to jump bigger and better. Those who qualify for jump-offs often become fiendishly competitive as they dart around the generally shortened and raised courses in their attempts to win. The various riding styles emanating from different countries are fascinating to watch; in international classes, this is as interesting as the jumping itself. For example, there is the classical style of American riders, trained by the great Bert De Nemethy, which can be contrasted with the very disciplined and powerful German style, or the rather relaxed approach of the British riders. Other countries which have riders who excel in this sport are Australia, Ireland, France, Austria, Holland, Brazil, and Canada.

Classes

In show jumping there are classes catering for all stages and standards of jumping, as well as for the different age groups of children, juniors, young riders, and seniors.

Each country has its own set of national rules designed to encourage horses to reach the top levels successfully. All international classes fall under FEI rules for show jumping,

on which most national rules are based, and are adapted to suit the locality. In Britain and Germany, courses are graded A, B, or C according to their height and difficulty, with the amount of prize money won deciding the move up to the next grade. In France, it is more the horse's age that determines the class. This is fine if you have a young horse and can start in the bottom class. The French system is not always so successful, however, if you have an older horse new to the sport.

The American system has warm-up and schooling classes with no prize money for

heights up to approximately 3 ft. 6 in. (1.07 m). They then progress to preliminary standard which includes fences up to 4 ft. 6 in. (1.40 m) and intermediate with fences up to 5 ft. (1.5 m). Once sufficient prize money has been won at this stage, the big time lies ahead.

Although each country has its own national competitions and championships, there are the same FEI championships as for dressage and eventing. Olympic and World championships occur every four years, with European, Pan-American, Asian games, and others slotted in every two years in between.

The jumping saddle

padded
knee roll   long, deep seat

These have team as well as individual status.

Apart from the more serious classes at the top, there are also some for amateurs and professionals. They include several fun classes such as relays and fancy dress. Special competitions also take place, such as six bars, fault and out, top score, power and out, puissance, and knockouts, each with their special rules relative to the type of class. Except for some of these special classes, which have their own rules, the FEI scoring system is almost always used.

A panoramic view of a large and colorful arena. There are many superb outdoor arenas such as this in the U.S.A., Europe, and Australia.

There are classes for ponies and juniors, as well as for horses of all different grades and standards, which are designed to encourage a gradual progression from novice level up to the very top levels. Ponies are amazingly quick and agile, and many of today's star riders learned the basics in pony competitions.

Many of the specialized classes have their own scoring systems; otherwise, the FEI system is used universally.

Scoring

The different classes are judged under various rules, mostly related to the jump-offs. How many there are depends on the particular type of class. Usually these are based on a "table system," and each class will set out clearly which of these it is to run under. The "table" rules will be written on the course plan, which is always pinned up in the collecting ring.

Most classes have a raised, but shortened, course in the jump-off, which may be against the clock, or if there are two jump-offs, the last may be against the clock with the fastest clear round winning. Sometimes there are two jump-offs with prizes being divided equally between those who jump clear rounds if there is still no clear winner.

Many of the special classes may have separate scoring systems, but for the majority of national and international show jumping classes, the following penalties apply:

Penalties

- **First disobedience (refusal)** three faults
- **Second disobedience (refusal)** six faults
- **Third disobedience (refusal)** elimination
- **Knockdown** four faults
- **Fall of horse and/or rider** eight faults
- **Exceeding the time allowed** 1/4 fault for each second or part thereof
- **Exceeding the time allowed in a timed jump-off** One fault for each second or part thereof
- **Exceeding the time limit** elimination

Schooling at home is most important to teach the horse the basic necessities of how to cope with the different problems which it is likely to encounter when it reaches the show ring. All sorts of equipment can be used as suitable jumping material, but always check beforehand that it is absolutely safe.

Further training

The show jumper requires experience around as many different courses as possible. As the horse progresses and becomes confident with the rules of one standard, it can then be moved up to the next class. All the time the horse has to improve its general way of going on the flat, and there is no reason why the show jumper cannot continue its training along similar lines to that of the dressage horse. It should be capable of some lateral work, with the shoulder-in and even the half-pass, turns on the forehand and haunches, half pirouettes, and counter canter, as well as flying changes, obedient halts, rein back, and increase and decrease of pace, particularly at the canter.

Suppleness and obedience is as vital to the show jumper as to the dressage horse if it is to cope with the big fences and tight turns encountered at the more advanced levels. The horse must stay down on the bit consistently, be totally obedient to the rider's aids, and always be going forward. It has to jump when asked to do so, though this can be quite difficult to achieve with horses of certain temperaments.

Constant repetition of an exercise is one of the best ways of teaching an impetuous or difficult horse, gently but persistently asking for what is required, such as a quiet jump over quite low single or double fences, until you achieve what you want. Once the basics have been mastered, you can build up to the required height and amount of fences.

Combinations and related distances

A series of two or three fences with one or two strides in between is collectively known as a combination and may consist of an upright, spreads, or a combination of the two. If the distance is between three to six strides away – a horse's canter stride is 12 ft. (3.7 m) on average – it becomes a related distance. Sometimes to increase the difficulty of the course, distances may incorporate an extra half a stride. The rider will have to decide whether to increase the pace and so lose the extra distance or to slow down sufficiently to put in an extra stride. It is therefore worthwhile practicing jumping fences with combinations and related distances which may require shortening or lengthening the stride. The distances jumped will vary slightly according to the types of fence being jumped, that is, spreads or uprights.

Distances between the different types of fences

With the fences at approximately 4 ft. (1.2 m) high.

- **Upright to upright**
  24 ft. (7.3 m) one non-jumping stride

- **Upright to upright**
  33 to 35 ft. (10 to 10.7 m) two non-jumping strides

- **Upright to spread**
  23 ft. (7 m) one non-jumping stride

- **Upright to spread**
  32 to 34 ft. (9.8 to 10.4 m) two non-jumping strides

- **Spread to upright**
  25 ft. (7.6 m) one non-jumping stride

- **Spread to upright**
  35 to 37 ft. (10.7 to 11.2 m) two non-jumping strides

- **Spread to spread**
  24 ft. (7.3 m) one non-jumping stride

- **Spread to spread**
  33 to 35 ft. (10 to 10.7 m) two non-jumping strides

The course This will need a thorough and careful assessment on the preliminary walk round, for the rider must decide how each fence and combination should best be tackled, taking into account a number of points: the horse's stride, the ground and whether it will affect the horse's way of going, the size of the fences, and the degree of technicality of the course as a whole.

Dealing with problems

Inevitably there will be times when things do not go according to plan. You will need to assess the situation to find out what is going wrong and whether the reason is something to do with the horse or the position or approach of the rider.

Refusals The most common problem is the horse refusing to jump – the refusal – which can happen for many reasons. It might be because of overfacing or attempting to jump the horse over fences it cannot cope with. This is a common fault at the lower levels of show jumping, but also occurs due to bad rider position or technique at any level. If a horse at an advanced level of jumping refuses, this is more likely to be because the horse and rider are not quite in agreement about their approach. (In this case, all may go well the next time.) Other reasons may be

The different types of show jumping fences

Vertical: planks

Vertical: colored poles

Vertical: rustic poles

Vertical: gate

Spread: parallel poles

The coffin

Water jump

The bank

If the horse has been well schooled and brought on sensibly, few problems should arise. However, things can go wrong, so first analyze the reasons.

because of jarring, for instance, or a back strain or a virus affecting the horse. If nothing seems obvious, and bear in mind that horses do not enjoy jumping big fences on hard ground, a blood test would be a wise precaution.

For the young horse it will be necessary to backtrack a little in training to rebuild its confidence by starting a gradual build-up program over smaller fences. If the problem lies with the rider, getting too far forward or being too restrictive with the hands are common faults, for instance, set out to improve your technique.

Rushing The horse may rush at fences. This may be because of fear, or anticipation or overexuberance, or because of the rider's style of riding. Being relaxed and allowing the horse complete freedom when jumping over fences are vital to build up the horse's confidence. If the animal is in any way restricted, it may well dash at fences in an effort to break free from the rider. Softness of the hand is vital if this fault is to be corrected. Jumping single fences with poles on the ground in front (approximately 9 to 10 ft. (2.5 to 3 m)) may help here. Jumping parallels on a circle trying to create a good pace and rhythm may also be a good idea.

Some horses are simply disobedient. They will need better brakes with a different bit and must be made to obey the rider. Extra schooling on the flat usually helps. Bitless bridles or hackamores can be quite effective (but only as a last resort), especially if the horse is afraid of its mouth and liable to rush because of or in anticipation of pain.

Hitting fences Most horses which have been correctly schooled do not enjoy hitting fences, but they may do this if they jump in poor style. It is essential to get the horse to the correct takeoff spot for jumping if it is to be given a fair chance. It will need complete freedom to be able to use itself over the fence. The rider's position will influence the style of the horse enormously; even if this is only slightly incorrect, it may be enough to unbalance the horse enough for it to touch a fence.

It may be that horse and rider are not using the correct approach and takeoff point to clear the fence at the right height. Ask your trainer to study your approach. Or it could be the pace that you are approaching fences at that is causing trouble; if it is too slow, the horse may be "dwelling" in the air and not completing the jump correctly, or if it is too fast, it may be tapping the fence in front on the way up.

The rider may need to sit up more on approach, use the body less over the fence, or be softer in the arms; the pace may need regulating; or the takeoff point may need to be adjusted.

Some horses will be sharper and neater if ridden on more strongly. It is often better not to overprotect the horse with brushing boots, but to use the open-fronted type which protect the back of the tendon but still leave the horse sensitive to a knock if it gets a bit casual about the fences.

The horse

Show jumpers come in all shapes and sizes. Outstanding stars include the British horse Stroller, only 14.2 hh, yet the Olympic silver medalist in Mexico, and more recently the little French horse Jappeloup de Luze. The horse should have the correct conformation with short cannons and good feet. The quarters should be round and strong with good hocks, and there should be a definite look of strength and power. The favored horses for show jumping tend to be the warmblood types which are specifically bred for competitive work. The Dutch Warmbloods, Hanoverians, and Britain's native ponies crossed with Thoroughbreds have all proved excellent show jumpers. In the U.K. the hunter type is favored, which is probably three-quarters to seven-eighths Thoroughbred, while in the U.S., even lighter horses are preferred, such as pure Thoroughbreds.

Jumping ability is what really counts, along with that indefinable little bit extra that turns a good horse into a star. There are thousands of show jumpers around the world, and a wide variation can be found in type, breed, and size.

Dress

The dress for show jumping should always be neat and tidy with the horse clean and well turned-out. For bigger shows, its mane and tail should be plaited or braided. For small shows, riders may wear tweed coats with a colored hunting tie, but blue or black coats with white stocks or ties are always worn at bigger shows. In international classes, those eligible may wear coats of national colors, such as green for Ireland, red with blue collars for the U.S., and red for the U.K. Those who have represented their country are also eligible for the coveted national flag or emblem above the breast pocket. Calientes with a safety harness are compulsory, with either black or navy blue covers. Jumping whips must not be more

The care and preparation that goes on behind the scenes is just as vital to the horse's success as its training and rider.

The importance of walking the course carefully cannot be overemphasized. Much is at stake here; very often it pays to walk around with a more experienced rider or with your trainer to find out about any likely trouble areas. Watch others ride the course and see where adjustments are taken and whether the combinations are riding long or short. When warming up, try to use your normal routine, especially on young horses who may get a little overawed by the occasion and need stronger riding.

There are various rules relative to the warm-up area which you must take great care not to infringe, such as jumping between the flags in the correct direction, the use of poles, etc.

than 30 in. (75 cm) long. Spurs must not in any way be capable of wounding a horse and must have the shank curving downward and directly back from the center (see p. 122).

Warming up in the collecting ring

Always make full use of the warming-up period to loosen up and make the horse fully supple before it has to jump its best. It is most important the horse is well motivated and ready to go before entering the arena. Always check the number of riders and be prepared to be the first to jump off.

Try to use the same warming-up routine at the show as you would at home, especially with young horses. Have a helper with you to alter the fences. Do not overface the inexperienced horse in the warm up, but build up its confidence. Some animals get a little overawed by the sense of occasion and do not go well, while others will rise to it and perform very well on the day.

There are various rules about warming up; be careful not to infringe these. Never jump practice fences the wrong way. Keep red flags or standards on the right, white on the left. The use of placing poles is restricted, as are any poles wedged in such a way that they will not fall easily. There should be an upright and parallel provided in the collecting ring, so make the most of these without unduly tiring the horse. Some horses need several preliminary jumps, while others will require only one or two before going into the ring.

In the ring

Once in the ring, the sole aim should be to achieve the best possible round. A clear round takes precedence over everything else. Start by saluting the judges, and use this as an obedience test for the horse as you bring your mount to a halt, often with a couple of steps in rein back before breaking straight into canter. Then set off, concentrating entirely on the course. Think of each and every approach to the fences. Remember that balance and impulsion have to be consistent throughout and that the horse must be given every chance to do its best. If you can, watch

a couple of rounds before your own to assess any trouble spots, especially in a speed class or before the jump-off. Only you can judge just how many risks to take in a jump-off and how fast you dare go if jumping against the clock. Every stride missed out will save vital seconds. If you can do related distances in four strides instead of five, or can angle the fence to take out a stride or even to gain more room for the next fence, you will be halfway toward a place in the final line-up. All the months of schooling will have paid off as you twist and turn around the arena, with the horse responding confidently.

EVENTING AND HORSE TRIALS

Eventing requires very versatile horses, and when reaching the standards required for a full-scale three-day event, a horse should be schooled sufficiently to cope with every aspect of this sport. Originally devised as a test for military riders and their horses to test for toughness and all-round training, the sport was subsequently adapted and is now controlled internationally by the FEI.

Condensed versions of the three-day event are used as training and qualifying events and are known as one-day events. They consist of dressage, cross-country, and show jumping, designed to suit horses and riders at various different levels. Sometimes two-day events are arranged with dressage and show jumping on the first day and a short steeplechase, roads and trails, and cross-country on the second. They are an excellent introduction to the three-day event.

The dressage phase requires obedience and suppleness as always – but these become very difficult to achieve as the horse is expected to go flat out in the speed and endurance tests. The fine line drawn between obedience and control can be particularly difficult to assess and maintain.

The speed and endurance phases consist of four different tests. Phases A and C are Roads and Tracks, which test the horse's endurance and are also a valuable warm-up and "let down" before and after the steeplechase (phase B). There is then a compulsory ten-minute halt to refresh and assess the horse before the cross-country (phase D).

Show jumping Following a fitness test by the inspection panel, there is one round of show jumping to prove the versatility of the horse. The horse with the lowest number of penalty points gained during the competition wins.

Dress for eventing

Clothes for the dressage and show jumping phases are as for those sports in general. Tweed coats are permitted in novice events for both phases, but at higher levels blue or black coats are the normal attire. Top hats and tail coats are only worn in Advanced tests. Gloves and spurs are compulsory for FEI and Advanced tests. For jumping, only calientes with navy blue or black silks are allowed.

For the cross-country phase, calientes and back protectors are compulsory, and long-sleeved cross-country sweaters are usual, often in the rider's or the stable's colors.

The dressage phase

Speed and endurance; phase B: steeplechase

Phases A and C: roads and trails

The horse

The eventer has to be a strong but athletic horse, capable of galloping for considerable distances. It must be bold and a good jumper, and also tough and sound. The seven-eighths bred or Thoroughbred horse are usually considered the best for this demanding sport, though some of the lighter breeds and warmbloods have done well. The stamina required for the three-day event does not get fully tested until the horse reaches that stage, so it is quite difficult to assess how it will cope at the top until it actually gets there. Horses have to be supremely fit to meet the very demanding requirements.

Size does not really seem to matter, as there have been several superstars both big and small over the years. The really big horse is probably at a greater disadvantage than a very small one because of the tight distances sometimes encountered in combination fences. Mark Todd's dual Olympic winner Charisma was only 15.3 hh.

Correct conformation with clean limbs and good feet, along with an ability to get out of trouble and enjoy the sport, are the main requirements for the horse.

Training

The eventer has to be a good all-rounder. At the top level, a medium standard of dressage is required, including half-pass and counter canter and differences in pace from working to medium and extended as well as collected. It is important that the horse is even and supple on both reins. A one-sided horse will not respond well when obedience to the aids is so important.

Phase D: cross-country

Grid work The event horse has to be very supple and athletic to cope with the tight and varied combinations met on cross-country courses. One of the best methods of training for this is through grid work, where the rider should interfere as little as possible, leaving the horse to work out things for itself.

Grids are a line of fences with poles on the ground set at different heights and distances to exercise the horse mentally and physically and to encourage it to shorten and lengthen its stride as and when necessary. They should never be set to trap the horse, but should be built up gradually in difficulty and set to suit each horse's natural stride. A bounce whereby the horse jumps two fences without a non-jumping stride in between can be incorporated into the grid.

The three-day event is the ultimate ambition of all serious-minded event riders. Thorough training for this demanding sport is vital if the horse is to be fully prepared for the widely different demands of all the different phases. The dressage day demands obedience and suppleness. The endurance day consists of riding along roads and tracks to test stamina, while the steeplechase and cross-country test speed and jumping ability. The show jumping on the third day is to prove the horse's training and wellbeing.

Show jumping

cross-country is generally a normal course for the standard of the event.

Three-day event

The ultimate test for the event horse is the full three-day event. Despite the name, it is usually spread out over a period of four or five days, depending on the number of runners.

The test starts with a compulsory examination for fitness carried out the day before the dressage by an inspection panel which usually consists of one veterinary surgeon, plus two other experienced persons, one of whom is president of the ground jury as a dressage judge. The horses are walked and trotted up in hand in front of the panel and will not be allowed to start the competition unless passed fit and sound. Depending on the number of starters, one or

Fitness

Fitness for the eventer needs to be built up slowly and gradually, together with its endurance ability. The essential fitness training will be much the same for all types of horse, slow to start with and building up gradually day by day.

Interval training This is a human training method adapted for use with horses. The idea is to build up the ability to cope with repeated demands (see p. 72).

Galloping If you do not use interval training, the horse will need to clear its wind with some fast work and exercise its lungs.

Galloping flat out is unnecessary for the event horse, but as the animal nears peak fitness, it is most important that it works hard to build up stamina.

One-day event

The one-day event is designed to introduce the horse to eventing at various different levels and provides courses to teach and qualify the horse for higher levels until it becomes proficient enough to qualify for the three-day event. Each country has a slightly different range of classes catering for the novice horse up to advanced standard. In the U.K., show jumping is generally held before the cross-country in the one-day event to enable as many horses as possible to be accommodated. This means, however, that riders miss experiencing the feel of a horse which is a bit tired after completing its cross-country the previous day, which happens in the three-day event. The horse will not be as sharp or probably as neat over its jumps after the cross-country, as it will have probably gotten a little low and flat over its fences. The times and speeds for cross-country increase with each higher grade, as do the

There are official inspections to test the horse's soundness before the start of the three-day event, and before the show jumping, as well as during the endurance phase.

height and width of the fences.

Eventing in earnest starts at preliminary (or novice in the U.K.) level, at about 3 ft. 6 in. (1.07 m). At intermediate level, the size in-creases to 3 ft. 9 in. (1.15 m). Courses become more difficult, and the dressage test requires a more advanced outline. For the advanced level, the courses may contain fences at a maximum height of 3 ft. 11 in. (1.49 m) and are likely to be as difficult as anything encountered in a three-day event.

Many one-day events are used as qualifiers for entry to a three-day event. There are also various championships at one-day event standard catering for the different grades, mares-only classes, regional championships, etc. Some one-day events are run under the FEI regulations and include a veterinary inspection at the start. The number of these events is usually limited to one or two per country. They often have generous prize money.

Two-day events

Some two-day events are run to provide valuable experience for up and coming combinations. They usually consist of dressage and show jumping on the first day, followed by a speed and endurance section and passing a veterinary inspection panel before the cross-country phase on the second.

The speed and endurance section usually includes short roads and trails phases with a correspondingly short steeplechase. The

two days of dressage follow, with those horses not performing having a day off. This allows the judges to judge all the horses competing. The maximum number of horses judged in one day is never more than around forty. The speed and endurance phases follow on the next day. The last day starts with another inspection, and the remaining competitors still in the competition do a single round of show jumps.

Scoring

Scoring for horse trials is done on a penalty basis. The marks from each phase are added together at the end, and the combination with the lowest score wins.

The dressage test is marked for individual movements, with any error of course marks subtracted. The average score is found by adding the good marks of the judges together (if there is more than one) and dividing by the number of judges. The total of good marks is then subtracted from the maximum attainable to convert these into penalties. To guarantee that dressage exerts the correct influence, a coefficient is applied which varies according to the test used, ranging from one-third to two-thirds. In all FEI tests this is two-fifths at present – 0.6 for three-day events.

For the cross-country and show jumping, the following charts show the penalty points given for the various faults likely to occur. Note that the show jumping faults at horse trials are not calculated on the usual basis.

Hill work is an extremely valuable means of fittening the horse, and slow cantering as well as trotting up and down hills works wonders.

Cross-country penalties

- First refusal, run-out, circle of horse at obstacle
  20 penalties

- Second refusal, run-out, circle of horse at same obstacle
  40 penalties

- Third refusal, run-out, circle of horse at same obstacle
  elimination

- Fall of horse and/or rider at obstacle
  60 penalties

- Second fall of horse and/or rider
  elimination

- Error of course not rectified
  elimination

- Omission of obstacle or boundary flag
  elimination

- Retaking an obstacle already jumped
  elimination

- Jumping obstacle in wrong order
  elimination

- Every commenced period of 3 seconds in excess of the optimum time
  1 penalty

- Exceeding the time limit
  elimination

Show jumping penalties

- Knockdown
  5 penalties

- Foot on lath, tape, strip, or in water
  5 penalties

- First disobedience
  10 penalties

- Second disobedience in whole test
  20 penalties

- Third disobedience in whole test
  elimination

- Fall of horse and/or rider
  30 penalties

- Error of course not rectified
  elimination

- Omission of obstacle or boundary flag
  elimination

- Retaking an obstacle already jumped or jumping an obstacle in the wrong order
  elimination

This sequence of photographs shows a horse which is jumping a "fan" fence. These are narrow at one end and wide at the other. This particular horse looks a little hesitant on the takeoff and so has not gained as much momentum over the fence as would one who had used a bolder and more adventurous approach.

Each standard of event will have its cross-country run at a certain speed, and the rider will need to achieve this within the optimum time so as not to acquire penalties. Going faster than the optimum does not gain marks, but it does tire the horse unnecessarily. Exceeding the optimum time incurs penalty points at the rate of one time penalty for every period commenced of three seconds. Exceeding the time limit (which is twice the optimum time) results in elimination.

Penalty zones

In three-day events and in all events in the U.S., there are penalty zones surrounding the steeplechase and cross-country fences. These consist of an area around every jump of approximately 33 ft. (10 m) in front and 72 ft. (20 m) after each jump in which faults will be incurred. Anything happening outside this area is not penalized. It is however likely that these penalty zones will be abolished in the future when the FEI next reviews its rules for the sport.

Weighing

The second or third day is very important, and the most exciting, with so much at stake. To compete at this level, riders have to carry a minimum weight of 165 lbs. (75 kg). They have to be officially checked before starting and also at the end together with their saddle and weight cloth if this is required. If underweight at the finish (it is possible to lose several pounds on the way around), the bridle can be claimed. An official form must be signed by the competitor on both occasions.

The three-day event course

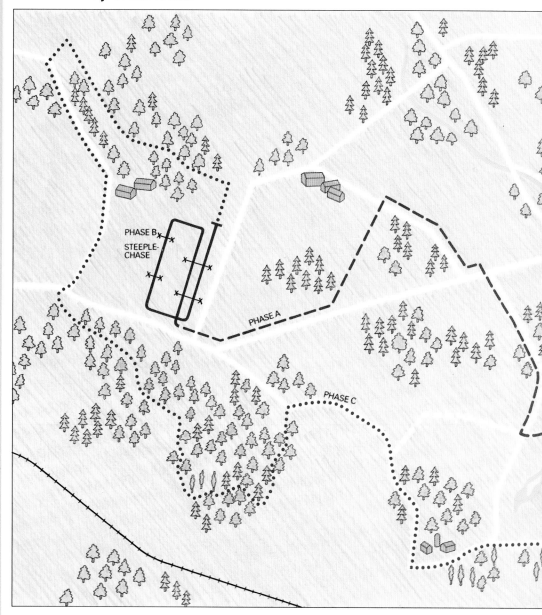

Phase A is the warm-up period, generally ridden at a steady trot or canter. It must be carried out at 220 m.p.m.

Phase B: the steeplechase varies in speed according to the standard of the event. it is usually between 630–690 m.p.m. over 6–10 fences.

KEY

- — — — PHASE A (roads & tracks)
- ──── PHASE B (steeplechase)
- • • • • PHASE C (roads & tracks)
- — · — · PHASE D (cross-country)
- Roads
- Footpaths
- ╫╫╫ Railway lines

DRESSAGE ARENA

PRACTICE AREA

HOW MPING ENA

PRACTICE AREA

FINISH

START

PHASE D

Phase C is the recovery period, and the longer it is, the better for the horse. Like Phase A, it is ridden at 220 m.p.m. in steady canter.

Phase D: the cross-country is the most demanding of all and follows a compulsory 10-minute halt and veterinary check.

Times

Your times are vital to success as each phase follows on consecutively. Once you are given the official times, work out your own, based on four minutes per kilometer for the roads and trails, which should leave a bit extra at the end of each phase to allow time to check the girths, etc. Your steeplechase needs to be worked out so that you finish just within the optimum time for no penalties. You are then on phase C, and this should be geared to allow a little time for the horse to recover its breath up until the first kilometer mark. Then once more stick to the four minutes per kilometer guide. Try to arrive a minute or two before the given finish time of phase C in as relaxed and calm a state as possible, so that the horse has a little more time than the compulsory ten-minute halt to relax and be refreshed.

Steeplechase

Before a three-day event, the horse should have had training over steeplechase fences. The animal must know how to gallop on into these without wasting time. The rider should shorten the stirrups a couple of holes and sit up more coming into the fences to be in a safer position to balance the horse should the unexpected happen or should it peck on landing.

The rider should not give too much with the reins over the fences, but keep the horse supported between hand and leg at this faster speed. Too loose a rein might be disastrous. It might well be a good idea to ride beside a professional steeplechase jockey, who can watch you ride and advise on how to improve your technique, especially if you have not done much steeplechasing before. Practice timing yourself over a measured distance at your event speed to get to know what is required.

Road and trails

The roads and trails phases make up the endurance element of the three-day event. The more you can encourage your horse to

Jumping into and through water presents various problems. It is essential for the rider to assess these carefully to determine the speed and balance of the approach, how to adjust the striding between elements, if necessary, and to be in balance over drop landings and throughout the obstacle. This sequence of photographs shows a rider successfully negotiating a multielement water obstacle, which requires the horse to jump out with a nonjumping stride over the final part. There are often alternatives to how these fences can be tackled, designed to assist the least experienced combinations. The picture opposite shows World and European champion Ginnie Leng jumping a big drop into water.

relax, the better state it will be in at the end of the day. To start with some people mostly trot, others canter around, depending on the terrain. The aim is to warm up the horse during phase A in order to be ready for the steeplechase. A short, sharp canter at some stage along the route, which may be anything from 1¾ to 3½ miles (3 to 6 km) long, will put the horse right on course with its adrenalin flowing and ready to go at steeplechase speed.

The roads and trails phase after the steeplechase acts as a very useful let down, and the longer it is the better, as this gives the horse more time to recover from the exertions of the steeplechase. Gradually pull up on phase C and let the horse walk for a bit. Then let it trot on so that you stick to your times.

Practice out on long rides trotting and cantering along measured distances if you are not sure of the speed. This phase is run at 240 yd. (220 m) per minute at all levels, and it requires a fairly constant trot or slow canter speed to cover each kilometer in just over four minutes.

Cross-country

Your start time for the cross-country will be ten minutes after the given finish time of phase C. If you know where the half or quarter way marks are on the cross-country well and good, but these can only be a guide, as the ground, terrain, and nature of the fences will greatly influence the time taken to get to different parts of the course. It may be best to know your finish time for no penalties and just keep galloping in a good rhythm, keeping the horse in balance, until you know how easily your horse copes with time limitations.

Preparation

For the speed and endurance phase, it is vital to have everything prepared and ready, with your helpers well briefed on what you expect them to do. Feed the horse four or five hours before your start time, and then do not let it eat anything. It may be necessary to tie the animal up or even muzzle it if it is on straw. Allow free access to water until one hour before the start.

Cleats should be put in, and boots or bandages put on within an hour of your start. Most people put a bootlace into the top plait behind the ears and then tie it to the bridle to prevent it from slipping over the ears should you fall. Try to keep the horse as relaxed as possible and avoid fussing.

You need to get up to the start to weigh out so be there at least 20 minutes before the phase begins. It is not necessary to ride your horse before you start, as phase A is a warm-up period. Your helper should take all the equipment you will need in the ten-minute halt to the start. This should include washing

down kit and scraper, halter and rope, grease for the legs, a bucket with a hoof pick, coolers, sweat blanket and warm blanket as well as spare shoes and tack, and a drink (non-alcoholic), and extra gloves for the rider. As the starter starts you off, remember to click your watch or stopwatch and set off at a good trot or canter, whichever is most suitable to settle your horse.

Care in the ten-minute box At the ten-minute box, you are required to see an inspection panel, which will advise on the horse's condition and check the heart and lung rate as well as the temperature. These checks provide vital indications of the horse's state of health and are particularly important in hot weather. Cool and refresh the horse with a washdown, and scrape off excess water two or three times. Iced water can be used with discretion in hot weather. Check the shoes, cleats, and bandages or boots, and walk the horse quietly, preferably in the

Success at the top is the reward of comparatively few people, but with determination and that all-important will to win, a good horse and rider, well-trained for the job, can join the numerous riders who compete at the highest levels. Careful attention to detail, both for the training of the horse and in its care and welfare, are essential elements for success. Split-second timing, and being prepared to take the occasional risk when others hold back, can make all the difference between coming first and being unplaced.

shade if it is hot. Grease the fronts of the horse's legs to help prevent scrapes and knocks, but keep the grease well away from the reins! The rider should have something to drink and change gloves if necessary during this time. The horse should be mounted two minutes before the start to allow it time to get into gear and to make sure its mind is on the cross-country. Move into the start box 10 to 15 seconds before the signal to go, and give the horse a good jump over the first fence to set you on your way.

Finishing

At the finish, you have to weigh in. Until this is done, only the weighing official is allowed to be in contact with you. Once it is over and the horse has been seen by the vets, wash it down quickly and then keep it quietly walking until it has cooled off and stopped blowing. This will take about 20 to 30 minutes. The horse can then return to the stables and have a thorough check and have its legs attended to and the cleats removed. Once settled, it should be given a small feed with an electrolyte supplement and left to relax. It is important to keep giving small but frequent drinks as soon as it has stopped blowing until its thirst is quenched. Later lead it out and trot it up to check for soundness. Check frequently to make sure it is relaxed and comfortable, and if you have any doubts, discuss them with the vets.

Final inspection

On the last day, there is first of all another compulsory inspection, and the horse has to be thoroughly loosened up before this and have any poultices completely washed off. A good walk for twenty minutes, followed by ten minutes trotting and cantering to loosen up, will usually be all that is required, but do keep the horse warm and walking until the inspection.

The show-jumping round

This round is designed to show that the horse has maintained its suppleness and

usefulness after the exertion of the previous day. Walk the course properly dressed as soon as you can. The horse will need to loosen up without becoming tired. Remember that it may feel quite tired after the cross-country. Make sure the horse is really loose and supple on the flat before jumping, and then go into the arena and do your best.

There is nothing better than finishing the three days with a good clear round.

Afterward

After any three-day event, whatever the standard, the horse will need a rest period of around a month to allow it to settle. It is worth having your vet check the horse over, paying particular attention to the legs. A blood test will confirm that all is well and that it has suffered no ill effects. The horse usually feels extremely pleased with itself after a three-day event and will know it has done something special. It will probably be a much more confident ride afterward if things have gone well. Prepare for the rest gradually over several days, either walking the horse out or turning it out for a few hours. Then either let it down altogether, or keep it up and fed and in at night for a few weeks before resuming work again.

Conclusion

For any rider to be really successful at his or her chosen sport, it is necessary to have a total commitment to wanting to succeed. This motivation forms the basis for whatever the future holds. There will inevitably be ups and downs, and it is very important always to keep looking ahead and aiming higher. Good is not good enough; if you want to be a champion, you can always be better. Learn as much as you can from as many people as possible, and then decide what is right for you. Set about achieving greater success as

The show-jumping phase has been the downfall of many a would-be champion, but for the horses at the end of a long hot day, there is nothing more refreshing than a washdown before the journey home.

you improve your knowledge and learn how to put it to its best possible use. How you prepare yourself mentally is just as important as how you achieve physical fitness. You have to be positive in your approach, confident that you can succeed, yet sensitive to your equine partner, and you have to assess how best you can bring out the horse's talents at a time when it really matters.

Never be tempted to rush basic training, but spend time getting the technique right, whether for dressage, show jumping, or riding cross-country. A lot of time spent on training always pays off in the end, though it may be frustrating to see fellow competitors snapping up the prizes early on. Remember, though, that even though horses may go well in one-day events, many do not survive the pressures of three-day events.

Above all, be a sport. The real stars are those who give back to fellow competitors what they have picked up from others. There is always so much to learn, and your help and experience will be invaluable to the next generation. We all have a great deal for which to thank our friends, above all, the horse. Its companionship, generosity, outstanding ability, and the sheer pleasure and fun it provides so willingly, in so many ways, is unique. We owe the horse our understanding and support in every possible way and must make sure that at every level rules and regulations are maintained. It must never be put under unreasonable stress or expected to perform at heights or standards for which it is not suitable or fully prepared.

GLOSSARY

Acting master a person appointed temporarily to organize and hunt the hounds, either for a day, or for a longer period pending the appointment of a permanent master.

Aged a horse which is ten years old or more.

Aid a signal used by the rider to give instructions to his horse. See also Artificial aids, and Natural aids.

Airs above the ground any of the various high-school movements performed either with the forelegs or with the fore and hind legs off the ground. See also *Ballotade, Capriole, Courbette, Croupade, Levade.*

Albino a color type without pigment rather than a breed, comprising colorless hair, pale skin, and pale translucent eyes.

Anvil (a) a heavy iron block with a smooth flat face, usually of steel, on which horseshoes are shaped. (b) (Western U.S.) a horse, particularly one which is shod, which strikes the forefeet with the hind feet.

Apron a covering made of strong horsehide worn by farriers to protect the front of the body while shoeing a horse.

Artificial aids include whips, spurs and martingales.

Back hander a polo stroke in which the player traveling forward hits the ball backward in the opposite direction.

Badge of honor an award presented by the FEI to riders competing in a specific number of Championships and Olympic Games.

Ballotade an air above the ground in which the horse half rears, then jumps forward, drawing the hindlegs up below the quarters, before landing on all four legs.

Bang-tail a tail which is cut parallel to the ground approximately 6 in. (15 cm) below the point of the hock.

Bed down to put down a bed for a horse in a stable or box stall.

Bend the slight curve in the horse's neck or body required for certain dressage schooling movements.

Bit a device, normally made of metal or rubber, attached to the bridle and placed in the horse's mouth to achieve control and steering.

Bitless bridle any of a variety of bridles used without bits; pressure is exerted on the nose and curb groove instead of the mouth.

Blemish any scar left by an injury or wound.

Blinkers a pair of leather eye shields fixed to the bridle or on a head covering, used to prevent a horse from looking anywhere other than in front of it.

Bloodstock Thoroughbred horses, particularly race and stud animals.

Body brush a tightly-packed, soft, short-bristled brush used to remove dust and dirt from a horse's coat.

Bounce two fences close together. The horse takes off for the second immediately after landing over the first without a nonjumping stride in between.

Borium tungsten steel welded into the fullering of shoes to improve grip.

Bran a by-product of the wheat grain, which when freshly ground and dampened acts as a mild laxative and aids digestion.

Break the initial training of a horse for whatever purpose it may be required.

Break down to lacerate or badly strain the tendons and ligaments of the leg.

Breastplate a device attached to the saddle to prevent it from slipping backwards.

Breeder (a) the owner of a mare which gives birth to a foal. (b) the owner of a stud farm where horses are bred.

Bridle the item of a horse's saddlery which is placed on the head as a means of control.

Bronc riding one of the standard rodeo events. The only piece of tack worn by the horse is a wide leather band around its middle, from which a leather handhold protrudes.

Browband the part of the bridle which lies across the horse's forehead below the ears.

Brush the tail of a fox.

Bull riding one of the standard events in a rodeo, in which the contestant has to ride a bull equipped only with a rope around its middle.

Bye-day an extra meet held by a hunt, usually during the Christmas school holidays or to compensate for days lost through bad weather.

Calf-roping one of the standard events in a rodeo, in which the rider ropes a calf and then swiftly dismounts to tie the calf by three legs.

Cap the fee payable by a visitor for a day's hunting.

Capriole an air above the ground in which the horse half rears with the hocks drawn under, then jumps forward and high into the air, at the same time kicking out the hind legs with the soles of the feet turned upward, before landing collectedly on all four legs.

Cavalletti a series of small raised poles used in the basic training of a riding horse to encourage it to improve its balance and strengthen its muscles.

Chaff meadow hay or oat straw cut into short lengths for use as a feedstuff.

Check a halt in hunting when hounds lose the scent.

Chef d'equipe the manager of an equestrian team responsible for making all the arrangements, both on and off the field, for a national team competing abroad.

Chukker a period of play in polo lasting 7½ or 8 minutes, depending in which country the game is being played.

Classic any one of the five chief English flat races for three-year-old horses: that is, the Derby, the Oaks, the St. Leger, the 1000 Guineas, and the 2000 Guineas.

Clear round a show-jumping or cross-country round which is completed without jumping or time faults.

Cob a type rather than a breed with a maximum height of 15.1 hh, it has the bone and substance of a heavyweight hunter and is capable of carrying a substantial weight.

Colic sharp abdominal pains, often the symptom of flatulence, an obstruction, or inactivity of the bowel which can lead to a twisted gut.

Collection shortening the pace by a light contact from the rider's hands and a steady pressure with the legs to make the horse shorten its frame and bring its hocks well under it so that it is properly balanced and prepared to perform specific movements.

Colt an ungelded male horse less than four years old.

Combination obstacle an obstacle consisting of two or more separate jumps which are numbered and judged as one obstacle.

Combined training competitions a comprehensive test of both horse and rider, consisting of the following three phases: dressage, cross-country, and show jumping, held over a period of one, two, or three days depending on the type of competition. Also known as Eventing and Horse Trials.

Contact the link between the rider's hands and the horse's mouth made through the reins.

Conformation the make and shape of the horse.

Corn bruising of the sole in the angle between the wall of the hoof and the heel, usually caused by pressure from the shoe.

Corral a pen or enclosure for animals, usually made of wood and always circular in shape, so that the animals cannot injure themselves.

Courbette an air above the ground in which the horse rears to an almost upright position, and then leaps forward several times on its hind legs.

Course (a) a racecourse. (b) in show jumping and cross-country, a circuit consisting of a number of obstacles to be jumped in a particular order within a specific time limit. (c) for hounds to hunt by sight rather than by scent.

Course builder the person responsible for designing and building a show-jumping or cross-country course.

Course designer (a) (U.K.) a person who designs a show-jumping or cross-country course, who may or may not actually build it as well. (b) (U.S.) course builder.

Covert a hunting term for a thicket or small area of woodland.

Cow horse the horse which a cowboy rides while working cattle.

Croupade an air above the ground in which the horse rears, and then jumps vertically with the hind legs drawn up toward the belly.

Cry the noise made by hounds when they are hunting their quarry.

Cub a young fox.

Curb bit (a) any bit used with a curb chain. (b) used in conjunction with a bridoon snaffle in the double bridle.

Curb chain a metal chain which is fitted to the hooks of a curb bit and lies in the curb groove in the lower jaw just behind the lower lip.

Curry comb a piece of grooming equipment used to remove dirt and scurf from a body brush. It has a flat back, while the front consists of several rows of small, usually metal, teeth.

Cut to geld or castrate a colt or stallion.

Cutting horse a horse especially trained for separating selected cattle from a herd.

Dam the female parent of a foal.

Dandy brush a hard long-bristled brush for removing the surface dirt or dried-on mud from the horse's coat.

Declaration a statement made in writing by an owner, trainer, or his representative a specified time before a race or competition declaring that a horse will take part.

Den the lair of a fox which it digs below ground level or in the side of a bank.

Dirt track a race track, the surface of which is a combination of sand and soil.

Dope to administer drugs to a horse, either to improve or hinder its performance in a race or competition. It is an illegal practice and carries heavy penalties in all forms of equestrian sport.

Double bridle a bridle consisting of two bits, a curb, and a bridoon, either of which may be operated independently. Used particularly in advanced dressage and show classes.

Drag an artificial scent for a hunt made by trailing a strong smelling material such as a piece of sacking impregnated with aniseed or a fox's dropping over the ground.

Draghunt a hunt with a drag or artificial scent.

Dressage the art of training horses to perform all movements in a balanced, supple, obedient manner, enabling them to compete in dressage competitions at various levels.

Electrolytes essential body salts, potassium, and ions usually given to horses in hot and humid conditions to replace those lost through sweat and dehydration.

Elimination the excluding of a competitor from taking further part in a particular competition.

Engaged the extent to which a horse's hocks create impulsion and balance.

Equine (a) of, or pertaining to, the horse. (b) a horse.

Farrier a blacksmith, a person who makes horseshoes and shoes horses.

FEI the Fédération Equestre Internationale (International Equestrian Federation) which is the governing body of international equestrian sport and was founded in 1921 by Commandant G. Hector of France. It has its headquarters in Switzerland. The FEI makes the rules and regulations for the conduct of international equestrian sports including the Olympic Games: all national federations are required to comply with these rules and regulations in any international event.

Field (a) the mounted followers of a hunt. (b) in racing, (i) all the horses running in a particular race; (ii) all the horses not individually favored in the betting.

Filly a female horse less than four years old.

Foal a young horse up to the age of 12 months.

Foal slip small adjustable halter for foals.

Forehand the part of the horse which is in front of the rider: that is, the head, neck, shoulders, withers, and forelegs.

Foxhunting the hunting of the fox in its natural state by a pack of foxhounds, followed by people on horses or on foot.

Full horse a stallion or ungelded horse.

Full mouth the mouth of a horse at six years old, when it has grown all its teeth.

Gag bridle a severe form of bridle: the shank-pieces are made of rounded leather and pass through holes at the top and bottom of the bit rings before attaching directly to the reins.

Gall a skin sore usually occurring under the saddle or girth.

Gelding a male horse which has been castrated.

Girth (a) the circumference of a horse measured behind the withers around the deepest part of the body. (b) a band, usually of leather, webbing, or nylon, passed under the belly of the horse to hold the saddle in place.

Gone to ground a fox having taken refuge in a den or drain.

Green a horse which is broken but not fully trained, an inexperienced horse.

Green hunter an American show class, including the jumping at hunter pace of a course of rustic fences.

Groom (a) any person who is responsible for looking after a horse. (b) to clean the coat and feet of a horse.

Gymkhana mounted games, most frequently for children, many of which are adaptations of children's party games.

Habit the dress worn by a woman riding side-saddle, consisting of a jacket and matching long skirt or shaped "apron" which is worn over the breeches and boots.

Hand a linear measurement equaling 4 in. (10 cm) used in giving the height of a horse.

Haute Ecole the classical art of equitation.

Hog's back in show jumping, a spread obstacle in which there are three sets of poles, the first being low, the second at the highest point of the obstacle, and the third low on the far side.

Hood (a) a fabric covering which goes over the horse's head and ears and part of its neck, and is used most in cold weather. (b) blinkers.

Hunt button buttons with the symbol or lettering of a particular hunt on them, presented only to worthy members of that hunt.

Hunter trials a type of competitive event held by most hunts and other organizing bodies during the hunting season, in which horses are ridden over a course of obstacles built to look natural and similar to those encountered out hunting. The course has to be completed within a specified time.

Hunting horn a cylindrical instrument, usually 9-10 in. (23-25 cm) long, made of copper with a nickel or silver mouthpiece, used by huntsmen to give signals, both to hounds and to the field.

Hunt secretary a person who carries out the normal duties of a secretary in connection with the hunt. The hunt secretary is also responsible for keeping close contact with farmers and landowners within the area of the hunt, and collects the cap money at the meet.

Huntsman the person in charge of hounds during a hunt, either the master or someone employed by the master.

In-hand class any of various show classes in which the animals are led, usually in a show bridle or halter, but otherwise without saddlery (except for draft horses which are often shown in their harness), and are judged chiefly for conformation and/or condition.

In the book accepted for, or entered in, the General Stud Book for Thoroughbreds.

Jiggle the ordinary gait of cow horse averaging about 5 m.p.h. (8 km/h).

Jog a short-paced slow trot.

Keep a grass field which is used for grazing. Known as pasture in the U.S.

Levade a high-school movement in which the horse rears, drawing its forefeet in, while the hindquarters are deeply bent at the haunches and carry the full weight.

Livery stable an establishment where privately owned horses are kept, exercised, and generally looked after, for an agreed fee.

Long rein a training method using two lunge reins to teach the horse to go forward, turn, and back without a rider on its back.

Lunge rein a piece of cotton or nylon webbing, usually about 1 in. (2.5 cm) wide and 25 ft. (7.5 m) long, which is attached by a buckle and leather strap to one of the side rings on a cavesson and is used for lungeing and training horses.

Maiden a horse of either sex which to date has not won a race of any distance.

Mare a female horse aged four years or over.

Martingale a device used to prevent the horse's head from coming up too high and out of the angle of control. It generally consists of a neck strap and another strap fastened to the girth at one end and passed between the forelegs and, depending on the type, attached at the other end to the reins or noseband.

Master the person appointed by a hunt committee to have overall responsibility for the running and organization of all aspects of a specific hunt.

Match a race between two horses, on terms agreed by their owners. There is no prize awarded.

Meet (a) the place where the hunt servants, hounds, followers, etc., assemble before a hunt. (b) the hunt meeting itself.

Mustang a wild horse.

Nap a horse is said to nap if it fails to obey properly applied aids, as in refusing to go forward or to pass a certain point.

National Federation the governing body of equestrian affairs in any country affiliated to the FEI.

Natural aids the body, hands, legs, and voice as used by the rider to give instructions to the horse.

Near side the left-hand side of a horse. This is the usual side to mount a horse.

Noseband the part of a bridle which lies across the horse's nose consisting of a leather band on an independent headpiece. There are four main types: cavesson, drop, flash, and grakle.

Numnah a pad cut to the shape of an English saddle and placed underneath it to prevent undue pressure on the horse's back.

Oats a cereal crop used as the main part of a horse's feed. May be given either whole, crushed, or boiled.

Off side the right-hand side of a horse.

One-day event a combined training competition consisting of dressage, show jumping, and cross-country and completed in one day.

Opening meet the first meet of the regular hunting season.

Pace (a) a lateral gait in two time, in which the hind leg and the foreleg on the same side move forward together. (b) the four different gaits: walk, trot, canter, and gallop.

Pacemaker in racing, a horse which takes the lead and sets the speed for the race.

Passage one of the classical high-school airs, which is a spectacular elevated trot in slow motion. There is a definite period of suspension as one pair of legs remains on the ground with the diagonal opposites raised in the air.

Piaffe a classical high-school air, a spectacular trot with great elevation and cadence performed on the spot.

Pirouette in dressage, a turn within the horse's length, that is the shortest turn it is possible to make. Performed in walk or canter.

Polo a mounted game, bearing a resemblance to field hockey, played between two teams of four a side.

Racing plate a thin, very lightweight horseshoe used on racehorses, usually made of aluminum alloy.

Racing saddle a saddle designed for use on racehorses, which may range from the very light type of less than 2 lb. (1 kg) used for flat racing, to the heavier, more solid type used for hurdling and steeplechasing.

Rack the most spectacular movement of the five-gaited American Saddlebred, it is a very fast, even gait in which each foot strikes the ground separately in quick succession.

Rein back to make a horse step backward while being ridden or driven.

Resistance the act of refusing to go forward, stopping, running back, or rearing.

Ride off in polo, to push one's pony against that of another player in order to prevent him from playing the ball.

Saddler a person who makes, repairs, or deals in saddlery and/or harness.

School (a) to train a horse for whatever purpose it may be required. (b) an enclosed area, either covered or open, where a horse may be trained or exercised.

Schoolmaster an experienced and well-schooled horse on which riders can learn and get the feel of what is required for certain · disciplines.

Service the mating of a mare by a stallion.

Shankpiece the sides of the bridle to which the bit is attached at one end and the headpiece at the other.

Sidesaddle a saddle designed for women, on which the rider sits with both feet on the same side, normally the nearside. On that side, the saddle has two padded projections placed diagonally one above the other. The rider hooks her right leg over the upper one and place the left leg under and against the lower one resting her left foot in the single stirrup iron.

Slow gait one of the gaits of the five-gaited American Saddlebred. It is a true prancing action in which each foot in turn is raised and then held momentarily in mid-air before being brought down. Similar to the rack and also called the single foot.

Stallion an ungelded male horse aged four years or over.

Starter's orders when the starter of a race has satisfied himself that all runners are present and ready to race, a flag is raised to show that the horses are "under starter's orders."

Steeplechase a race over a certain course of a specified distance on which there are a number of obstacles to be jumped.

Stock class a show class for stock or ranch ponies.

Stock saddle the high-pommeled, high-cantled Australian cowboy's saddle which has long flaps.

Surcingle a webbing belt usually 2½-3 in. (6-8 cm) wide, which passes over a racing or jumping saddle and girth and is used to keep the saddle in position, or to hold a blanket securely temporarily.

Sweat scraper a metal, rubber, or plastic blade used to scrape sweat from a horse.

Teaser a stallion used to determine whether the mare is receptive before being covered by the stallion of choice. Often an unfashionable stallion.

Trail horse a horse trained, bred, or used for cross-country rides.

Treble in show jumping, a combination obstacle which consists of three separate jumps.

Triple bar in show jumping, a wide spread fence which consists of three sets of poles built in a staircase fashion with the highest at the back.

Vixen a female fox.

Walking Horse class any of various competitions held for Tennessee Walking Horses at horse shows.

Walkover a race in which only one horse has been declared to start. To qualify for the prize money, the horse has to be saddled, paraded in front of the stands, and then walk past the winning post.

Water brush (a) a brush used to wash the feet and to dampen the mane and tail. (b) in show jumping, a small, sloping brush fence placed in front of a water jump to help a horse take off.

Weigh in in certain equestrian sports where a specified weight has to be carried, such as racing, advanced eventing, and show jumping, the rider has to be weighed immediately after completion of the race or competition to make sure the correct weight was carried throughout the event.

Weigh out in certain equestrian sports where a specified weight has to be carried such as racing, advanced eventing, and show jumping, the rider has to be weighed before the race or competition to make sure the correct weight is carried.

Weight cloth a cloth carried under the saddle on a horse. It is equipped with pockets in which lead weights may be inserted to achieve the correct weight.

Windgall a puffy elastic swelling of a horse's fetlock joints caused by an over-secretion of synovia, a fluid similar to joint oil, following hard work or concussion on hard ground. Sometimes known as wind puffs.

Windsucking a harmful habit in which a horse draws in and swallows air, causing indigestion and unthriftiness. A notifiable vice when selling.

Wing one of a pair of upright stands with cups or similar fittings used to support the poles or other suspended parts of a show jumping obstacle.

Withers the highest part of a horse's back: the area at the base of the neck between the shoulder blades.

*I*NDEX

ACKNOWLEDGEMENTS

I would like to thank the following:
Bob Langrish for his patience and care when taking the superb photographs for this book, Lord Patrick Beresford for so kindly contributing the section on Polo, and Eleanor Ward for writing the section on Showing in the USA, two sections I felt ill-equipped to write myself, and to Sandra McCallum for her painstaking efforts typing on the word processor from my handwritten notes. I would also like to thank Nigel Howes D.W.C.F. for his help on farriery, and I am deeply indebted to Darrell Scaife for his research into the breeds section and for his help with photographs, as well as the patience and time given for these by Carol Cavegn, Sharon Mordaunt, Pam Cary Croton, Kristin Kosowan, Jo Thomas and Cheryl Grubb. Finally, I would like to thank the horses who acted as such excellent models, including 24-year-old Warrior, former Badminton and Burghley winner, Above the Clouds, Light Entertainment, Flatteur, Secret Weapon, Hannibal, Sijama, Gemma, Funny Business and Coloured Classic.

Jane Holderness-Roddam

The publishers would like to thank the following who were involved in the preparation of this book:
The Fédération Equestre Internationale; Midge and Richard Roberts and staff at the Forest Lodge Equestrian Centre, Motcombe, Dorset, for the use of their facilities and their horses: Eric, Ben, Specs, Monarch, Leggitt, Wizard, Dunnit, Oliver, Amber and Darkie; Rawles & Son Ltd., London, for providing various pieces of equipment, and Margaret Allison for her help and assistance.

Photographic acknowledgements

All the photographs in this book have been supplied by Bob Langrish with the exception of those appearing on the following pages:
The pictures appearing on pages 1, and 9, top left, are reproduced by courtesy of the Trustees of the British Museum.
Action-Plus Photographic/Chris Barry 150; Ardea/Jean-Paul Ferrero 95 bottom, 103 bottom; British Library 9 centre right; ET Archive 10 top; Mary Evans Picture Library 14; Hulton-Deutsch Collection 10 centre left, 10 bottom; Mansell Collection 8, 14-15; Octopus Publishing Group Ltd/Kit Houghton 52, 67 top, 69 centre left, 69 centre, 69 top right, 94 bottom, 96 bottom, 101 bottom, 102 bottom, 128-129, 131 bottom left, 131 bottom right, 136 left, 136 right, 137 top, 141 bottom, /Alyson M. Kyles endpapers, 19 top, 25 bottom, 26 top left, 26 top right, 26 bottom, 27, 28 bottom left, 28 bottom right, 29 left, 29 top, 33 centre top, 33 centre bottom, 33 bottom, 36 right, 38 top, 38 centre, 38 bottom, 42, 47 top, 47 centre, 47 bottom, 48 bottom, 49 top left, 49 top right, 49 centre left, 49 centre, 49 centre right, 54, 56 top, 59, 60 right, 65 centre left, 65 centre right, 65 bottom left, 65 bottom right, 66 top, 66 bottom, 67 bottom left, 67 centre bottom, 67 bottom right, 69 bottom left, 77, 79 bottom; /Ross Laney 109 bottom, Bob Langrish 24 right, 44-45, 49 bottom, 64, 85 bottom, 104 left, 139, 154-155, 158 left, 159 bottom right , 161 top, 161 bottom, /Sally Anne Thompson 84 bottom, 98-99; Peter Roche 74 top left, 74 bottom left; H Roger-Viollet 11 top; Staatliche Museen Berlin Antikenabteilung/Bildarchiv Preussischer Kulturbesitz 9 top right.